Beating the S&P with Dividends

How to Build a Superior Portfolio of Dividend Yielding Stocks

MERGENT, INC.

PETER O'SHEA
AND JONATHAN WORRALL

WILEY

John Wiley & Sons, Inc.

Contents

PREFACE V

ACKNOWLEDGMENTS VII

CHAPTER ONE 1
Introduction

CHAPTER TWO 5
All About Dividends

CHAPTER THREE 19
A New Tax Environment

CHAPTER FOUR 27
Dividend Stocks Make a Comeback

CHAPTER FIVE 41
The Evidence Is In: Dividend Stocks
Really Do Perform Better

CHAPTER SIX 51
What Makes a Good Dividend Stock

CHAPTER SEVEN 67
Yields and Ratios Unraveled

CHAPTER EIGHT 81
The Mergent Dividend Investing Strategy

CHAPTER NINE 91
Dividend Investment Options

CHAPTER TEN 121
Real Estate Investment Trusts

CHAPTER ELEVEN 125
Selected Dividend Achievers

APPENDIX 201
Dividend Actions of Dividend-Achieving
    Companies

NOTES 225

INDEX 229

Preface

This book has been compiled to give the average investor a path through the quagmire and confusion with which he or she is confronted when attempting to obtain a low-cost and reliable way to build an investment portfolio. It provides an uncomplicated method to identify companies that will bring solid long-term returns at low risk. In other words, it is for you and me and, in particular, for anyone concerned about building a worthwhile fund for the future. Above all, it is simple.

Who is the "average investor?" you may ask. You may say that this cannot possibly include me with my unique objectives, my family, my aims and my risk outlook. Well, we believe that unless you are a day trader, this does include you and, furthermore, that this book might just change your perspective on investing.

This book is about companies that have been shown, over a considerable time period, to regularly pay dividends to their shareholders and increase them every quarter. This means that, despite changes in the economy, through downturn or boom, through different administrations, or through war and peace, these companies have steadily grown the return that they make to their shareholders year after year.

You will hear stockbrokers, market analysts, and fund managers use technical phrases such as "growth stocks" or "value stocks" and recommend investment according to certain profiles that they have contrived. Alternatively, they may recommend that due to a lower tolerance for risk you only invest in "large caps" or, if you are over 50 years old, that you start investing increasingly in bonds. We believe that if you take a relatively small amount of time to dip into this book and consider the facts that we have uncovered in conjunction with our colleagues and others, you will have a simple platform from which to question those recommendations or sales pitches.

Of course, risk comes into play with regard to your decreasing ability to accept loses as you get older and the inability to wait long enough for any losses to be recovered because you may need to take income. However, it also applies to those much younger, even the newborn who needs a fund for college, or the recent graduate in his or her first job who needs to save for that first mortgage down payment—or even for those that dream of a Ferrari!

We all have a different tolerance for risk and constantly find our financial advisors talking about it and telling us that, due to our profile, we need to invest in a particular set of financial instruments and to diversify our investment. Often, the end result of these discussions is a very complex set of recommendations with a significant cost associated with it. This is a major reason why we complied this book. We believe we can show that the answer is a simple one and that in fact you don't even need a broker to execute a plan to meet you needs. Most of the companies identified herein will take investments directly and, thus, even further increase your return through the savings incurred by not having to pay commission on the purchase of the shares.

In many ways this is a very simple and, we hope, readable book about a very simple solution to investing that we feel everyone should know about. Our conclusion is that investing in dividend achievers, either through a fund or directly ourselves, is an efficient way of building an investment portfolio for almost everyone. It is a way to cheaply invest; it generates regular cash returns that can be withdrawn or reinvested; it brings a relatively high rate of return; and yet it can done at very low risk with relation to almost any other type of financial investment. And now you even have the government helping through the reduction of tax on dividends!

We hope that you personally benefit from this book, particularly if you have never before read a book about investing. Please use it and tell your friends; we should all be investing this way.

Jonathan Worrall
November 2004

Acknowledgments

In researching, compiling data and writing this book there are several people whose efforts were critical. Many thanks go to Mergent's Index Team whose efforts to create the Mergent dividend indices were central to this project. Particularly, thanks are due to Kevin Heckert and Bill Rogers without whose meticulous and painstaking research and data skills this project simply would not have been possible. Thanks are also due to Lynn Tilton of Patriarch Partners LLC without whose vision of the business environment—Mergent, and many other successful companies—would not exist today.

CHAPTER ONE

Introduction

*Do you know the only thing that gives me pleasure? It's to
see my dividends coming in!*

—John D. Rockefeller

Dividends are back. Soaring stock prices, dot-com millionaires,
and day traders are things of the past. Many people remember
the boom days of the late 1990s and early 2000s fondly and wish those
days would return. But many others wished them good riddance when
their investments disappeared as quickly and as surely as night followed
day. The period from March 2000 to October 2002 was one of the worst
in the U.S. stock market's history, with stocks in the Standard and Poor's
500 index losing around 49% in value.

At the end of the 1990s, when people talked about making money in
the stock market, they really meant the amount of money they made from
their shares having appreciated in value. Value tended to be defined in
terms of capital growth, not income growth. But we all know that's not
correct, right? The reality is—and always has been—that there is much
more to wealth creation than growth in value. Stocks are one of those
investments that provide both capital appreciation as well as income. In
fact, if you had invested in leading dividend-yielding stocks 10, 20, or 30

1

years ago, chances are you would have made more money than if you had invested solely in leading stocks such as those on the S&P 500 index.

More specifically, if you had invested $10,000 in Mergent's index of dividend-yielding stocks 10 years ago, you would have almost quadrupled your money (to around $38,000). But, wait, you say, there are many stocks whose value has appreciated over this period of time. This is true; however, 10 years ago you would not have known which of those stocks would have appreciated based on capital growth alone.

This book shows you how to be almost certain about it. The reason is that dividend-yielding stocks on Mergent's index are there because they have a long-standing history of consecutive dividend achievement. The important word here is "consecutive." In other words, if companies have not increased their dividends consistently year after year, they don't get on the index. At the same time, companies that are on the index but miss a consecutive year's increase fall off the list for the next quarter.

That's a fairly harsh call, but the outcome is that the stocks on the index are almost sure bets for future income. Some of the companies on the index have increased their dividends for 50 years in a row! The added beauty of investing in stocks that increase their dividends consecutively is that not only will you be able to depend on the income, but you can look forward to growing income year after year.

Sure, you could gamble and try to beat the returns that consistent dividend investment will provide. Undoubtedly there will be another bull market somewhere in the next decade. However, we are only just recovering from one of the worst periods in stock market history (in terms of annual returns). The markets saw a very marked downward turn at the end of the last century, a moment in time marked by the dot-com bust, corporate scandals, and the effects of adverse national and world events. Taking a gamble on the fact that stocks will keep growing created a lot of disappointed investors in the late 1990s. In fact, IRS figures show that the amount of money people made from stocks fell markedly over the last couple of years.

Dividend investing, however, is not new. In the 70 years prior to 2002 the payment of dividends contributed around 40% of the average annual return of stocks provided by the companies on the S&P 500 index, whereas in the decade from 1980 to 1990 the payment of dividends accounted for only 16% of the average annual return for stocks.

However, with the falls in the stock markets of the last two years, investors have looked to other ways to make money and companies have provided other ways to return value to shareholders. Many investors who held onto their stocks over the last few years have begun to wonder whether investing in stocks is worthwhile. Many have wondered what the point is of investing in assets whose value falls or, at best, fails to appreciate. Many have found that fixed-income investments (such as term deposits) have delivered greater returns than the stock market over the last few years.

The stock market is central to the national economy and with falling values and poor returns in mind, congressional legislators made a significant change to tax laws in 2003. The change significantly altered the way dividends are taxed. Previously, there was a built-in disincentive in the tax system to buy dividend-yielding stocks. In a nutshell, many dividends were the subject of double taxation. How, you ask? Dividends are part of the profits that companies have made and are handed out to their investors. But those company profits are taxed before they are handed out. And then when they are given to investors in the form of dividends, the individual investor pays tax as part of his other overall income tax assessment.

It's true that some dividends are not effectively taxed twice; these include those paid to nonprofit institutions and foundations, pension plans, 401(k) plans and other individual retirement accounts, as well as dividends paid to local, state, and federal governments.[1] However, most dividends paid to individual investors are indeed effectively taxed twice.

Companies have been well aware of this and, particularly over the last three decades, have chosen to create shareholder value not so much by paying dividends, but by focusing on strategies that build stock value. Other strategies include share buybacks, in which companies buy back shares on the market, a move that often makes money for the individual shareholder, who more often than not bought his or her shares some years previous at a cheaper price. Many companies have given stock options to employees (a move that in many cases has diluted the shareholdings of other investors).

This situation led to a dramatic turnaround in 2003. More companies, such as Microsoft, began issuing dividends for the first time and more companies increased their dividends compared to previous years, and average dividend yields, which had been down since the 1990s, slowly started to creep back up. Dividends really do matter and now more so than ever. Furthermore, with a changed tax environment in the United States they are set to be more important.

In the current environment, investing in dividend stocks has never looked so good. The following chapters discuss how investing in dividend-yielding stocks can generate greater returns than investing in leading companies on the major indices, including the S&P 500. They also explain why such stocks are good investments, what to look for, and how dividends have been achieved.

CHAPTER TWO

All About Dividends

WHAT ARE DIVIDENDS?

Companies generally provide returns to their shareholders in two ways: through capital appreciation or dividends (or both). A dividend is, in its most rudimentary form, a payment a company makes to its shareholders. The most relevant definition is perhaps that offered by the Internal Revenue Service (IRS), which after all, has the most interest in your income after yourself. The IRS defines dividends as "distributions of money, stock, or other property paid to you by a corporation." These may be received through a partnership, an estate, a trust, or an association which is taxed as a corporation. Ordinary dividends are the most common type of distribution from a corporation and are received from holdings in common or preferred stocks unless the corporation says otherwise.

WHAT IS COMMON STOCK?

Common stock is a slice of ownership in a company. There are different classes of share ownership, and each comes with different rights. These may or may not include voting rights and other rights, although most common stock does come with full voting rights. This is usually provided as the right to vote in the election of company directors and on major decisions that are put to a shareholder vote. Common stock ownership also is subject to relevant laws, including bankruptcy-related laws. One drawback of common stock ownership is that owners of common stock are not high up the food chain. In the event that the company gets itself in trouble with creditors, owners of any bonds the company may have issued and owners of preferred stock get priority. Preferred stock is essentially stock that comes with greater rights, including the right to be paid first in the event of company liquidation. The advantage to a company of common stock is that it allows companies get capital from the market with few obligations. Investors can vote, but their votes must be subject to rules that the company sets down. A company does not have to pay the money back to investors and it does not have to pay dividends if it doesn't want to.

Most dividends are paid quarterly and are usually in the form of cash; however, payments in stock are increasingly common, especially when it comes to employee stock options. Dividends are usually paid out of the earnings and profits of the company, and they are treated as income by the IRS, unless they are in the form of stock. If they are in fact in the form of stock, they are not taxed until they are sold, in which case they are subject to capital gains tax, not income tax. In the United States, most corporations use the IRS Form 1099-DIV, Dividends and Distributions, to show the distributions during the year. Dividends are usually defined in terms of dividend per share, and the return is usually expressed in terms of the dividend yield or simply the yield. We will show in Chapter 7 what these mean and how they are used to invest in dividend (and nondividend) stock.

WHY COMPANIES PAY DIVIDENDS

There are a number of reasons people invest in businesses—investing to make profits is obviously the main one. There are a number of ways, however, to profit from an investment in stocks; capital appreciation is one and dividends are another. Thus, there are companies that tend to focus on building shareholder value by driving stock value up and those that focus on distributing dividends. They tend to fall into two separate camps, largely because doing one or the other generally involves running a business differently and seeking growth in different ways.

The reasons why one company will be a "dividend company" and why another may not are complex. Management obviously has a big say, but shareholders do too. Ultimately, shareholders look for value, and it is up to management to determine the best way to provide it. You could say there are two ways to provide insight into this issue: broadly, by highlighting the ways companies provide value to shareholders, and on a micro level, that is, by looking at the trigger events or the motivations of company executives at the time. Let's explain this further.

Broadly speaking, when companies are growing, the best way to provide value to shareholders is to keep up with competitors, to reinvest cash, and to take a larger slice of the market as quickly as possibly. Companies that are growing quickly tend not to pay dividends, but rather reinvest the money to boost their ability to access cash. However, companies that are well established and do not need to grow aggressively are the ones that do tend to pay dividends. They tend to be larger, more mature companies that sell lots of product to lots of people.

We go into more detail later as to the nature of dividend-paying companies, but consider that the Dow Jones Industrial Average stocks—the largest companies in the United States—all pay dividends. They are established and have regular and reliable revenue bases. Most of them are not going through phases of rapid expansion and growth. Most have large piles of cash and strong cash flow and have ample room to provide value to shareholders in this way.

When a company is growing quickly, it is also often in the throes of fending off competitors—which also tend to be growing just as quickly. It is more often than not tapping opportunities in new markets—opportunities that often disappear as quickly as they appear. Consider that once a dividend is declared (usually at an annual meeting), the total amount reserved for payment becomes a liability on the company's balance sheet. The company's assets are reduced and the money is paid, usually straight out of the company's bank account. Although paying a dividend at times when a company is growing can be popular with shareholders in the short term, it can restrict the company's options for accessing cash when it needs it.

Perhaps the best example of this is one of the largest companies in the world. When Microsoft was growing quickly in the 1980s, demand for its product was strong. It was entering new territory and its products were evolving quickly. Potential competitors like IBM and Apple were hanging around, wondering how to respond, and Microsoft couldn't afford to sit back and hand out cash to shareholders. It would have opened the way for others to move in and take the limelight. Indeed, in terms of its growth, a quick look at Microsoft's quarterly revenue growth since 1985 reveals the company's revenue increased almost every quarter consistently right through to 2004 (see Figure 2.1).

Something changed for Microsoft in March 2004—it issued its first dividend. When doing so after 17 years of being a public company, Microsoft said it based its decision after assessing the company's "potential future long-term capital requirements relating to research and development, investments and acquisitions, dilution management, and legal and business risks." In other words, it made an assessment at the time as to whether profits were best distributed to shareholders or best retained in the company for its growth needs. Indeed, Microsoft's decision to implement a dividend policy in 2003 also coincided with President Bush's announced tax reform plan, which involved a change in the way dividends were taxed, even though Microsoft said the two decisions weren't related.

Similarly, in February 2003, Qualcomm issued its first dividend. Here's what it told its shareholders about the reasons behind doing so, and the reason it planned to do so in the future:

> *We believe that returning capital to stockholders is an important part of stock ownership. It is also an indication that Qualcomm is a successful*

FIGURE 2.1   MICROSOFT REVENUE GROWTH, QUARTERLY
1985 TO 2003

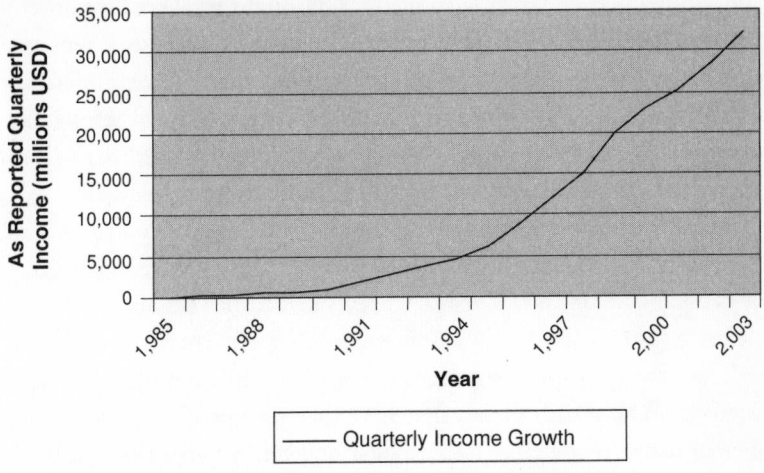

SOURCE: Microsoft Corporation. Raw data taken from Microsoft website.
http://www.microsoft.com/msft/history.mspx

company. Subject to continued capital availability and a determination
that cash dividends continue to be in the best interests of the Company
and its stockholders, it is the intention of the Board of Directors to pay a
comparable quarterly dividend on a going forward basis.

Qualcomm has been generating increasing amounts of free cash
from operations as a result of the success of CDMA technology, particularly with increasing third generation (3G) CDMA network deploy-
ments around the world. In declaring the first dividend in our history,
Qualcomm's Board of Directors has determined that the Company can
return some of its cash to stockholders without impacting future revenue and earnings growth or restricting strategic opportunities.

Another major consideration for companies is the taxation dividends
are subject to. As discussed earlier, in the 1980s and 1990s most dividends
were effectively subject to double taxation. Companies were taxed on the

profit and then shareholders paid tax as part of their income tax assessment. As a way to build shareholder value and a way to increase the value of the company overall, many companies felt that they were best off buying back the shares shareholders owned in share buybacks. Companies were not (and still are not) taxed on this transaction and shareholders usually paid only capital gains tax—if they made money from selling their shares back in the transaction. Share buybacks helped build the value of companies because their shares on the market became fewer in number.

The other way (on a micro level) to provide insight into the reasons why companies issue dividends is by looking at the motivations of particular companies. Across the board, a number of academics and students of finance have tried to identify common reasons why companies pay dividends and the corresponding trigger events. Unfortunately, the task hasn't turned out to be as easy as they may have thought initially. A discussion of the circumstances that lead to particular dividend payments by particular companies could be a book on its own.

Several studies have found that the key beliefs among company executives about dividend payments are that it is better for investors to pay smaller amounts of tax on dividends than larger amounts of capital gain when they sell their stocks; that it is less costly to provide value to shareholders by paying dividends than by other methods, such as share buybacks; and that a company's share price will respond positively to the announcement that a company intends to pay a dividend.

It's certainly the case that stock prices usually rise after a dividend announcement. This has been the finding of a number of studies. It's also certainly the case that dividend announcements do send a positive message to the market. However, there is not much evidence to suggest that dividend announcements themselves—or any other of these key beliefs—have a positive effect all of the time. At the end of the day, experts are unable to find any solid and consistent motivation.[1] Essentially, the reasons vary from company to company.

In fact, sometimes a sudden dividend increase actually can send negative messages to the market. Many investors are wary of companies that change their dividend policies to suit the current mood. A study by University of Georgia Professor Kathleen Fuller and Babson College Professor Michael Goldstein in 2003 found that investors actually respond positively to a lack of change in dividends during a down market.[2] The study findings suggest that they don't take a lack of change in dividend policy as a sign the company is lagging behind but rather that the company is on track as planned.

In their simplistic form then, dividends are a way to provide value for companies that can afford it and when it's good for investors. For example, Microsoft paid its first dividend from a huge cash surplus. Shareholders received 8 cents per share. Later, in July 2004 Microsoft announced a special dividend of $3 per share along with a share buyback, saying that "these steps would represent a combined total value to shareholders of up to $75 billion over the next four years, if quarterly dividends continue at the new level." In this distribution, Chairman Bill Gates, the software maker's largest shareholder, received a dividend of $4.8 billion. Now that's a dividend and rather good value to its key shareholder!

WHY ARE DIVIDENDS IMPORTANT?

DIVIDENDS PROVIDE CURRENT INCOME

Most investors want money and most investments provide it. The real drawing card for many investors is that dividends provide income—not just occasional income, but regular income. Because most dividends are paid on a quarterly basis, they supplement many Americans' annual salary or wage or other investment income—even when a salary or wage stops. In 2002, even though salaries and wages provided most income that Americans as a whole brought into their households, dividends comprised 5% of the total individual income reported to the IRS. As a whole this doesn't sound like a lot, but many investors are elderly and it represents a greater proportion of total income to them (see Figure 2.2).

A PROFILE OF STOCK OWNERSHIP

A revolution has taken place in stock ownership in the United States in the last decade. In the 1990s alone, the number of stockholders jumped by over 50 percent in the United States. One of the most respected and

FIGURE 2.2   DIVIDENDS AS A PERCENTAGE OF
              INDIVIDUAL INCOME (IN TRILLIONS OF
              U.S. DOLLARS).

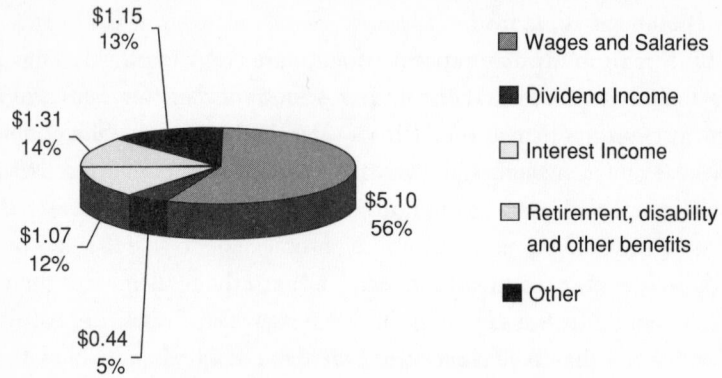

NOTE: Seasonally adjusted annual rate as of November 2002.
SOURCE: U.S. Commerce Department.

widely used sources of data on stock ownership is the Survey of
Consumer Finances, which is conducted by the Survey Research Center
at the University of Michigan for the Federal Reserve Board every three
years. The 2001 survey found more than half (52%) of all U.S. households
owned stock in some form. This was 3% higher than the 48.8% that held
stock in the 1998 survey. In fact, the level of stock ownership has been
increasing steadily for some time, and it picked up significantly in the
mid-1980s. Other more recent studies, however, have put the figure of
stock ownership in the United States even higher. A survey by the
Investment Company Institute and the Securities Industry Association in
January 2002 estimated that 52.7 million U.S. households and 84.3 million investors owned equities in individual stocks or mutual funds. It also
found the levels of ownership increased from its 1998 survey.[3] This
broadening of what has been dubbed "The Investor Class" contributed
significantly to U.S. savings and the bull market of the late 1990s.

The change has been attributed to a number of factors: the prolifera-
tion in the number of mutual funds and the increase in investment in
them, reforms to the way savings and investments are taxed, and an

emphasis on price stability by the U.S. Federal Reserve, which has resulted in lower interest rates and hence more savings.[4] Most of the growth, according to a congressional Joint Economic Committee study in April 2000, has come from retirement savings plans provided by companies, including individual retirement accounts (IRAs) and 401(k) plans. These allow employees to contribute a portion of their wages to a retirement account and, since the IRS issued rules regarding them in 1982, they have grown substantially. Another form of stock ownership that has contributed significantly to the growth in stock ownership is employee options plans.

Most people who invest in stocks fall into the baby boomer generation. According to a study by the Investment Company Institute and the Securities Industry Association in 2002, generation X investors (people born in 1965 or later) represented 25% of all equity investors, and baby boom generation investors (born between 1946 and 1964) accounted for 48%. Silent generation and GI generation investors (born between 1926 and 1945, and in 1925 or earlier, respectively) together represented 27% of equity owners. However, even though baby boomers are the biggest buyers of stocks, their portfolios are not worth as much as those held by silent generation and GI generation investors. However, ownership of dividend-yielding stocks is another matter. Overall, the Federal Reserve figures from 1998 show that around 17% of Americans received dividends from stock investments. Although dividend investors are often regarded as being senior citizens, they are not. According to these figures, 25.6 percent of American households headed by someone aged 65 or older received dividends in one form or another, according to the Federal Reserve figures from 1998. We say "one form or another" because this also means dividends from mutual funds and other investments, not necessarily direct holdings in stock.

In fact, most dividend investors are middle- to high-income earners. One analysis of the Federal Reserve data, by tax experts and authors Leonard E. Burman and David L. Gunter, shows that about 3.8% of families with incomes above $200,000 received 47% of all dividends, and families with incomes over $100,000 accounted for 72%. And how much did they receive? According to the same data, about 11% received more than $500 in dividends, and fewer than 9% received more than $1,000.[5]

DIVIDENDS ARE A VALUABLE FUTURE INCOME SOURCE

The fact that a quarter of American households headed by someone aged over 65 receive dividend income has very significant implications for the future. The fact is that America, as a nation, is aging. The percentage of the U.S. population aged 65 and over is rising rapidly. In 2000 the percentage of the U.S. population aged over 65 was 13%. However, that percentage has been forecast by the U.S. government to rise much further by 2030. This is in line with trends not only in other developed countries, but also in the world generally. The causes are varied and complex and relate to life expectancy rates, fertility rates, rates of suicide, infant mortality, accidental deaths, and a fall in mortality rates for diseases such as cardiovascular disease. Further, the life expectancy for both men and women at the age of 65 is rising (see Figure 2.3).

Although this means there are more people aged over 65 who can pay taxes, it also means there are more people who require income support, either in the form of pensions, their own savings, or other forms of income. The baby boomer generation has now begun to enter retirement age. This is becoming a greater problem for policy makers than it has been in the past because the figures show that Americans are more reliant on Social Security and pensions than asset income and earnings than they have been in the past (see Table 2.1 and Figure 2.4 and Figure 2.5).

Approximately 69% of the aged received Social Security benefits in 1962, whereas in 2001, 91% of the aged received them. According to government figures, most of the increased dependence on Social Security occurred in the 1960s. The proportion of the aged who received what the Social Security Administration calls "asset-related income" dropped in

FIGURE 2.3 LIFE EXPECTANCY IN THE UNITED STATES AT AGE 65

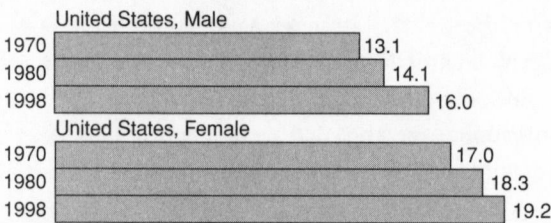

SOURCE: U.S. Census Bureau.

TABLE 2.1A   PERCENTAGE OF POPULATION AGED 65 AND
OLDER AND 85 AND OLDER, 1900 TO 2050,
ACTUAL (TABLE A) AND PROJECTED (TABLE B)

YEAR	65 +	85 +
1900	4.1	0.2
1910	4.3	0.2
1920	4.7	0.2
1930	5.4	0.2
1940	6.9	0.3
1950	8.2	0.4
1960	9.2	0.5
1970	9.9	0.7
1980	11.3	1.0
1990	12.6	1.2
2000	12.4	1.5

TABLE 2.1B

	65 + MIDDLE PROJECTION	65 + HIGH PROJECTION	85 + MIDDLE PROJECTION	85 + HIGH PROJECTION
2010	13.2	13.0	1.9	1.9
2020	16.5	15.9	2.1	2.1
2030	20.0	18.5	2.5	2.5
2040	20.5	18.3	3.8	3.5
2050	20.3	17.8	4.8	4.3

NOTE: Population projections are based upon the 1990 census and data refers to the resident
population.
SOURCE: U.S. Census Bureau.[6]

the 1990s from about two-thirds in the 1980s to about 55% in the 1990s.
It should be noted that this class of income also includes investments such
as property investment income, that is, rental income and income from
managed funds, and so on. The Federal Reserve's Annual Survey of Consumer Finances in 2000 showed that about one-quarter of families
headed by someone over age 65 reported earning dividends that year.

FIGURE 2.4   PEOPLE AGED 65 OR OLDER BY AGE GROUP
1900 TO 2050

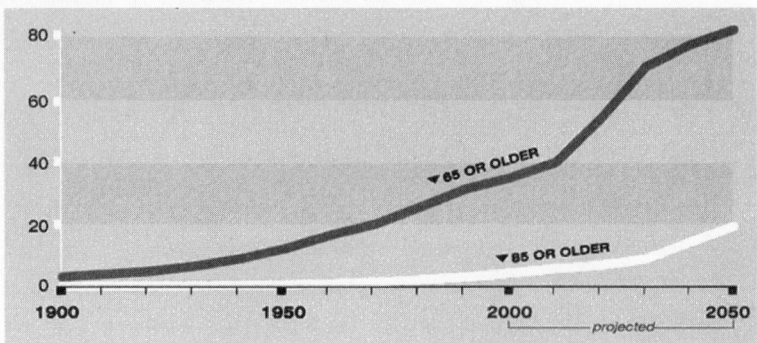

NOTE: Data for the years 2000 to 2050 are middle-series projections of the population.
REFERENCE POPULATION: These data refer to the resident population.
SOURCE: U.S. Census Bureau.

However, the Social Security figures show that there is a greater
dependence on Social Security and a falling dependence on other income
sources—to such a degree that dependence on Social Security among the
aged is now almost universal. The number of aged people receiving earnings (or salaries and wages) also dropped since the 1980s, from about 32%
to 22%, and the proportion of people getting pension income also
dropped. This reversal can be attributed to a number of factors, but the
decrease in average dividend yields from companies issuing dividends is
among them.

This situation should send alarm bells to policy makers, many of
whom are nevertheless very much aware of the pressure to provide Social
Security support. Not only is there greater dependence on Social Security,
but a number of studies have forecast that the aging of the population is
likely to result in a slowdown in the growth of number of people entering
the workforce, labor shortages, particularly in some industries, and slower
economic growth.[7]

Since fewer people in their retirement years are earning salaries and
pensions, income from other sources is what the aged need. This is where
dividends can play a more important role. Investors who invest in growth
stocks do so because they see their value rising over time. But time is
not as abundant for people aged over 65 as it is for younger investors, nor
is income.

FIGURE 2.5   CHANGE IN PERCENTAGE RECEIVING INCOME
FROM MAJOR SOURCES, SELECTED YEARS

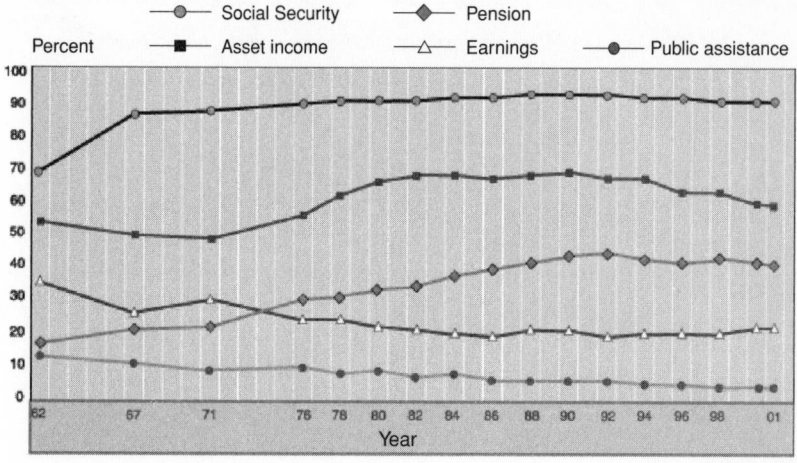

SOURCE: Social Security Administration.[8]

As society ages and there are more people aged over 65 looking for income such as dividends, this could have an impact on the way companies provide value to shareholders. Companies may be under greater pressure from investors to provide returns that they can depend on.

DIVIDENDS INDICATE STABILITY AND LOWER RISK

People like stability in their lives and investors like stability in their investment portfolios. Stability allows people to manage their lives effectively in the present and plan for the future. It thus allows investors to make projections. Arguably, the best way that companies can provide this stability is by consistently paying dividends. The payment of dividends tends to indicate that a company is less risky than other companies.

Mergent Inc. has many years experience of analyzing the benefits of dividend paying stocks. Bill Rogers, Manager of Equity Analysis at Mergent, has identified two particularly important aspects with regard to stability and risk:

As well as providing a steady cash flow to the investor, dividend stocks
have historically generated higher total returns than stocks that are

purchased principally for capital appreciation (commonly known as "growth stocks"). From December 31, 1974, through to August 31, 2004, large capitalized dividend stocks had an annualized return of 14.43% versus 12.28% for large capitalized growth stocks. However, of perhaps greatest interest to the investor is that this extra return has come with considerably less volatility (14.90% versus 16.81% for the growth stocks) as measured by standard deviation. This return premium also appears in mid-cap and small-cap stocks.

Secondly, we have found that companies that have a history of increasing their dividends on a regular basis provide the added benefit of shielding the investor's cash flows from the effects of inflation. This is especially true for companies whose dividends are growing at a rate higher than inflation.

DIVIDEND PAYMENTS LEAD TO GOOD CORPORATE MANAGEMENT

There is strong evidence to support the notion that when a company initiates or continues with a strategy of making regular dividend payments, the outcome is good corporate governance. Dividends are items that need to be included in cash flow projections for the quarter or year, and certainly a plan to increase dividends consecutively requires very close attention to cash flow and overall cash management. For most companies to maintain their payout ratios at stable levels, a regular dependable cash flow is required. This focus on cash leads to fine tuning in respect to corporate governance, according to a number of studies. One recent study, by Luis Correia da Silva, Marc Goergen, and Luc Renneboog in the United Kingdom, found a link between corporate control and dividend payouts, i.e., that companies with solid dividend payouts tend to have good controls in place and vice versa.[9]

HIGH-YIELD DIVIDEND COMPANIES ARE UNDERVALUED

Many investment specialists and fund managers believe that a high-yield dividend company or a dividend increase, particularly in a company consistently paying dividends, is an indication that the company is undervalued and is ready for price growth.

CHAPTER THREE

A New Tax Environment

Astute investors are always aware of not only their dividend yields and the rate at which their investments appreciate, but also the tax rates on their income. In most countries around the world the rate at which dividends are taxed and the tax rate on capital gains differ. This was certainly the case in the United States, up until 2003 when the law was changed.

The Jobs and Growth Tax Relief Reconciliation Act of 2003, which passed on May 23, 2003, covered a range of tax reforms and aimed to lower tax rates for individuals and businesses. The changes to the law had a number of intentions. On the broadest level, the changes were designed to stimulate the economy and it was expected they would give a boost to the stock market. On the individual investor level, the changes to dividend and capital gains taxes aimed to lower these taxes.

Prior to the passage of this act, dividends and capital gains were taxed at different rates, a situation which has had a big impact on the way companies in the United States distribute profits to shareholders. The tax on net capital gains was lower than the tax rates most investors paid on dividend income. Prior to the change, net capital gains on stocks held for more than one year attracted a maximum tax rate of 20%. The rate was just 10% for gains made by people in the 15% or 10% tax brackets. Further, stocks held for more than five years attracted even lower rates. It should be noted that several exceptions and exemptions applied to these rates.

FILING DIVIDEND INFORMATION WITH THE IRS

In the United States, most corporations use the IRS Form 1099-DIV, Dividends and Distributions, to show the distributions during the year.

However, more importantly for people investing for income from dividends, as mentioned previously, most dividends were subject to double taxation. Dividends are the proceeds of a corporation's profits—profits that have already been taxed before being distributed to shareholders. The more profits a company makes, the more tax it pays. After it pays its company tax, there is money left over to distribute (or reinvest in the company, depending on the company's strategy). The income distributed to shareholders was not, until the changes in the law, treated any differently than most other forms of income. Thus, the tax people paid on their dividends depended on their income bracket. Investors in the top income bracket, for example, paid 38.6% on the dividend income they received. Of course, people in lower tax brackets paid lower rates.

The fact that the money made from selling a stock was taxed at a lower rate than the money made from holding it and receiving dividend income not only created a substantial disincentive for companies to build value other ways for shareholders, but it contributed to the popularity of day trading. This was especially the case because many investors in the stock market were people in the top tax brackets.

CHANGES TO THE WAY
DIVIDENDS ARE TAXED

After much debate, Congress approved legislation which effectively increased the after-tax income investors receive from investments in stocks. The new laws have lowered the taxable rate on income from most dividend stocks to 15%. Those investors who would otherwise have been taxed at a regular rate of 10% or 15% are now taxed at just 5%. As a bonus, the cuts were retroactive to January 1, 2003, and apply to ordinary dividends received between then and December 31, 2008. There is a catch to these changes, however. The reduced rates for dividends end at the end of 2008.

In the meantime, the law also changed the capital gains rate, lowering the rate on sale or disposition of stocks after May 5, 2003, to the same 15% and 5% rates. Again, it should be noted that there are exceptions and exemptions. To qualify for the 15% or 5% rates, the dividends must be qualified dividends, as defined by the IRS, the dividends must have been paid by a U.S. corporation or a qualified foreign corporation, and stocks must have been held for certain specified holding periods.

QUALIFIED DIVIDENDS

The Internal Revenue Code at the time of writing defines dividends as distributions made from current or accumulated profits and earnings. According to many tax professionals, this means interest from some investment funds that are not generally referred to as dividends could be eligible for qualified dividend income relief. It also means, however, that some other forms of income, such as credits paid to insurance policyholders, for example, may not be eligible. The exact definition is outlined by the IRS, not by what *is* a qualified dividend, but what is not. Table 3.1 shows the IRS explanation of what is *not* a qualified dividend.

In terms of defining a qualified corporation, it should be noted that dividends from shares held in companies in other countries are normally treated by the IRS as dividend income as well. They are subject to tax in the United States as long as they are "qualified foreign corporations."

TABLE 3.1   IRS EXPLANATION OF WHAT IS NOT
            A QUALIFIED DIVIDEND

CATEGORY	IRS EXPLANATION
Capital gains	Capital gain distributions.
Some income funds	Dividends paid on deposits with mutual savings banks, cooperative banks, credit unions, U.S. building and loan associations, U.S. savings and loan associations, federal savings and loan associations, and similar financial institutions. These amounts are reportable as interest income.
Tax-exempt organizations	Dividends from a corporation that is a tax-exempt organization or farmer's cooperative during the corporation tax year in which the dividends were paid or during the corporation's previous tax year.
Employee stock plans	Dividends paid by a corporation on employer securities that are held on the date of record by an employee stock ownership plan (ESOP) maintained by that corporation.
Similar stocks	Dividends on any share of stock to the extent that the shareholder is obligated (whether under a short sale or otherwise) to make related payments for positions in substantially similar or related property.
Payments in lieu	Payments in lieu of dividends, but only if the shareholder knows or has reason to know that the payments are not qualified dividends.

These are defined as companies incorporated in the United States, companies in countries with which the United States has a tax treaty, a list of which is published by the IRS on its website,[1] or companies whose stocks are tradable on one of the following securities markets in the United States:

- The New York Stock Exchange
- The NASDAQ Stock Market
- The American Stock Exchange

- The Boston Stock Exchange
- The Cincinnati Stock Exchange
- The Chicago Stock Exchange
- The Philadelphia Stock Exchange
- The Pacific Exchange

One of the most popular dividend investments is the real estate investment trust (REIT). However, these trusts are the subject of special tax legislation. One of the features of the legislation is that REITs generally do not pay corporate taxes, so dividends from the majority of REITs will continue to be taxed at a maximum rate of 35%—nevertheless a drop from 38.6%. However, according to the National Association of Real Estate Investment Trusts, about one-third of all dividends handed out by REITs will qualify for the lower 15% capital gains rate in 2003. The association has advised that REIT dividends will qualify for the lower rate under the following circumstances:

- When the individual taxpayer is subject to a lower scheduled income tax rate
- When a REIT makes a capital gains distribution (15% maximum tax rate)
- When a REIT distributes dividends received from a taxable REIT subsidiary or other corporation (15% maximum tax rate)
- When, as permitted, a REIT pays corporate taxes and retains earnings (15% maximum tax rate)

It's best to consult a tax professional about which income is subject to the new lower taxes and which is not.

HOLDING PERIODS

The holding periods differ for different types of stocks, but for ordinary stock, according to the IRS, "Investors must have held a stock for more than 60 days during the 121-day period that begins 60 days before the ex-dividend date." The ex-dividend date is the next day after the declaration of a dividend. When determining the number of days a stock is held, the IRS includes the day on which the stock is disposed, but not the day it was purchased. In respect to preferred stocks, the stock must be held for more than 90 days during the 181-day period that begins 90 days before the ex-dividend date if the dividends are from a stock held for 366 days or more.

This may sound a little confusing, so the IRS has offered some examples to clarify the differences. The following three examples have been published on the IRS website.

Example 1

You bought 5,000 shares of XYZ Corp. common stock on July 1, 2003. XYZ Corp. paid a cash dividend of 10 cents per share. The ex-dividend date was July 9, 2003. Your Form 1099-DIV from XYZ Corp. shows $500 in box 1a (ordinary dividends) and in box 1b (qualified dividends). However, you sold the 5,000 shares on August 4, 2003. You held your shares of XYZ Corp. for only 34 days of the 121-day period (from July 2, 2003, through August 4, 2003). The 121-day period began on May 10, 2003 (60 days before the ex-dividend date) and ended on September 7, 2003. You have no qualified dividends from XYZ Corp. because you did not hold the XYZ stock for more than 60 days.

Example 2

Assume the same facts as in Example 1 except that you bought the stock on July 8, 2003 (the day before the ex-dividend date), and you sold the stock on September 9, 2003. You held the stock for 63 days (from July 9, 2003, through September 9, 2003). The $500 of qualified dividends shown in box 1b of your Form 1099-DIV is all qualified dividends because you held the stock for 61 days of the 121-day period (from July 9, 2003, through September 7, 2003).

Example 3

You bought 10,000 shares of ABC Mutual Fund common stock on July 1, 2003. ABC Mutual Fund paid a cash dividend of 10 cents per share.

The ex-dividend date was July 9, 2003. The ABC Mutual Fund advises you that the portion of the dividend eligible to be treated as qualified dividends equals 2 cents per share. Your Form 1099-DIV from ABC Mutual Fund shows total ordinary dividends of $1,000 and qualified dividends of $200. However, you sold the 10,000 shares on August 4, 2003. You have no qualified dividends from ABC Mutual Fund because you did not hold the ABC Mutual Fund stock for more than 60 days.

THE IMPLICATIONS FOR INVESTORS

The changes to the law have big implications for the way companies return value to shareholders. A significant disincentive for companies to pay dividends and, hence for investors to invest in dividend stocks, has been eliminated. This is particularly the case for higher-income investors, many of whom are active stock market players. The tax changes mean that investing in dividend stocks is not only more attractive, but also that companies will almost certainly change the way they look at dividends in the future.

There is strong evidence that companies have already taken note. According to the American Shareholders' Association, there was a jump in what it calls "favorable" dividend activity after the passage of the legislation. It estimated that in the 12 months from June 2003 to May 2004, the number of companies in the S&P 500 which increased and initiated dividend payments was 55.2% higher than the number of companies which did so between June 2002 and May 2003. Anheuser-Busch (NYSE: BUD) and Qualcomm (NASDAQ: QCOM) have actually attributed their increases in dividends to the tax cuts.

In a study on the 100 days after the passage of the legislation, the association also claimed that the tax relief had had a greater impact on the market than the capital gains reductions in 1997. Although the previous tax reforms certainly furthered the interests of individual shareholders, there is no doubt that the new laws have had some effect. A number of companies initiated dividends for the first time—and these include technology companies that have been "growth" companies.

Since more stocks will now be paying dividends, the changes encourage corporate management to allocate a greater proportion of a company's earnings to paying them. Companies now view dividends as a more viable way to build shareholder value. There are indications that this may be more the case since the changes. For example, Best Buy Co Inc (NYSE: BBY) declared a cash dividend of 40 cents per common share in October 2003 while at the same time announcing a share buyback. Similarly, Yum! Brands Inc. (NYSE: YUM) in May 2004 announced the company's first-ever quarterly dividend of 10 cents per share of common stock and a share buyback. A dividend taking place at the same time as a share buyback would have been very uncommon under the old tax law.

In the future, more investors may even begin to expect dividends, even in some cases when companies did not pay them previously. The lower rates should also have an effect on day or short-term trading. Previously, short-term trading was effectively rewarded with lower tax rates, but now short-term and long-term trading will be at similar tax rates.

It should be kept in mind that the legislation is primarily intended for individuals; that is, dividends paid to corporations do not attract the lower rate. Corporations, such as mutual funds and other investment companies, do not get the benefit of lower dividend tax rates. This has implications not so much for individual investors, but for dividend-paying companies whose shareholders are mainly institutional investors. These companies are not likely to change their dividend policy just because tax rates have changed because their institutional shareholders cannot expect any tax benefit.

CHAPTER FOUR

Dividend Stocks Make a Comeback

In the 1980s and 1990s investor attention focused on making money through capital appreciation, with the late 1990s delivering annual returns of up to 30%. In March 2000, the U.S. stock markets were at a peak but as the year went on, the party that has become known as the dot-com boom began to fizzle. The environment began to change and many markets shuddered as investors lost confidence in many of the technology-based companies that had captured so much attention. As expectations failed to materialize, stock prices began to fall; overall in the year 2000 the NASDAQ Market Index declined by nearly 40% after several years of spectacular growth. A series of adverse events followed. In 2002 a wave of accounting scandals emerged in the United States; a number of leading companies admitted to misstating their accounts, in several cases to the tune of billions of dollars. Major companies such as Enron and Worldcom subsequently became involved in fraud cases and even names such as Freddie Mac, which had previously been seen as staples of the economy and beyond such scandals, later admitted irregularities in their accounts. The situation was further worsened by disappointing economic figures and extraordinary adverse events such as the terrorist attacks on the World Trade Center and the Pentagon.

In bull markets people tend to think short term and can see that, even though there may be short-term fluctuations, their stocks are appreciating in value. However, when investors feel that expected returns are not going to come to fruition, they exit. Thus, as capital flowed out of equities in late 2000, individual and institutional investors began to look elsewhere. Many turned to other markets—property and fixed income, for example—a normal progression that follows a downturn in the economic cycle.

In falling markets, such as in 2000 and 2001, companies tend to look at ways to maintain investor interest and hence create shareholder value, apart from share buybacks and moves which drive up their share price. In such environments, investors tend to turn to dividend stocks. The key attraction is that they provide certainty, and in an uncertain market in which pessimism or low expectations prevail, certainty is a valued commodity.

Over the last few years, more and more companies have issued dividends and more and more companies have begun to issue dividends, some never having done so. As a result, average dividend yields, which fell in the 1990s, have begun to creep up. Some companies have issued special dividends, that is, a special bonus to shareholders designed to send a positive message to current and potential investors.

WHY THERE WAS GREATER FOCUS ON DIVIDENDS IN THE PAST

Although dividend stocks now attract more attention, they are certainly not a new phenomenon. Dividend stocks were, to many people of previous generations, the only stocks. When people bought stocks, they did so in order to get the income stocks provided. General Electric has paid a dividend each quarter for over 100 years. The fact that it pays dividends is one of the main reasons many investors have bought its shares. If it stopped paying them, investors would be horrified.

To put this discussion into perspective, let's take a step back in time. It is clear from a number of perspectives that the emphasis on dividends has subsided in the last few decades. The last three years, particularly, have seen poor returns for shareholders. The real U.S. stock market return on an annual basis from the beginning of 2001 to the end of 2003 was −2.5%. This compares to, according to various estimates, between 12% and 14% in the 1990s and 2% to 3% in the 1980s.[1]

The environment of the last two decades differed from previous decades in a number of ways. First, in the past dividends contributed a much greater proportion of the total return of stocks to shareholders. Since 1926 dividends have represented 43% of the total return of the S&P. In contrast, in the two decades between 1980 and 2000, dividends represented around 20% of the total return of the S&P.

Second, the 1990s were also a historical anomaly when it comes to the number of companies that paid dividends. As of 1999, 20% of companies in Standard & Poor's 500 Composite Index had paid dividends, compared to 40% two decades earlier. Another study in 2001 found that 20.8% of nonfinancial and nonutility companies listed in the NYSE, AMEX, and NASDAQ exchanges in 1999 paid dividends compared to 66.5% of companies listed on those exchange in 1978.[2]

Third, the average dividend yield, or the average dividend paid by companies, was higher earlier in the twentieth century. From 1911 to 1920 the average annual dividend yield of the stock market was around 6.1%. In the 1920s it averaged around 5.2% a year. A number of data sources show that average dividend yields have been falling for some time, both for the overall U.S. stock market and the S&P 500.

More recently, in the 1970s and 1980s, average yields dropped to around 4.1% and then down to 2.1% in the 1990s. Throughout the 1990s, dividend yields continued to fall, reaching a low of 1% in 2000.[3] Since then, yields have crept up slightly, but the average is still not where it used to be decades ago. Even though there are many companies that provide yields up to 10, 12, and 15%, at present a yield of around 1.5 to 2% is average and 4% is good. A quick analysis of the dividend yields of all the S&P 500 companies shows the average as of August 25, 2004, was 1.53%.

WHY INTEREST IN DIVIDEND INVESTING SUBSIDED

The fall in the number of public companies paying dividends in the 1980s and 1990s has been attributed to a number of factors. They range from political reasons to the taxation environment. The decrease has been attributed by some to a rise in the number of companies that have never paid dividends. These companies tend to be newer and smaller companies with low earnings and larger investments relative to earnings—companies which tend to be still in their growth phases. The number of new firms listed on the key NYSE, AMEX, and NASDAQ exchanges over the last 10 years has risen dramatically—information technology (IT) stocks and other technology-related companies like biotechnology firms are just some of them.

The drop in dividend yields from previous decades to the 1990s and, more recently in this decade, has been attributed also to a change in many companies' dividend policies and a change in the thinking of the day. Until the late 1970s and early 1980s, most companies paid dividends. But, during the long bull market (1982 to 2000), emphasis shifted toward capital appreciation through rising share prices. This shift was due at least in part to the popularity of share buybacks and the way dividends were taxed (at least until 2003).

At the beginning of the 1970s, popular finance theory taught that management should not focus on dividends and increasing dividends because earnings would be taxed twice, once at the corporate level and once at the investor level. So it became more and more accepted that it was better use of the capital to buy back shares and support growth long term and that the stock would respond to that and that the investor would make money from increased value. So that was the mentality that management, analysts, and academics possessed from the late 1970s pretty much up to the change of the tax laws in 2003.

SHARE BUYBACKS CAPTIVATED ATTENTION

Share buybacks were favorable for a number of reasons. They still are popular and are employed as a good way to return shareholder value. The problem is that there are pitfalls and many of these have not been realized until recently. Share buybacks can be initiated in two ways: by tender offer (in which shareholders are given a tender offer and have the option to submit some or all of their shares, usually at a higher price than they paid for them) or by open market buybacks (in which companies buy the shares available for sale on the open market).

When stock prices are rising for some time, say for 3, 5, or 10 years, this usually means the investors who decide to sell their shares back to the company make money. In the course of doing this, the number of shares available for purchase on the market at any one time is reduced. This often has the effect of increasing the share value for investors who hold the shares. The effect is sometimes exaggerated when companies announce that they intend to buy back a large number of shares. Reducing the number of shares on the market also has the effect, often, of increasing the company's earnings-per-share ratio. Even if a company's revenue is not growing, a share buyback should increase this ratio, giving the impression it is more profitable.

The reasons for companies initiating share buybacks in the 1980s and 1990s were (and still are) varied but followed a common thread. The major reasons cited in one survey of chief financial officers of public firms listed on the NYSE in the late 1970s were "a good investment of excess cash" and "use in employee bonus or stock option plans."[4] In another survey of chief financial officers in 1989 the two most important motives cited were "to acquire undervalued stock" and "to signal investors that managers are confident about the company's future."[5] Many companies give these reasons when declaring dividends. When People's Bank reported its twelfth consecutive annual dividend increase in April 2004, the company's president and CEO John A. Klein said it was a "strong indicator of our confidence in the bank's future direction." Other studies have found that the most important trigger to initiating a share repurchase have been "low stock price" and that a decision to issue a dividend has been related to a desire to boost it up.[6]

The problem is that share buybacks are not guaranteed. The outcome is not predictable at all. In fact there are many companies whose share prices have fallen following a share buyback announcement, but more on this later.

More broadly, there are other reasons why dividend companies lost their shine, one of which was a long bull market. The 1980s and 1990s saw one of the longest bull markets in history. This was assisted by, and also coincided with, the emergence of new technologies such as advanced telecommunications and the Internet, the fragmentation of media, far-reaching changes to the regulatory environment, and changes to tax structures.

THE BULL MARKET OF THE 1980s TO 2000

In the three decades after the Vietnam War the world went through a period of almost unprecedented uninterrupted political stability as well as a number of significant reforms to the U.S. financial system. Throughout the 1980s and 1990s many markets were deregulated and new opportunities for large and small investors were opened. The high inflation that was seen in the 1970s has also been credited with driving many investors back to the stock market, as many individuals' savings accounts were eroded away. The economic growth that ensued provided the right fuel for these changes to take effect.

The 1980s in particular saw the wide-spread introduction of computers—into business, industry, and eventually individuals' homes. This led not only to innovations in telecommunications and media, but to the introduction of new technologies into a range of manufacturing and service industries. Of course, the last few years of the last decade saw the emergence of the Internet as a powerful tool that would impact on and change virtually every industry in every country on the planet.

The Internet and faster communications bought more information to more people more quickly, and empowering individual and institutional investors, expanding the number of investors, and changing the nature of investing itself. It also led to emergence of a whole new breed of companies, a lot of which were computer-, software Internet-, and information technology-based stocks.

The NASDAQ exchange is a monument to the wide-ranging developments that shared the last few decades. Take the NASDAQ 100. It is an index that covers a range of major industry groups including computer hardware and software, telecommunications, retail/wholesale trade, and biotechnology companies, but not financial services companies. It is an index that didn't exist 25 years ago.

Many of the computer and software technology giants on the index have leap-frogged their way into history and rank among some of the world's largest companies. They include companies such as Microsoft, Intel, Qualcomm, and Cisco. However, the NASDAQ also includes other technology stocks such as Amgen, one of the world's leading biotechnology companies. It is, by its very nature, an index of newer companies. At the end of the 1990s, growth was not a concept unfamiliar to many people.

THE DOT-COM DAZE

In the 1990s, there was hype and optimism about technology and communications-related stocks, with many dot-com stocks providing three-digit returns and seemingly soaring higher and higher. How many of us were blinded by the lights? Most of these companies—as with similar companies launched on the world's leading exchanges—were based around the assumption that the Internet would change our lives, which, to a large degree, it has. There were also a lot of lessons to be learned, however, not only about investing in the new breed of companies but how the Internet and information technology would evolve. Of course, as it turned out, the assumptions upon which many business models were based were flawed. Essentially, the demand for many companies' products and services was yet to be established.

Stories of young entrepreneurs who got rich quickly captivated public attention. Many made their money by establishing companies that attracted venture capital and went public. The company shares soared through the roof, and accordingly, the entrepreneurs made a fortune, either by leveraging the value of their new-found portfolio or, in some cases, cashing in their shares. Who wouldn't want to invest in companies just like these? However, many companies were based on business models whose projections were untested. They included projected Internet adoption rates, projected revenues from online advertising, projected license fees, and projected demand. There was little shortage of believe and faith; unfortunately, there was a massive shortfall in reality. There are a number of lessons that came out of it all. One is that projections are projections and forecasts and forecasts.

THE DAY TRADING PHENOMENON

Another development that characterized the turn of the century was the emergence of the day trading phenomena. The Internet brought with it the fragmentation of media. Television—and cable television after it—brought a new medium for people to get news and information in the 1960s, 1970s, and 1980s. In the 1990s, the Internet split the channels through which people get news and information even further, diversifying the way information was presented. A plethora of stock market news, information, and data sources flooded the market. At the same time, the cost of personal computers plummeted. The number of Internet connections in households skyrocketed, not only in the United States but in other countries with stock markets that interact heavily with the markets in the United States.

2003 USHERS IN A CHANGE IN MOOD

The end of the last century saw, to a large degree, the end of a party. As discussed, fewer leading companies paid dividends, overall returns were down, and dividend yields were down. However, as sure as night follows day, the markets turned around. In 2003 dividend stocks began to attract attention. The tax cuts which came into effect in May 2003 and lowered the rate at which dividends were taxed had an immediate impact on the market.

A number of large companies increased their dividends substantially and other companies that had never issued dividends did so for the first time. In 2003, according to the American Shareholders' Association, 1,630 companies increased their dividends, which was a 14.4% increase from 2002 and a 20% increase from 2001. The number of S&P 500 companies that increased their dividends was up 43%.[7]

In 2004, a number of very high profile companies set the pace with significant dividend increases in 2003. Previously mentioned Microsoft, for example, doubled its dividend from 8 cents a year to 16 cents in September 2003, while other notable increases included Citigroup's jump from 20 cents a share in May 2003 to 35 cents in August. Energy pipeline company Kinder Morgan Inc (NYSE: KMI) increased its dividend by 167% and Waste Management Inc (NYSE: WMI) announced a raise in its annual payout from 1 cent a year to 75 cents, citing its "confidence in the company's cash generating ability." Wells Fargo increased its dividend by more than 50%, saying "in view of the strength and consistency of our results, as well as the recent changes in tax laws, we are evaluating our dividend policy." For a detailed list of recent dividend actions of dividend-achieving companies as of September 2004, see the Appendix.

Dividend Yields Are Up Again

Since 2000, at the height of the dot-com boom, dividend yields—although still at low levels relative to the 1920s, 1930s, and 1940s—have been creeping up again. Based on one source of credible data, average dividend yields of U.S. stocks in 2003 are up, slightly, to 1.7% from 1.6% in 2002 and 1.2% in 2001. Furthermore, Standard & Poor's expected a 9.8% for 2004.

More Companies Increase Dividends on a Consecutive Basis

In addition to more companies issuing dividends and slightly higher dividend yields, there are strong indications that more companies are now increasing their dividends on a yearly consecutive basis. An analysis of the dividend data of leading U.S. companies reveals that 2003 was the year in which a significant turnaround took place.

In the last 10 years, the number of companies that consistently increased their dividends on a quarterly basis fell at the beginning of 1999, as many companies became subject to the effects of a downturn in the equities markets and suffered from falling revenues and tighter cash flows. In 1994, according to data from Mergent, which tracks the dividends and dividend payment records of leading U.S. and Canadian companies, 31 companies were added to its index of consistent dividend achievers and 22 companies were removed. In 1995, 21 companies were added to the index and an equal 21 were removed. In 1999, just 17 companies were added and 33 companies were removed. This negative trend continued throughout 2000, 2001, and 2002, but in 2003 things changed: the number of companies increasing their dividends rose again. A total of 35 companies were added to the index and 31 were dropped, indicating that the market has again turned around. In fact, Mergent's 2004 Dividend Achievers

FIGURE 4.1 NUMBER OF COMPANIES ADDED AND
DROPPED FROM MERGENT'S INDEX OF
CONSISTENT DIVIDEND ACHIEVING
COMPANIES, 1994–2004

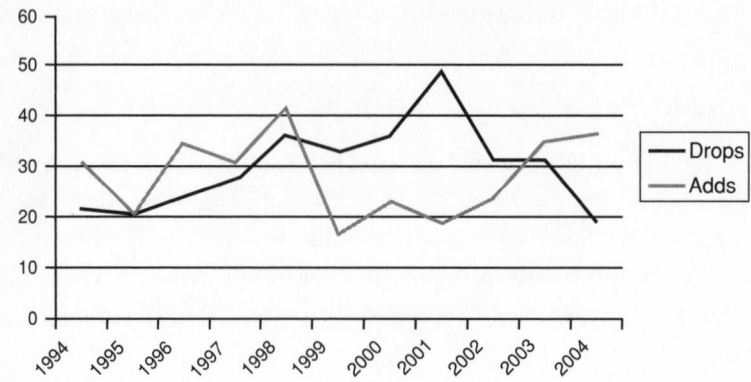

SOURCE: Mergent Inc.

Index includes 303 stocks—a net rise of 17 companies—up from 286 companies in 2003. This net increase is the largest in more than 10 years. It would seem that, again, more companies are not only recognizing the importance of issuing dividends on a consistent basis but are able to do so (see Figure 4.1).

DIVIDEND FUNDS COME BACK IN VOGUE

A new era in dividend payments by leading companies has ushered in a renewed mood in organized dividend investing. Higher dividend payments by more companies, combined with higher dividend yields, have driven up interest in dividend funds once again. In the heady days of the 1990s, fund managers were written off as boring, unimaginative, and risk averse, but now they are many investors' best friends. Even though many dividend funds lost money in the 1990s, these days it is not uncommon to see dividend funds providing average annual returns of between 8% and 9%. With many fixed-income returns providing between 4% and 5%, dividend funds have come back in vogue. A number of fund managers have launched new dividend funds in the last year, and at least three have gone public.

These include two funds launched by BlackRock–Dividend Achievers Trust (NYSE: BDV) and the Strategic Dividend Achievers Trust (NYSE: BDT). The first was launched on December 23, 2003, and raised $720 million in its IPO. Both are closed-end funds and focus solely on dividend achieving stocks in Mergent's Index of Dividend Achievers (this index is quoted on the AMEX under ticker symbol DAA). The latter launched on March 30, 2004, and has a slightly different composition but follows the same basic investment strategy.

Both trusts aim to provide both current income and long-term capital growth and comprise investments in stocks that have had at least 10 consecutive years of dividend payment growth. In mid-2004 the BlackRock Dividend Achievers Trust had a yield of 6.13% while the BlackRock Strategic Dividend Achievers Trust had a yield of 6.34%. Mergent's proprietary Indicated Annual Dividend projected dividends of $0.90 for both funds showing that such yields will likely be sustained in the future.

Similarly, the Dreman/Claymore Dividend and Income Fund, managed by Dreman Value Management LLC, which launched on the NYSE on January 28, 2004, under the symbol DCS, plans to invest mostly in dividend-paying stocks. Its stated objective is to provide "current income with a secondary investment objective of capital appreciation, when consistent with current income." The IPO was co-led by Merrill Lynch & Co. and A. G. Edwards & Sons, Inc. and raised $810 million. In mid-2004 the fund had a 7.13% return, again Mergent's Indicated Annual Dividend showed a projected dividend of $1.30 and thus sustainability. Some of the funds focus more on particular industries. The John Hancock Tax-Advantaged Dividend Income Fund (NYSE: HDT), which went public on February, 27, 2004, holds more than 50% of its investments in utility companies.

WHY THE CHANGE?

THE IMPACT OF NATIONAL AND WORLD EVENTS

The stock markets heavily interact and are arguably at the epicenter of the increasingly globalizing world. Certainly the market has reacted poorly to adverse world events over the last three years. The World Trade Center attack of September 11, 2001, and subsequent terrorist attacks such as those in Bali and Madrid, sent shivers through the market. In each case, the market has rebounded, but it is the fear of what could happen to the market in the future that has left a legacy in the mind of investors.

COOKED BOOKS SIZZLED THE MARKET

Such events took place at a time when financial scandals involving "cooked books," imprudent management excesses, and audit failures were also popping the investor confidence balloon. A number of high-profile corporate collapses, such as WorldCom and Enron, were instrumental in eroding confidence. Such scandals have shaken investor confidence and alerted investors to the degree to which companies can lie and get away with it. High-profile corporate collapses of this nature seldom do much to boost confidence, and a lack of confidence is all that it takes for investors to make the decision to sell or not to buy.

SHARE BUYBACKS DISCREDITED

Share buybacks have lost their shine to some degree. Many experienced investors, including Berkshire Hathaway chairman Warren Buffett, have recognized the value of share buybacks in the right circumstances. Buffett, in his 1984 letter to shareholders, commented that share buybacks when stocks were undervalued were "encouraging and rewarding" because they not only increased the value immediately but because they showed management was "given to actions that enhance the wealth of shareholders, rather than to actions that expand management's domain." There have been many companies whose value has risen substantially and many investors who have made large windfalls in share buybacks.

The big drawback with share buybacks is that the outcome is not guaranteed. There are pitfalls and there have been losers. The reality is that companies do not always wind up buying back the amount of shares they say they will. Also, there are plenty of cases in which companies have announced buybacks and, rather than enjoying rising stock prices after the event, their stock prices have tumbled. This can lead to losses for investors who keep their shares or only sell some of their shares in the buyback. The bottom line is that, like any purchase, companies have to be able to afford it. If they can't (and analysts and investors can see it), the market's response is not likely to be favorable. Of course, there are plenty of companies out there that don't act sensibly. They gamble that their actions will be viewed as positive and risk a little more than they should.

There are a number of other issues that have emerged with share buybacks, particularly over the last two decades, which have contributed to a great deal of skepticism about their usefulness in creating value for shareholders. One issue is that if a company buys back its shares, the IRS has a set of rules to determine whether the redemption of stock will be treated as a dividend or as a capital gain. Capital gain treatment may result, particularly if there is a "substantially disproportionate redemption of stock." There is also a general rule that redemptions that are not essentially equivalent to a dividend will be treated as capital gains. Additionally, in some cases, the companies would have been better off spending the money they planned to spend on share buybacks on giving dividends to their investors. There is some evidence that initiating a share buyback is more costly than issuing dividends.[8]

There has also been criticism that stock repurchases are great for the company executives that issue them. They tend to own substantial shareholdings in the companies they manage and, with the benefit of inside information about the company's future directions, are in a better position to profit as a result. This is not just a cynical accusation: studies have confirmed that there tends to be increased insider activity when stock repurchases are announced.[9] One of the other issues that has emerged is that the stock option plans many companies initiated at earlier stages to provide employee benefits have turned out to be very costly. When employees hold stock for 10 or even 20 years, the value of their shareholdings usually rises—in some cases quite substantially. The cost to companies of buying those shareholdings back off their employees (or former employees) can be very costly.

Skepticism over share buybacks is only one reason that dividends have made a comeback. A change to tax laws is the other, and that is dealt with in the next chapter.

Conclusion

Many investors, large and small, are still licking their wounds from investments that went bad during the dot-com years. Investors lost money and many saw the high risk involved in investing in fast-growing stocks come to fruition. Despite the fact many people made a lot of money in the dot-com boom, a lot of everyday investors lost money, or at the very least, failed to make it. The mom and dad investors may not have the clout of the big players in the market—the institutional investors—but they represent the bulk of it. While the dot-com phenomena sizzled along, many other traditional companies were written off as uninteresting.

CHAPTER FIVE

The Evidence Is In: Dividend Stocks Really Do Perform Better

I f you are investing in the market for a quick return, then the stock you choose to buy might be different than if you were taking a longer-term approach. If you are looking at the stock market to provide returns and income, then it is critical to consider your goals. Short-term or long-term? High-risk or low-risk? These are critical questions to answer before you start; otherwise investment in equities is nothing more than a wait-and-see gamble.

It just so happens that in terms of returns, dividend-paying stocks perform better over longer periods of time. In this respect they are a little like property. To get the full benefit, you should hold the investment over 5, 10 or 20 years. Picking the winners over the longer term (or shorter term) really requires knowledge and understanding. When you have those, you can employ a strategy.

DIVIDEND STOCKS PERFORM BETTER OVER TIME

It is a common misconception that most of the returns to investors who invest in stocks have come from capital growth. However, since 1926 nearly half of the 10.3% annual stock market return has come from dividends and dividend reinvestment.[1] As an example, over the past 70 years, ending December 31, 2002, dividends contributed almost 40% of the average annual return of stocks on the S&P 500 Composite Index.

There are a number of formal studies that have found dividend stocks provide higher returns. For example, one study of monthly returns by S&P 500 companies over 31 years found that dividend-paying companies significantly outperformed non-dividend-paying firms by 0.37% per month. The sample of companies used in the study was based on returns in 217 months during which the S&P 500 had a positive return (what were defined as *up markets*) and 155 months where it did not (defined as *down markets*). The study mentioned earlier by University of Georgia Professor Kathleen Fuller and Babson College Professor Michael Goldstein, found similar results for other periods examined, namely from January 1970 to December 1979, January 1980 to December 1989, and January 1990 to December 2000.[2]

Although stock prices tend to fluctuate more wildly, dividend returns tend to be more consistent, providing returns more silently but surely over time. As such, it's not a surprise that when the market is bearish, dividend stocks outperform their non-dividend-paying counterparts. The study above, for example, found that dividend-paying companies provided 0.9% more return than non-dividend-paying companies during down markets. It is at these times that investors turn their attention away from growth stocks and toward other alternatives. Overall, in the just over three decades examined by the above study, the difference between dividend-paying firms and non-dividend-paying firms was more than 20 times larger in down markets than in up markets.

The interesting thing is, however, that even in up markets, stocks held in dividend companies can still provide better returns that non-dividend-paying stocks. This study again found that (over the particular period examined, at least) dividend stocks were returning 0.16% more than non-dividend-paying companies during up markets. Although this obviously depends on the state of the market at the time and the time period examined, it suggests that dividend stocks are in the background performing for their shareholders, while most attention is focused on stocks whose share prices are rising. The simple reason is that most people are captivated by the possibilities of their stocks doubling or tripling over short periods of time and most people sell and buy much more frequently in times like these.

DIVIDEND COMPANIES CAN OUTPERFORM MAJOR INDEXES

Formal studies are one thing, but they are not necessarily conclusive, you say. Let's consider dividend stocks against major indices. We have mentioned Mergent's dividend index—arguably one the most recognized indices of dividend stocks around. Its core large-cap index tracks companies that have consistently increased their dividends. An analysis of these companies and their dividend history shows that these stocks as a whole outperformed both the S&P 500 and Dow Jones Industrials over a long-term basis. Mergent has a number of indices, including indices of large-cap, mid-cap, NASDAQ, Canadian, and American Depository Receipts companies, and we go into more detail a little later about the composition of these.

In respect to the index of large-cap companies, an analysis reveals that these companies outperformed the S&P 500 by more than 1.5% per year on average from 1993 to 2002. Dividend-paying companies are not only as good an investment as the S&P 500 stocks, but they are better! Given that most investors invest in the larger companies, that is, the companies listed in the S&P 500, most investors would have done better to have invested in companies in the index Mergent created. For the 10 years ended April 30, 2004, the annualized total returns were as shown in Table 5.1 and Figure 5.1.

TABLE 5.1   TOTAL RETURN KEY INDICES,
            APRIL 1994–2004

INDEX	TOTAL RETURN, %
Mergent's Large-Cap Dividend Achievers	14.88
Dow Jones Industrial Average	13.00
S&P 500	11.36

SOURCE: Mergent Inc.

What this translates to, of course, is more income. In other words, if you had invested solely in Mergent's index of large-cap dividend, achieving companies at the beginning of 1993, you would have made about 19% more money than if you had invested in just S&P 500 companies. As Figure 5.2, shows, that's $7,399!

FIGURE 5.1   DIVIDEND ACHIEVERS TOTAL RETURN
             VERSES S&P RETURNS OVER 10 YEARS
             (BASED ON MARKET CAPITALIZATION)

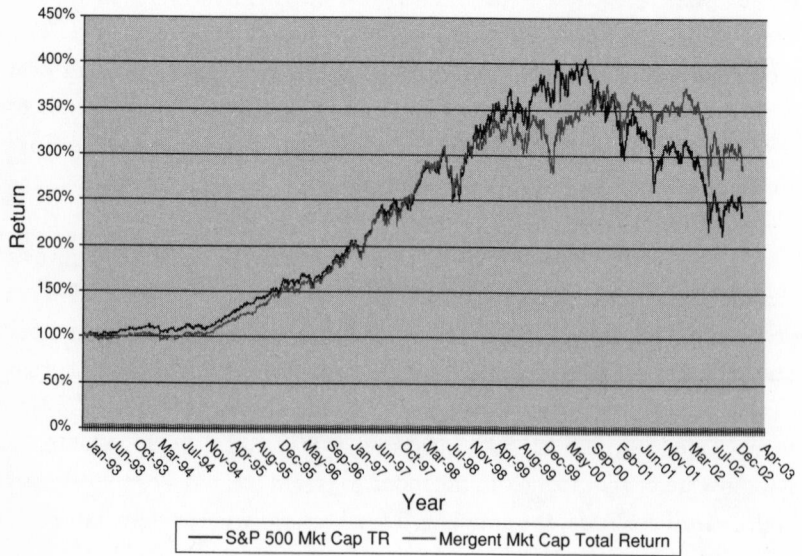

SOURCE: Mergent Inc.

FIGURE 5.2   A $10,000 INVESTMENT OVER 10 YEARS IN MERGENT'S LARGE CAP INDEX

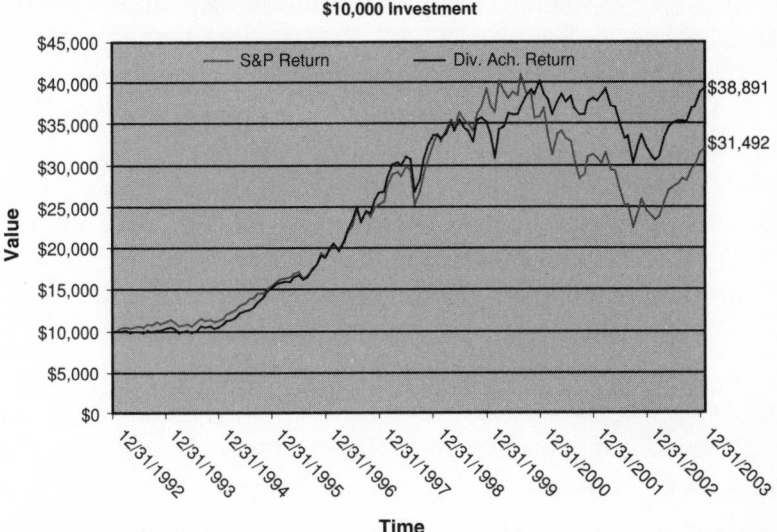

SOURCE: Mergent Inc.

Table 5.2 suggests that in the short term you may have been better off investing in the S&P 500 companies or the companies in the Dow Jones Industrials (of course, many companies are in both indexes). However, as we all know, good times don't necessarily last forever. In the down market that followed the boom in the 1990s, both the S&P and DJI began to

TABLE 5.2   CUMULATIVE MARKET-CAP WEIGHTED TOTAL RETURNS WITH DIVIDENDS REINVESTED

AS OF 3/31/2004	MERGENT'S DIVIDEND ACHIEVERS, %	S&P 500, %	DJI DOW JONES INDEX, %
1 Year	15.96	18.33	17.61
3 Years	3.10	−6.22	−0.57
5 Years	16.45	−7.53	5.91
10 Years	297.62	193.97	230.73

SOURCE: Mergent Inc.

provide negative returns, as evidenced by the calculation of three-year returns in Table 5.2. However, in the longer term—the 5-year and 10-year periods—the compelling case for investing in dividend-paying companies becomes obvious.

Over a five-year period the cumulative total returns of consecutive dividend payers would have been 16.45%, compared to a −7.53% with your investments in the S&P 500 and just 5.91% with your investments in the Dow Jones Industrials. Over a 10-year period, the returns are stark: a 297.62% total return versus a 193.97% return from the S&P 500 and 230.73% from the Dow Jones Industrials.

Additionally, short-term investing in dividend stocks can also provide greater returns than investments in nondividend stocks. A case in point is that as of the summer of 2004 the Dividend Achievers large-cap index total return was 2.31%—greater than the S&P 500's modest total return of 1.10% and that of the Dow Jones (DJI) Industrial Average which fell by 1.57%. When considering that investors get an extra 30% in income as a result of the recent tax law changes cutting the tax on dividends, the 2.31% return is even more attractive.

DISPELLING THE MYTH: DIVIDEND STOCKS DON'T GROW

It is a common myth that dividend stocks don't grow. Many investors believe that you are either in one camp or the other: growth stocks or value stocks. If you are in value stocks, so the myth goes, your capital doesn't grow (not very much anyway). And if you are investing in growth stocks, then you're essentially waiting for capital appreciation—and dividends are just cream to go with the main meal.

But this assumption is wrong. We've already seen that selective investing in dividend-achieving companies listed on major exchanges can deliver greater returns than investing in indices such as the S&P 500. It's also possible to show that many of the stocks that are regarded as growth stocks are not only dividend-paying companies in disguise, but they are capable of outperforming both the S&P 500 and the DJI index.

NASDAQ-listed companies tend to be regarded as growth companies, and, this is the case with many of them. However, it is an often overlooked fact that many of the companies on this technology-laden exchange are not only dividend-paying companies—and generous dividend-paying companies (take Microsoft for example)—but have a long history of dividend payment going back many years. Many of the best dividend companies in the United States are not on the NYSE, but the NASDAQ. SJW Corporation (NASDAQ: SJW), a water utility, water treatment, and commercial property company based in San Jose, California, has a history of 37 years of consecutive dividend increases (as of summer 2004). Fifth Third Bancorp (NASDAQ: FITB), a diversified financial services company based in Cincinnati, Ohio, has a history of 31 years of consistent dividend increases (as of summer 2004). And Trustmark Corporation (NASDAQ: TRMK), a financial services company which provides banking, investment, and insurance products, has a history of 30 years of consistent dividend increases.

Many NASDAQ dividend companies have outperformed their non-dividend paying counterparts over time, just as many of the dividend stocks on the NYSE have outperformed their non-dividend paying counterparts. For those NASDAQ investors who bought their stocks in the mid- or later 1990s and kept them through the dot-com bust and into 2001, this would not be hard. The NASDAQ 100 lost 43% of its value from January 2000 to January 2002[3] (see Table 5.3)—incidentally, the NYSE lost just 1% of its value over these two years.

However, dividend stocks on the NASDAQ exchange hung in there. In the 10 years from March 1994 to March 2004 the total returns from the S&P 500 doubled. However, the total returns of Mergent's index of dividend achieving NASDAQ stocks more than tripled (see Figure 5.3).

TABLE 5.3   NASDAQ MARKET VALUE (MONTH END)

JAN-00	JAN-02	DIFFERENCE	DIFFERENCE
$5,048,404,519	$2,872,865,856	$2,175,538,663	43%

SOURCE: Nasdaq

FIGURE 5.3   A $10,000 INVESTMENT IN THE NASDAQ
DIVIDEND ACHIEVERS COMPARED TO THE
QQQs AND S&P 500

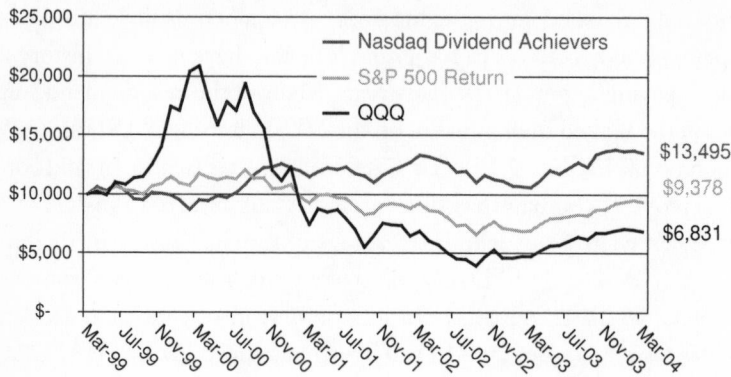

SOURCE: Mergent Inc.

A closer look at some the stocks on Mergent's index of NASDAQ achievers reveals why. The rate at which some of NASDAQ's dividend-paying companies have increased their dividends over the last 10 years and more is truly impressive. People's Bank (PBCT), which as of March 2004 had increased its dividends for 10 years in a row, increased its dividend by 43.97% per year on average during this period. That's at least 10% per quarter! Paychex (PAYX), which of at March 2004 had increased its dividend for 15 years in a row, did so at an annual rate of 39.78%. And Courier Corporation (CRRC) as of March 2004 had increased its dividend by 35.65% per year on average for 10 years in a row.

We talk in a later chapter about the stocks in the Mergent NASDAQ dividend index; however, it is clear that a strategy of investing in dividend stocks on the NASDAQ would have put you in a better financial position than investing in S&P 500 stocks. And, not surprisingly, this would be true had you invested in just the leading NASDAQ stocks themselves. Although many investors sold at the peak of the NASDAQ's dizzy heights in March 2000 (when the QQQ price was around $117 a share), others were not so lucky. If you had invested $10,000 in the QQQs just before the NASDAQ's fall in 2000, you would still have been behind five years later with a valuation of $6,381 (as of March 2004). Similarly, an investment in the S&P 500 stocks would have you wishing you had gone on a vacation instead with just $9,378. But an investment in Mergent's

NASDAQ dividend-achieving companies would have made you $13,495—and all with much lower risk attached and with lower levels of volatility (see Figure 5.3).

As demonstrated by the below table the dividend yield would have been higher with such an investment.

2004 NASDAQ DIVIDEND ACHIEVERS		S&P 500
Stats	Mkt Cap	Mkt Cap
Price/Book Ratio	3.23	3.11
Return on Equity	14.73	16.27
Price Earnings Ratio	21.91	21
Dividend Yield	1.77	1.46

SOURCE: Mergent Inc.

Put the QQQs and other indices aside for a minute. If you take a selection of individual dividend-paying companies on other exchanges, you will find that many have done better than the S&P 500 as a whole. Take Citigroup (NYSE: C), for example, a company which as of April 2004 had increased its dividend for 17 consecutive years and whose ten-year annual compound dividend growth rate was 29.70%. In addition to this, its stock price has surpassed the S&P 500 over the same ten-year period.

HAVE YOUR CAKE AND EAT IT TOO

The moral of the story is that generally speaking, in either a strong or weak market, dividend-paying companies—over the longer term—are better bets than those companies that do not pay dividends. This is likely to come as a shock for many investors who believe that you cannot have your cake and eat it too. Many investors still believe that you have to choose one or the other: a stock you make money from by sitting tight while its value appreciates or a stocks that appreciates little but provides dividend income. Almost all of the stock on key indices such as the S&P 500, the NYSE Composite 100, and the Dow Jones Industrials pay dividends, so it's a matter of picking the right mix. That's where a strategy comes to play and this is discussed in coming chapters.

CHAPTER SIX

What Makes a Good Dividend Stock

Almost everyone who has invested in the stock market for some time has a favored strategy for maximizing their investments. Some of it is the result of experience; some is the result of study. The reality is that the market is a huge one; some investors fail where everyone else succeeds, and some succeed where everyone else fails. In the same way, some companies fail as being investment-worthy where their counterparts have succeeded and others succeed against the odds.

Trying to find the best investment strategy and ranking them in descending order of their success—and finding companies and ranking them in descending order of future returns—are as problematic as a company predicting its own future. Companies don't know what the future holds for them because they are run by people and people can't predict the future.

We can, however, have a good shot at it. Investors who have perfected the art better than others tend to come out with better returns than those who have not. The game of investing is about understanding companies and the environment in which they operate and choosing worthy companies. It is also about understanding risk and not how to eliminate it, but manage it. As discussed previously, if you are in the business of investing to get rich quick, then a dividend investment strategy is probably not for you. Of course, it depends on what you believe to be quick. In the history of the stock market, 20 years is very quick indeed. Even in terms of the payment of dividends some well-known U.S. companies have a history of paying dividends that goes back hundreds of years. Several U.S. banks paid their first dividends in the late 1700s. Citigroup, which has consecutively increased its dividend for the last 17 years, paid its first dividend in 1816.

If you are considering investing for 20, 30, 40, or even just 10 years, then there is good evidence that a dividend investment strategy can generate better returns than a higher-risk growth stock strategy. As we discuss in a later chapter, Mergent's investment strategy is to choose companies that consistently increase their dividends. One option is to simply follow Mergent's index. It's easy—and it's been shown to outperform a number of key indices such as the S&P 500 and the Dow Jones Industrials over a 10-year period. Other options include choosing dividend companies as part of your retirement plan or investing in mutual funds that focus on dividends. You can also invest in a number of other types of funds including closed-end funds that also focus solely or mostly on dividend stocks.

Choosing Your Own Dividend Investments

Rather than following an index or buying a mutual fund, you can apply the principles involved and choose your own dividend investments. If you do this, then this chapter will help you identify what a dividend achiever might look like. A later chapter deals with the Mergent dividend investment strategy itself.

A golden rule of successful investing is to understand what you're investing in. The more you learn, the more you know, and the more you know, the better you understand. The reason for this is that there are a number of investment options, and different options most likely will give you different outcomes. You could invest in a mutual fund or another type of managed fund, in which case you will pay fees, some of which will be higher than others. Generally the rule is that the more you do yourself, the lesser the cost will be in terms of fees.

There are a number of arguments in favor of doing your own analysis—or at least part of it. The following extract is taken from Jack Schwager's *New Market Wizards*, published by Harper Collins in 1992:

- Markets are random. Academics who have argued the efficient market hypothesis are simply wrong; there have been too many examples of consistent outperformance over an extended period of time by investors who have a rational approach to markets.

- Markets can't be random because they are based on human behavior and human behavior, especially mass behavior, is not random. It never has been and it probably never will be.

- There is no Holy Grail or grand secret to the markets, but there are many patterns that can lead to profits.

- There are a million ways to make money in markets. The irony is that they are all difficult to find.

- The markets are changing and they are always the same.

- The secret to success in the markets lies not in discovering some incredible indicator or elaborate theory; rather, it lies within each individual.

- To excel in trading requires a combination of talent and extremely hard work (surprise!), the same combination required in any field. Those seeking success by buying the latest system or by following the latest hot tip will never find the answer because they haven't yet understood the question.

As with all information, however, it's crucial to pick your sources. So if you are doing some of your own research and even developing your own strategy and choosing your own investments, some sources are better than others. Obviously, they have to be accurate. There's no way to be sure about what you're reading, but reducing the changes of inaccurate information is the name of the game.

IDENTIFYING DIVIDEND ACHIEVERS

Identifying companies that pay dividends as part of a dividend investment strategy is one thing. Identifying good dividend-paying companies that are going to provide the stability and certainty that you would ideally like is another thing. Companies go through all sorts of changes, obviously because the environment in which they operate changes. Even the most stable and solid companies acquire, merge, or are acquired. In fact, their stability is often one of the features that make them a good merger or acquisition target.

Nevertheless, good dividend-paying companies tend to be a particular type of company and tend to have common business practices. Once you've found a good dividend-yielding stock—even if it has a strong track record—it isn't necessarily a safe dividend payer. That is, some companies are more likely to be consistent dividend payers than others. Companies pay dividends for different reasons and have a range of motivations and justifications for doing so.

THE TOP-DOWN APPROACH

There are generally two ways to look at a company: from the top down and the bottom up. In one respect, you could say you need two eyes, with each focused on different aspects of the company. Although it is not particularly attractive image, one eye should focus on the company's industry or the sector in which it operates and another on the company itself.

A top-down approach to analysis is surveying the big picture, that is, the current operating environment for a particular company and the factors that affect the sector as a whole. This is important because it helps establish expectations and the norm for a particular sector. There's not much point expecting huge dividends from a biotechnology company that has just started out. It's going to use all its cash developing its fledgling market, building alliances, or continuing its research and development program. Many biotechnology companies don't make profits, let alone have money left over to hand out to shareholders.

If you are interested in a mining company, then clearly world commodity prices are going to be of significance when assessing the company's outlook. If the demand for a number of commodities has been rising, you would think that the performance of mining companies generally would be good. However, if the company you are interested in has been doing badly, this might suggest something else is wrong. Industry-based analysis is also useful because companies in some industries are more likely to be dividend companies than companies in other industries. We talk a bit later in this chapter about what those companies might look like.

Additionally, this approach can consider even broader factors, such as the national economy and the world economy. If interest rates are rising, some industries are likely to be hit harder than others. For example, property and construction companies could expect to see slower growth, generally speaking. Some industries face greater regulation and a number of legislative changes may be on the horizon for a particular industry—changes that could dramatically affect all companies in a particular sector.

ANALYSIS FROM THE BOTTOM UP

At the same time, the other eye focused on the company itself should examine its fundamental data, cash flow, earnings (and stock) performance, history, current business practices, and recent company developments. Dividend yields, payout ratios, debt-to-equity ratios, and EPS ratio are all useful indicators that, when understood, provide an insight into a company's performance. This terms are discussed in more detail in Chapter 7.

This type of approach is also called *fundamental analysis* and it is something that, not surprisingly, is fundamental to investing. All investment professionals engage in it. Essentially, fundamental analysis involves examining a company's key stats and figures—its bare bones, if you will. There is also a related concept—*technical analysis*—which unlike its fundamental cousin tends to use a more superficial approach to stock market investing. It really focuses much more on stock movements, stock prices, and major market movements as a whole and less on the company itself. It's not for those serious about dividend investing.

Fundamental analysis is where access to good data sources is critical. Accurate and credible data is as important to investing as a foundation is to a building; it lays the stones for your future portfolio. Some of best source material is that reported by the company itself and this takes many forms. It includes a company's annual reports, its 10-K or 10-Q financial statements, its releases to the stock exchanges, SEC filings, investor relations presentations, press releases, and other key financial data. Additionally, reputable news sources, analysis reports, research reports, broker assessments, and fund advisories provide valuable information.

Many libraries have access to a number of valuable sources of company fundamental data. Many companies themselves provide this sort of data on their website (e.g., Microsoft has downloadable Excel spreadsheets going back to its inception as a public company). There are also a number of handbooks, magazines, and websites that provide this sort of material. Most companies' annual reports put the company's current year's performance in some historical context; that is, they carry a table with the current year's financials as well as the previous year's and maybe the year before. Most releases to the market, however, only present the current year or quarter's performance and the previous year's, but the more data you have, the more valuable it becomes. You can never have too much information! The longer you can go back into a company's historical performance, the better perspective you get on its performance. The key to the future is history.

WHAT DIVIDEND ACHIEVERS
HAVE IN COMMON

Virtually any company can pay a dividend, but true dividend achievers are a different story. A history of strong dividend payments—or, even better, a history of consistent dividend increases—requires a high level of discipline and planning that goes beyond one or two people in the organization. Dividend achievers often cite an entrenched company culture of dividend payments and have shareholders who invest in the company largely or even solely because they do pay dividends. In the cases of real estate investment trusts, however, they are required to pay dividends under U.S. law.

Generally speaking, dividend achievers have a number of features in common. They tend to be larger and more mature, they tend to be well past their growth phase of market expansion and don't have large expenditures on research and development, and they usually have strong cash flow and earnings growth (especially if they sustain consistent dividend increases). As a result of this they also tend to have good management and solid corporate governance—they need it to keep up dividend payments over a sustained period of time. The corollary of this is that they have a culture of good management. Look for a commitment to running a company properly!

DIVIDEND COMPANIES FOUND IN PARTICULAR INDUSTRIES

An analysis of the types of companies that are dividend achievers will bring up companies in particular types of industries. As mentioned previously, dividend-paying companies tend to be companies that sell lots of product to lots of people. Overwhelmingly, dividend payers are found in the finance and banking industry, such as Citigroup (17 consecutive years of dividend increases), Fifth Third Bancorp (31 consecutive years of dividend increases), Bank of America (26 consecutive years of dividend increases), and Cincinnati Financial Corp. (43 consecutive years of dividend increases). They are also found in the utilities industry, such as American States Water Co. (NYSE: ASW) (50 consecutive years of dividend increases), Emerson Electric (47 consecutive years of dividend increases), and California Water Service Group (36 consecutive years of dividend increases). The food and beverage industry is another likely location, including Coca-Cola (41 consecutive years of dividend increases), Heinz (40 consecutive years of dividend increases), and Hormel Foods Corp. (36 consecutive years of dividend increases). All of these companies have increased their dividends consecutively year after year as of summer 2004. Other major groups include pharmaceutical companies, insurance companies, and real estate investment trusts.

Most of the closed-end and publicly traded dividend funds invest in companies in these industries. A look at BlackRock's two dividend funds, which as discussed previously launched on the NYSE just in the last year on the basis of investing in dividend companies, typifies the breakdown by industry. The stocks that currently comprise the trust's dividend fund investments are mostly in the financial services industry, but energy and utilities, food and beverage, telecommunications, and other consumer categories figure prominently (see Table 6.1).

Having said this, dividend-paying companies—as well as dividend achievers—are found in virtually every industry. Even on the NASDAQ, which is known for high-risk and high-growth stocks, there are dividend companies with long histories of dividend increases. Although most of the companies with consecutive dividend increases on NASDAQ are in the financial services industry, they also include medical diagnostics company Meridian Bioscience Inc. (11 years of consecutive dividend

TABLE 6.1   ASSET COMPOSITION OF BLACKROCK
DIVIDEND ACHIEVERS TRUST (NYSE: BDV)
BY INDUSTRY, AS OF JULY 31, 2004

SECTOR	PERCENTAGE
Financials	43
Energy and utilities	17
Consumer products	17
Telecom services	9
Healthcare	6
REITs	4
Industrial	1
Computer and Office Equipment	2
Manufacturing	1

increases), transport technology company Quixote Corp. (NASDAQ: QUIX) (10 years of consecutive dividend increases), and science and lab equipment company Sigma-Aldrich (NMS: SIAL) (22 years of consecutive dividend increases).

DIVIDEND COMPANIES ARE LARGER AND MORE MATURE

A common trait is that dividend payers are almost always larger companies. Virtually all the companies on the Dow Jones Industrial index, for example, pay dividends. Typically middle to large in terms of their market capitalization, high-dividend-paying companies with high yields are usually well established. They have to be well established to be able to afford relatively large and regular payments. The fact that dividend-paying companies tend to be larger, older, and more profitable has been confirmed in a number of studies.[1] They also tend to have wide ownership structures; that is, they are owned by a larger number of investors. A number of studies have shown that companies that are controlled by a group of institutional shareholders tend to have lower-dividend payout policies than similar companies that have lower levels of institutional shareholdings. Companies with large institutional shareholders tend to generate value for their shareholders in other ways, for example, through share repurchases or large special dividends.

It has to be said that this is a general finding and certainly not the rule. A number of high-yielding dividend companies are in fact small-cap companies. National Security Group (NASDAQ: NSEC) is one example. With a market capitalization of just $57,234,400 and 2,467,000 shares outstanding (as of August 2004), this insurer has a history of 13 years of consecutive dividend increases. Its yield, incidentally, as of summer 2004 was a healthy 3.77% and it paid 0.21 cents per share in May 2004. United Mobile Homes Inc. (AMEX: UMH) was yielding a fairly high 7.09% in summer 2004. With a market cap of $120,577,600, it is not a high profile company. Yet it has a 13-year history of dividend increases, and its yield has not slipped below 5.45% over the last five years.

DIVIDEND COMPANIES ARE PAST THEIR GROWTH PHASE

We've established that dividend-paying companies tend to be larger and more mature, which means, typically, that they are also well established. When a company has been established for some time, say 20 or 30 years at least, they find that they have built up solid and fairly dependable customer bases. They've become known in their market segment and, more than likely, have dominated the segment (and/or have handful of key rivals). In one respect, they are now on autopilot. They don't need to come up with brand new ideas or revolutionary products to change the course of the market. Almost everything they can think of has been done in some way or other before; in other words, you could say they are struggling to think of new ways to provide value to shareholders. Typically, their share prices may be improving, but market analysts don't believe their share prices are going to rise as rapidly as they did before. It is in circumstances such as these that companies that have never issued a dividend before find themselves well placed to do so.

A good case in point is Microsoft which, as discussed previously, announced its first dividend in March 2003 after 17 years as a public company. Microsoft was established in 1975 and went public in 1985. Its revenues have been rising progressively since 1985 and, in fiscal year 2003, the company generated $15.8 billion in cash flow from operations on revenues of $32.19 billion. When it distributed its first dividend, Microsoft did so from a cash surplus of $43.4 billion. It's evident that the company was sitting on a pile of cash (and it still is). Dividend strategist Marshall Acuff explains Microsoft's situation:

> *If you're a small company in a fast growth stage and you want to rein-vest all your retained earnings into future growth and not focus on dividends, there is merit to that point. Where the shift is significant is when companies become larger and more mature, where management begins to recognize that their rates of earnings growth in the future are going to be lower than they have been in the past. At the same time, they don't see similar reinvestment opportunities, relative to what they saw when they were smaller companies, or the investment oppor-*

tunities are not large enough to have a big impact on the future growth of the company.

This is why Microsoft initiated a dividend. It was quite interesting because Microsoft will never grow as it once did. The management understands that and cash has been piling up and the pressure has been on to do something with that cash. There's been the odd acquisition and they can reinvest in R&D and so on. But the rate at which the cash is piling up can't be spent fast enough to generate a decent return for shareholders. So it makes good sense for Microsoft to accelerate the growth of dividends.

In fact, Microsoft has issued dividends quarterly—in each case from large amounts of cash. As of March 31, 2004, Microsoft had $56 billion in cash and short-term investments. In July 2004 it actually announced a special dividend of $3 per share, or $32 billion in total, recognizing the need to provide shareholder value in ways other than share price growth, with CEO Steve Ballmer saying, "As we looked at our cash-management choices, our priorities were to increase our regular payments to shareholders, increase our stock-buyback efforts given our confidence in the company's growth prospects, and distribute additional resources in the form of a special one-time dividend."

DIVIDEND COMPANIES HAVE LOW LEVELS OF RESEARCH AND DEVELOPMENT EXPENDITURE

Current growth rate is an important factor that affects a company's decision whether to pay a dividend. If a company is growing, it tends to spend more money on research and development; it needs to in order to keep ahead of its game. This helps it keep up with competitors or get to the top of its particular market segment. In the case of many biotechnology research companies, for example, research and development is critical to future success. Studies have shown that high R&D expenditure is closely related to low dividend payments. Even though many pharmaceutical companies—which typically spend big on research and development—are dividend achievers, their R&D expenditure does not tend to be high disproportionate to their revenue. In other words, their income can support their R&D comfortably. Pfizer, Merck, and Johnson & Johnson are examples.

DIVIDENDS REQUIRE STRONG CASH FLOW

To be in the enviable position that Microsoft has found itself in means that its accounting department has no shortage of work to do: it has strong cash flow—money coming in from all over the place. Dividend-paying and dividend-achieving companies have strong demand for their products and also tend to have diversified their revenue streams; that is, they have several different sales channels. They usually have piles of cash from which to pay dividends. There are a number of ways to assess a company's cash flow, and this is discussed later in the next chapter. When a company begins paying dividends, it is an indication that the company's earnings and cash flow have become less risky. A study in 1998 entitled "Why Do Public Companies Begin Paying Dividends? A Reevaluation of Dividend Signaling" found that a firm's earnings were less volatile following a dividend announcement.[2]

DIVIDENDS GROWTH REQUIRES STRONG EARNINGS GROWTH

Dividend-paying companies, because they tend to be larger and mature, are almost always profitable. A quarterly dividend distribution usually requires regular cash flow, and a regular dividend increase really should correspond to an increase in revenue. Earnings are the best way to fund this; otherwise, companies are cutting themselves short. The evidence is clear that earnings growth is a key feature of dividend achievers. In the Mergent index, for example, 96% of dividend achievers earned a positive total return in 2003. In the previous year 98% were profitable and 75% increased earnings over their 2001 figures. Additionally, the average revenue growth was 11.5% and average profit growth 8%. Some analysts look for certain earnings growth projections when identifying good dividend prospects and a 10% earnings growth projection is fairly healthy. A dividend increase that is not accompanied by earnings increases generally is not received very well. In a healthy company, this should trigger a rise in stock price and, when combined with a dividend yield, should provide a fairly good return.

DISCIPLINED MANAGEMENT IS CRITICAL

There are not a lot of companies that have a history of increasing their dividends year after year for half a century. American States Water Co. (NYSE: AWR), Diebold (NYSE: DBD), and Proctor & Gamble (NYSE: PG) can all claim this record (as of summer 2004). Almost any company that has cash in the bank is capable of paying a dividend. It may not be the right decision, but it can do it.

It is ultimately management that decides to issue a dividend at the end of the day. Good management is the key. Investment guru Warren Buffett is just one to have consistently espoused the importance of good management. In his book *The Warren Buffett Way*, he wrote: "The most important management act is the allocation of the company's capital.... [A]llocation of capital, over time, determines shareholder value." Deciding what to do with the company's earnings—reinvest in the business or return money to shareholders—is, in Buffett's mind, an exercise in logic and rationality.

Fifty years of consecutive dividend increases is a mighty feat and one that take a little more planning and discipline than just entering a figure into financial forecasts and hoping for the best. It requires planning and even more planning.

Parker Hannifin is a diversified manufacturer of motion and control technologies and systems. With offices in 44 countries and employing more than 46,000 people, the Cleveland-based company has around $7 billion in sales deriving from a wide variety of commercial, mobile, industrial, and aerospace markets. In July 2004 it issued its 217th consecutive quarterly dividend and had increased its dividend for 48 consecutive years. It prides itself as being among the top five companies with the longest-running dividend-increase records in the S&P 500 index and describes its dividend record as "something of great significance around here." Here's what CFO Tim Pistell has to say about how the company dividend record has come about:

> *I don't think 48 years ago they sat down and said let's have this goal to increase it for next 50 years. They started a long time ago, before any of us were around, but now it's a record. There hasn't been a CEO who has wanted to be the one to break that run. Interestingly we start with a premise that there is a record that we want to maintain. We know we have to do something to make that record go up each year. So it's like genetically built in. So we know it's got to go up every year but by how much.*
>
> *Then we look at what we need to do to be competitive. We trade in the diversified industrial group and we actually track 19 other companies very closely and along with Parker that makes 20. We look at those other 19 and we ask ourselves what kind of yield is competitive. Because those are the companies we are vying with for our shareholders.*
>
> *"What we try and do is maintain a dividend payout ratio of 25% of our earnings. We look over a 5 to 10 year span for that. When we go through a recession like we did—which lasted three years for the industrials—we were getting much higher than that. We were getting up to almost 50% there towards then end, and then in the 40%. In the expansion boom times we were down there to less than 20% but, over-all, we've told the investment community that too.*

Planning is central to dividend increases. Washington Real Estate Investment Trust (NYSE: WRS) is another consistent dividend payer. Required by law to issue dividends, REITs must plan for them. Typically, they have consistent dividend increases, but not all REITs do increase consistently. Like any other business, they are subject to the ebbs and flows of the economic cycle. The real estate market rises and falls and the rental and investment yields rise and fall accordingly. This means that the pressure is on to plan accurately. The Washington Real Estate Investment Trust has increased its dividend for 30 years in a row as of August 2004.

Here's what the Washington Real Estate Investment Trust's CFO Sara Grootwassnik has to say about it:

> *REIT earnings are relatively consistent and the only thing that would interrupt that would be if a lease expires and you don't renew and/or someone goes bankrupt. It's not like you're selling widgets; you can plan what you think your income is going to be. Certainly over the last two years our occupancy has been a little bit lower than it has been historically but we've gone ahead and increased our dividends more than what we've done in the past because we view our occupancy issues as temporary issues, whereas we believe our dividend policy should be a long-term policy.*
>
> *So one year our funds from operations might be up 1 or 2% and another year they might be up 8% or 10%. We're not going to increase our dividend 8% or 10% though; we are just going to keep it at that 5% because we think on average that's how we think our funds from operations will grow. We look at the situation every quarter, and the board votes on it, but dividends are a fundamental part of our thought process.*

CHAPTER SEVEN

Yields and Ratios Unraveled

There are a number of key figures and ratios that highlight a company's performance. Almost every analyst has his or her favorite ratio and many have their own methods of assessing a company's health. There are a few that are fairly well used across the board, including dividend yield, payout ratio, price-to-earnings ratio, return on equity, price-to-sales ratio, and debt-to-equity ratio.

INFLATION

Before we consider tools to assess a company's performance against your investment criteria, it is useful to discuss a factor against which all money is racing: inflation. It is important to consider inflation because if a dividend yield does not keep pace with inflation, then you are effectively losing money. Historically there have been times when inflation has been higher than the savings interest rates offered by banks, meaning that the money people invested actually fell in value over time. This has been credited as one of the reasons why the number of investors in the stock market rose in the 1980s.[1] Dividends, however, have generally kept up with inflation, providing returns when they were not seen in many other markets.

Given that investors essentially are racing against inflation, some investors and analysts prefer higher-yielding companies. They figure that you need to determine the return you want, add the projected inflation rate for the period over which you are investing, and then choose your yield. Thus, for example, if you wanted a 5% dividend yield from your investments over five years, and inflation was projected to be 3% over this period, you would choose a yield of 8% (which is quite high and not particularly common). Over the last four years, for example, inflation in the United States has hovered between 1.5% and 3.5%. Other analysts, however, consider the risk of inflation as just one of the many risks inherent in investing in the stock market. Whichever way you look at it, the effect of inflation on your investments is important to keep in mind.

Dividend Yield

Dividend yields are one of the most widely monitored valuation benchmarks and provide an idea of how expensive a stock is. Dividend yield is usually calculated two ways: either by dividing a company's total annual dividend payout by its stock price on a certain day, or a company's *projected* annual dividend payout by its stock price on a certain day. Dividend yield calculations usually exclude special (or extraordinary) dividend payouts. Dividend yields and payout ratios have fallen off in recent years for a number of reasons. In line with this, the focus of stock price evaluation has shifted somewhat toward earnings.

DIVIDEND YIELD CALCULATION EXAMPLE

If a stock pays a dividend of $2.00 and its shares are priced at $40, its yield is calculated as its dividend divided by its value; thus, $2.00 / $40 = 0.05. Thus, the dividend yield is 5%.

Around half a century ago, the average dividend yield was around 5% by a number of estimates. The average dividend yield of the U.S. stock market reached a high of 8% in the 1920s and these days the average dividend yield is barely above 1%. A quick look at the dividend yields of the 30 stocks on the DJIA, the oldest stock price measure in continuous use reveals just 25 companies have yields above 1%. On the S&P 500 index, 277 companies have yields above 1%.

Nevertheless, dividend yields are best used simply as a benchmark against which companies in a particular sector can be compared. It is fairly critical to compare yields to the industry sector in which a company is placed. For example, REITs, by their nature, are required to pay 90% of their dividends to shareholders, so they tend to have higher dividend yields overall. A yield of 6% is not uncommon for REIT. Based on closing share prices on March 31, 2004, Commercial Net Lease Realty Inc paid 6.48%, TEPPCO Partners LC 6.19%, United Dominion Realty Trust 5.96% and Healthcare Realty Trust 5.90%.[2]

A NOTE ABOUT CALCULATING DIVIDEND YIELDS

There are two ways to assess dividend yield: by dividing a company's total annual dividend payout by its stock price on a certain day, or by dividing a company's *projected* annual dividend payout by its stock price on a certain day. If yields are calculated the latter way, it's important to consider that a company's dividend may not actually turn out to be what it is projected to be. There are usually four dividend payments in a full year and they may all end up being quite different.

HIGHER YIELDS ARE NOT ALWAYS BETTER

Don't be misled by the notion that the higher the yield the better. It's important to remember that, as discussed above, yields are calculated by dividing total dividend payout by stock price. As stock prices fluctuate, so can the yield. Dividend-paying companies, especially mature and more established companies, don't tend to have wildly fluctuating prices; however, they do fluctuate in line with the market. As discussed previously, stock prices are also affected by market expectations relating to future dividend payments. If a company is expected to make a higher dividend than it actually does, its share price may fall.

Consider the following scenario. Company A has an annual dividend payment of $2 and a share price of $40. It yield is 5%. However, if its share price falls to, $35 because of a factor not related to its fundamentals, such as a key executive resigning or a failed acquisition, its yield rises to 5.71% ($2/$35). This makes the company more attractive as a dividend-yielding investment than it really is. Certainly the fall in stock price may level out before long and its yield will return to normal levels, but this shows how going only for high yields can be misleading.

This, however, is not the only catch. Because companies sometimes pay dividends when perhaps they are better off using the money for current operations, high yields can mask companies stretching themselves beyond what is sensible. Take the same company, but let's say it makes a payment of not $2 but $2.50. If its stock price is $40, then its yield is not 5% but 6.25%—quite a difference, and one that may be equally misleading. As Marshall Acuff advises: "When you're talking about dividends you're talking about growth, you're not talking about high yield. Sometimes high yield suggests high economic and financial risk. Sometimes they are better off focusing on the mathematics of growth and what that might mean for the longer term to shareholders.

Even so, there are a number of top yielding companies that have a history of dividend achievement. A history of dividend rises suggests that a company is quite capable of meeting its dividend promises and payments. As discussed above, it requires discipline and planning. Among the Mergent dividend achievers there are a number of companies whose dividend yields are way above the yields of the key indices. (see Table 7.1).

TABLE 7.1

RANK	COMPANY	DIVIDEND YIELD, %
1	Commercial Net Lease Realty Inc NNN	7.72
2	Universal Health Realty Income Trust UHT	7.56
3	Healthcare Realty Trust HR	7.09
4	TEPPCO Partners LP	7.05
5	Health care Property Investors Inc	6.99
6	EastGroup Properties Inc	6.63
7	Tanger Factory Outlet Centers	6.54
8	United Mobile Homes Inc	6.52
9	United Dominion Realty Trust	6.52
10	Camden Property Trust	6.00
11	Cedar Fair LP	5.78
12	Weingarten Realty Investors	5.74
13	Consolidated Edison Inc	5.48
14	Washington Real Estate Trust	5.48
15	NICOR Inc	5.47
16	Progress Energy Inc	5.38
17	Kimco Realty Corp	5.33
18	Federal Realty Investment Trust	5.29
19	People's Energy Corp	5.17
20	SBC Communications	5.02

Based on closing prices at April 30, 2004.
SOURCE: Mergent Inc.

PAYOUT RATIO

The payout ratio is the percentage of earnings paid to shareholders in the form of dividends. It shows the degree to which companies are distributing profits to shareholders or reinvesting them. There are a two ways to calculate the payout ratio:

$$\text{Payout ratio} = \frac{\text{Annual dividend per share}}{\text{Earnings per share}}$$

$$\text{Payout ratio} = \frac{\text{Total dividends paid}}{\text{Net income}}$$

Generally speaking, the larger and more established the company is, the better it is able to support dividend payments. Strong cash flow is also critical, and earnings growth is a sign that dividend payments can be supported. Thus, it is the larger companies that have higher payout ratios and the smaller companies that have to be a little more prudent.

A NOTE ABOUT DIVIDEND ANNOUNCEMENTS

Almost all companies are selective with the information they put in press releases and market announcements—and this includes dividend announcements. Earnings information is not always included in dividend announcements and not all companies raise their dividends even though their earnings may be higher than in the previous period. There have been a number of studies which have shown that an increase in dividends does not necessarily mean an increase in earnings.[3]

The answer may be more complex than just a fall or rise in earnings. What this means is that a dividend announcement is just that—just a dividend announcement. Investors will do well to delve deeper to find the reason why a dividend has been raised or why it has not. Further, it should also be kept in mind that dividend expectations are simply expectations and have no real correlation with the actual dividend issued. There have been a number of studies that have shown that what the market expects a company to pay is not necessarily what it does pay.

PRICE-TO-EARNINGS RATIO

The price-to-earnings (PE) ratio is commonly used as a tool to determine whether a stock is undervalued or overvalued. It represents what investors are willing to pay for a company's earnings. It is calculated by dividing a company's share price at a given time, usually when its financial results are released, by the company's earnings per share (EPs) at the time. Thus:

$$\text{Price-to-earnings ratio} = \frac{\text{Price per share}}{\text{Earnings per share (EPS)}}$$

For example, if the price of a stock is $30 a share and the company's annual earnings are to $2 per share, then its PE ratio would be 15 ($30 divided by $2).

Dividend-paying companies have historically had lower PE ratios and have been regarded as undervalued. A PE ratio of around 15 has historically suggested a reasonably valued stock. Anything under 10 is regarded as undervalued, and stocks with a PE ratio of 20 or greater tend to be regarded as overvalued. The PE ratio for the S&P 500 index at the end of 1993—when the market was up—was 21.31, a fall of 6.62% from the end of 1992. The PE ratio of the S&P 500 for its 2004 forecast earnings was around 17, suggesting the market is now a little overvalued.

A high PE ratio is not necessarily a bad thing. In fact, many dividend-achieving companies have high PE ratios because they are highly profitable but do not have wide shareholder bases. In other words, the number of shares outstanding is not overly high, compared to other companies that have tried to maximize the capital available to them by issuing large numbers of shares. The company whose figures are shown in Table 7.2 is such a company. Indeed, some of Mergent's dividend achievers have PEs well into the hundreds.

Often, a better indicator of risk and performance is a rising PE ratio. In the boom time of the late 1990s, when a lot of companies' share prices spiraled higher and higher, their PE ratios went up, even though their profits and share levels remained the same. Many analysts have cautioned that the higher the ratio, the higher the risk. This assumption is often based on a rising PE ratio, when compared to previous quarters, or a PE ratio that is higher than the average for the industry in which the company operates. For instance, consider what happens when a company's share price rises from $30 a share to $35 a share to $40 a share as shown in Table 7.3.

TABLE 7.2

Share price	$30
Shares outstanding	100,000,000
Earnings	$500,000,000
EPS	$5
PE ratio	6

TABLE 7.3   EFFECT OF A SHARE PRICE RISE ON PE RATIO

Share price	$30	$35	$40
Shares outstanding	100,000,000	100,000,000	100,000,000
Earnings	$100,000,000	$100,000,000	$100,000,000
EPS	$1.00	$1.00	$1.00
PE ratio	30	35	40

In this situation the company's earnings have remained the same; it is no more profitable, and thus there is no reason why its PE is higher other than the fact that its share price has risen. This could be due to a number of factors—not just the company's performance. It may be in an industry which has attracted a lot of attention from individual retail investors and thus demand for its shares is high. It is for this reason that some analysts caution about the use of the PE ratio solely to draw conclusions.

Once again, making generalized assumptions is not a good idea. A rising PE ratio does not *always* mean high risk. If a company has a higher profit than it did the previous quarter but the number of shares available remains the same, its PE ratio will rise. Similarly, if the company buys back some of its shares, thus reducing the number of shares on the market, its ratio will rise. Consider the scenarios in Table 7.4.

TABLE 7.4   THE EFFECT OF A SHARE BUYBACK AND AN EARNINGS RISE ON PE RATIOS

	NORMAL	SHARE BUYBACK	EARNINGS RISE
Share price	$30	$30	$30
Shares outstanding	100,000,000	75,000,000	100,000,000
Earnings	$500,000,000	$500,000,000	$750,000,000
EPS	$5	$6.67	$7.5
PE Ratio	6	4.5	4

In fact, the PE ratio is best considered in a similar light as dividend yield—as just one tool to assess a company's overall performance. As such, it's best to compare it to the rest of industry involved since each industry tends to have different average ratios. Companies in one industry may have higher share prices or higher shareholder bases than companies in another industry, and may operate in different ways.

There are a number of ways to define an industry and a number of different classification systems are used. So determining an average depends on how an industry is defined. Based on the way Mergent classifies industries, Table 7.5 shows some industry average PE ratios as of August 2004.

TABLE 7.5   PE RATIOS OF SELECTED STOCKS

INDUSTRY	NUMBER OF COMPANIES	AVERAGE PE RATIO
Accounting & Management Consulting Services	28	28.75
Advertising, Marketing, & PR	14	60.17
Apparel	33	18.89
Automotive	40	19.88
Automotive Repair Services	3	8.59
Aviation	36	22.47
Biotechnology	49	58.39
Building & General Construction	30	20.41
Chemicals	80	26.27
Coal Mining	6	59.98
Commercial Banking	416	21.96
Communications	110	37.13
Construction—Public Infrastructure	10	41.19
Consumer Accessories	37	25.00
Credit & Lending	26	50.02
Defense	4	19.92
Diagnostic Services	40	29.51
Earth & Rock Mining	6	25.88
Electrical	76	35.23
Electricity	58	19.80

TABLE 7.5 *(Continued)*

INDUSTRY	NUMBER OF COMPANIES	AVERAGE P/E
Engineering Services	29	45.13
Finance Intermediaries & Services	51	23.51
Food	68	28.34
Gas Utilities	33	17.98
General Construction Supplies & Services	7	29.83
Government Services	4	6.01
Hospitality & Tourism	83	35.95
Hospitals & Health Care	26	48.24
Human Resources Services	14	82.31
Industrial Machinery and Equipment	67	34.35
Instruments and Related Products	64	52.19
Insurance	124	16.75
IT & Technology	279	69.76
Leather and Leather Products	13	18.68
Machinery Supply Retail	10	28.42
Media	33	101.65
Medical & Health Related Services	4	32.51
Medical Instruments & Equipment	88	46.06
Membership Organizations	1	53.85
Metal Products	46	32.82
Metal Works	26	38.05
Misc. Transportation Services	8	39.38
Miscellaneous	19	29.43
Miscellaneous Business Services	60	30.28
Movies & Film	14	28.33
Non-Media Publishing	8	19.84
Non-Precious Metals	3	24.89
Office Equipment Supplies	34	79.83
Oil and Gas	125	39.64
Other Depository Banking	175	22.66
Paper Products	26	53.44
Personal Services	14	28.57
Petroleum and Coal Products	2	18.95
Pharmaceuticals	59	25.93
Plastics	16	46.46

TABLE 7.5   *(Continued)*

INDUSTRY	NUMBER OF COMPANIES	AVERAGE P/E
Precious Metals	4	110.54
Printing	16	21.68
Professional Health Care Services	3	19.14
Property, Real Estate, & Development	165	38.99
Purpose Machinery	13	25.04
Rail Transport	11	47.72
Retail—Alcohol & Tobacco	2	19.95
Retail—Apparel and Accessory Stores	39	28.50
Retail—Automotive	24	20.35
Retail—Food & Beverage	23	24.18
Retail—Fuel & Oil	3	18.73
Retail—Furniture & Home Furnishings	6	19.97
Retail—General	31	26.40
Retail—Hardware	8	25.31
Retail—Miscellaneous	52	80.73
Retail—Sporting, Toys & Hobby	14	27.51
Road Transport	33	31.38
Rubber Products	10	19.85
Sanitation Services	9	89.26
Schools and Universities	4	27.50
Shipping	12	27.06
Social Services	1	34.22
Sporting & Recreational	29	30.26
Stone, Clay, Glass, and Concrete Products	17	22.40
Textiles	7	15.99
Tobacco Products	2	15.76
Trusts & Holding Entities	469	45.88
Vocational Education Services	11	57.91
Water Utilities	10	28.64
Wealth Management	13	23.17
Wood Products	9	34.07
Total Number of Companies	**3785**	
Average PE Ratio Across All Industries		**37.39**

SOURCE: Mergent Inc.

RETURN ON EQUITY

Return on Equity (ROE) determines the rate at which shareholders are making income from their shares. It is not only an indicator of the level of returns to shareholders but an indicator of a company's profitability. It is most useful when comparing companies in the same or similar industries. For example, the beverage industry averages around 12% to 15% ROE. Anheuser-Busch, however, has a 72% ROE and is clearly an impressive earner for its shareholders. Coca-Cola (NYSE: KO) and Pepsi (NYSE: PEP) both have an ROE of an above-average 33%.

More specifically, ROE is a company's profits, when factors that mask its true performance are removed, divided by shareholders' equity or the company's overall book value. However, when calculating ROE, it has to be noted that different people use different figures when determining the company's profits. Some use net income, which is the company's revenues after the costs of doing business, such as interest and taxes are taken out. This is also often referred to as EBIT (earnings before interest and taxes), although another figure, EBITDA (earnings before interest, taxes, depreciation, and amortization), is also often used.

The return on equity figure sometimes includes stockholders' equity at the end of a declared financial year. However, it is a good idea to add the stockholders' equity at the beginning of the year and the end of the year and divide it by 2 to create an "average" over the year in which the dividend is provided. Table 7.6 has on example calculation of a company's return on equity. However, as in dividend growth itself, a positive ROE is one thing, but a historical pattern is more significant. A consistently high

TABLE 7.6   EXAMPLE RETURN ON EQUITY

EBIT	$30,000,000
Average stockholder's equity	$15,000,000 at the beginning of the year + 18,000,000 at the end of the year divided by 2 = $16,500,000
Return on equity	$\dfrac{\$30,000,000}{\$16,500,000} = 1.818182$

ROE is a sign that the company is consistently performing against its competitors and for its shareholders.

Essentially, the higher the ROE, the more profitable the company is. The higher the ROE, the more profit attributable to a shareholder's stake in the company. Given that income and net profits change every year, a consistent ROE indicates the company is consistently profitable, while a consistently improving ROE is a sign it is becoming more profitable. What this also means is that the company probably has a good management team.

PRICE-TO-SALES RATIO

Price-to-sales ratio is calculated in a similar way to the price-to-earnings ratio, except the stock price is divided by sales per share instead of earnings per share. The key difference between the two is that the price-to-sales ratio focuses on sales revenue or, in other words, the flow of cash through the door. Earnings can be volatile for a range of reasons, while revenue holds fewer variables. For this reason, the price-to-sales ratio is sometimes a better indicator than price-to-earnings. Sometimes companies don't make profits and in such cases, sales are a better indicator of performance. Typically, the price-to-sales ratio for dividend stocks is under 3.

DEBT-TO-EQUITY RATIO

The debt-to-equity ratio is another key analytical tool. Many investors prefer to see low levels of debt, because debt hampers earnings growth and undermines shareholders' equity. Although debt is a useful way to access capital when a company wishes to expand and grow, most dividend companies don't need to grow as quickly as "growth stocks." So a dividend-paying company with high levels of debt might be struggling to keep its dividend payments up to date. A high debt level compared to equity can make profits unpredictable because it restricts cash flow allocation. Additionally, it adds interest to the list of expenses.

The debt-to-equity ratio helps define the level of debt. A high debt-to-equity ratio shows that debt rather than equity is being used to finance operations, including dividends. The higher the ratio, the more concern there is. Some analysts use long-term debt (considered more than 10 years) instead of total liabilities. The debt-to-equity ratio is calculated as follows:

$$\text{Debt-to-equity ratio} = \frac{\text{Total liabilities}}{\text{Shareholders' equity}}$$

CHAPTER EIGHT

The Mergent Dividend Investing Strategy

Risk is inherent in all types of stock market investing. It cannot be eliminated, only managed. There is generally a trade-off; the more risk, the greater is the return. If you are not getting a good return with a high level of risk, then there could be something wrong. Even though there are broadly two types of investment strategies when investing in stocks—growth stocks or dividend stocks—it is not true to say that growth stocks have higher risk and dividend stocks have lower risk attached. Each can be unpredictable. If you are planning to invest over a 10-year period, you do not know, for example, to what degree your stocks' share prices will go up or down. You do not know whether your stocks will issue dividends and to what degree their management will keep their promises of dividends.

As discussed in earlier chapters, there are a number of unknowns in stock market investing and all add to the level of risk involved. When it comes to dividend investing there are a number of questions you would normally ask yourself when trying to determine the best stocks to put in your portfolio. Will it keep to its promise of a dividend? Will it increase its dividend? Will the increase be what the company says it will be? Will its earnings fall? And if its earnings do fall, will it keep to its promise of a dividend? Will the company overextend itself trying to meet its payment? How will its dividend payment impact on the company's operations and its future plans? Additionally, if you are also seeking capital growth from the stock, you may want to know at what rate it will grow. These are all pertinent questions and ones that really should be asked by all investors. Also, they are all questions to which you should have an accurate answer—or at least the closest thing to an accurate answer. You could look at it like this: the degree to which these answers (and others) cannot be answered represents a level of risk. In other words, if you can't answer these questions, then you would literally be risking it to invest in the company anyway, right?

There are a number of well-known dividend strategies which seek to do a lot of this work for you. One well-known strategy, the "Dogs of the Dow," is based on picking dividend yields. Popularized by Michael O'Higgins in his book *Beating the Dow* published in 1991, the strategy involves choosing the 10 most undervalued stocks on the Dow Jones Industrial Average and keeping the investments for a year. At this stage you assess the performance of your investments and repeat the same steps, choosing again the stocks with the best yields. The problem with this strategy is that yields rise and fall over time, and yields now tend to be different for different industries (this is especially the case with the emergence and preeminence of real estate investment trusts).

We've already looked at ways to interpret a company's historical performance by examining its key ratios and the other fundamental data that helps you see it for what it is. We've also looked at ways to analyze a company's position in the market by comparing it to other like companies and establishing some base expectations. Mergent's dividend investment strategy not only answers many of the questions above but has inherent in it a lower level of volatility than other dividend strategies may have.

MITIGATING RISK
BY IDENTIFYING CONSISTENCY

The Mergent dividend investment strategy mitigates the risk involved in dividend investing by minimizing one of the biggest uncertainties: an irregular dividend payment. It creates a higher level of certainty around the issuance of dividends by relying on history. Obviously, there is no way to know whether a company will or will not issue a dividend; however, history is more often than not the key to the future. It's at this point that we should establish the two central criteria for the strategy:

1. Dividend consistency
2. Consistent dividend increases

A consistent payment history suggests a company has built shareholder returns into its financial plan and has a commitment to making distributions to shareholders from its profits. Any company can issue a dividend, but not any company can issue a dividend that is higher than the previous dividend for 50 years in a row as American States Water Co., Diebold, and Proctor & Gamble had as of summer 2004. Coca-Cola has increased its dividends consistently for 41 consecutive years and Heinz for 40 years. General Electric has paid dividends for more than 100 years now and it has increased its dividends for the last 28 years. In its own words, the company is "committed to dividend growth in line with earnings growth."

As part of the strategy to establish consistency and consistent increases in dividends, the main condition that companies must meet to get on the Mergent index is that they must have increased their dividends for at least 10 years in a row. What this means is that if companies miss a dividend increase, they fail to get on (or fall off) the index. For example, if Company A increases its dividends every quarter but then suddenly drops its dividend for just one quarter, off the index it goes. This is a tough rule but it is in line with the objective of picking only the consistent dividend achievers.

The theory behind the Mergent dividend investment strategy is that companies ultimately aim to increase dividends. Indeed, many companies promise increases and to a large degree it is now expected of them. Some of them do so; others fail in their objective. Inclusion in the index, according to Mergent, shows that (1) the company has enough capability to sustain a 10-year cycle and is hence a worthwhile company in which to invest and (2) it has engaged in a strategy of dividend growth and return to shareholders. As Roby Muntoni, Director of Index Operations for Mergent says: "If a company has not been doing that well, it can pay dividends from reserves for maybe one, two, or three years. But over a ten-year period it has gone through the ups and downs of an economic cycle and hence is able to sustain that growth through those cycles and over the long-term. This means that companies which have sustained dividend increases over ten-year periods or more do not have the same risk and volatility that other stocks might have."

Thus, the risk of an uncertain dividend payment is reduced by creating the 10-year rule. The Mergent index also has a lower volatility profile when compared to other indices. A back study test by Northfield found that the dividend achievers index outperformed the S&P 500 at "considerably lower total monthly volatility" of 3.95% versus 4.48%.

ABOUT THE INDEX

In 1979 Mergent, formerly Moody's, began compiling and publishing a list of the top dividend-achieving companies in the United States in its *Handbook of Common Stocks*. The list has subsequently been developed into a formal index which, among other things, is used by two BlackRock investment trusts as the basis for investments.

The index is constructed based on market capitalization, meaning that companies are first ranked by market capitalization and then by their dividend achievement history. This means that there are companies that have consecutively increased their dividends for a longer period of time than other companies on the index. There are three indices: an index of large companies, another of medium-sized companies, and another of smaller companies. Mergent has also created an index of NASDAQ dividend achievers and companies based offshore whose stock can be purchased in the form of depository receipts.

Most indices are updated every three months and new companies are added or removed, depending on their recent dividend announcements. The large-cap index comprises U.S. companies whose regular dividend payments have increased for 10 or more consecutive years. The current index (spring 2004) includes 303 companies and features names such as Citigroup, Harley-Davidson, Wal-Mart, McDonald's, and Johnson & Johnson. The current companies in the index represent just 3% of the more than 10,000 North American publicly listed companies.

HOW CONSISTENCY
CAN OUTPERFORM KEY INDICES

There is an argument that some analysts have put forward that dividend increases are a negative because they show that a company is running out of ideas about ways to reinvest its profits. Although this may be true of some dividend companies, it does not detract from the fact that companies that consistently increase their dividends can provide better returns over the longer term. As evidenced in earlier chapters, an investment in dividend achievers can generate better returns over time than investments in some key indices such as the S&P 500 index or the DJI. This has been the case with all the indices created under Mergent's strategy (see Figure 8.1).

The large-cap index currently comprises 303 companies headquartered in the United States and U.S. territories. It includes companies in more than 50 industries, and its average annual compound dividend growth rate over the last 10 years stands at an impressive 11.4%. More than half of the companies (53%) have increased their dividends each year for 20 years or more. For the trailing twelve months ended March 31, 2004, 77% reported a total return of 20% or more.

**FIGURE 8.1   MERGENT'S DIVIDEND ACHIEVERS 2004
YEAR-TO-DATE TOTAL RETURN**

Index Comparisons

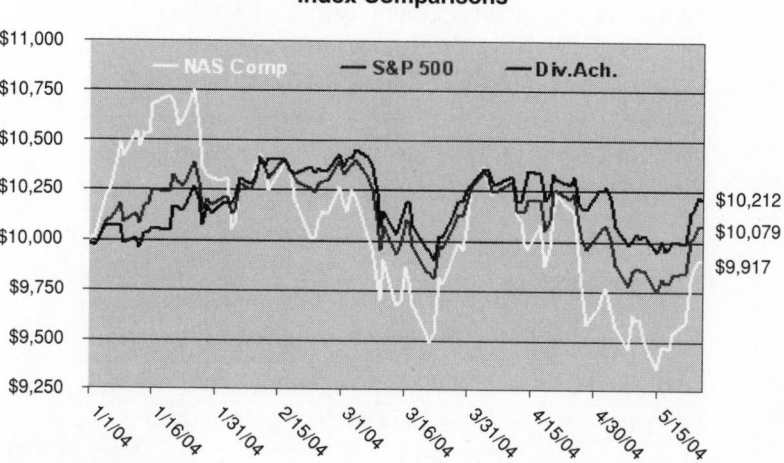

SOURCE: Mergent Inc.

THE NASDAQ DIVIDEND ACHIEVERS

The top consistent dividend-paying companies on NASDAQ would have earned you a lot more money if you had invested in just these companies over time than if you had stuck loyally to the QQQs—NASDAQ's key index of 100 top stocks, which includes heavyweights Microsoft, Qualcomm, Intel, Cisco, eBay, Nextel Communications, Dell, Amgen, Comcast, and Oracle—the darlings of the technology world. The index's current yield is 0.1%—not the sort of return dividend investors would want.

There are a number of pros and cons connected with dividend investing. One of the cons is that it leaves little opportunity to make money from capital appreciation. Although this may sometimes be the case, proponents of this argument fail to take into account that a growth stock strategy and a dividend investment strategy have fundamentally different levels of risk. In reality the two approaches, (i.e., investing in stocks whose share prices are projected to rise versus investing in dividend stocks whose dividends are projected to increase) cannot be compared.

In March 1999 many technology stocks were at their height and many new investors jumped in. What many failed to realize was the risk involved. A $10,000 investment in the QQQs, for example, would have

TABLE 8.1   A $10,000 INVESTMENT OVER
TEN YEARS IN MERGENT'S
NASDAQ DIVIDEND ACHIEVERS

DATE	NASDAQ DIVIDEND ACHIEVERS	QQQ
3/31/99	$10,000.00	$10,000.00
3/31/00	$9,475.26	$20,869.47
3/31/01	$11,515.08	$7,461.55
3/31/02	$13,265.88	$6,872.63
3/31/03	$10,603.81	$4,812.37
3/31/04	$13,494.79	$6,830.70

carried a vastly different level of risk than a $10,000 investment in Mergent's NASDAQ dividend achievers. If you had invested in the QQQs, you found that out before too long in a very cruel manner. In the five years between March 1999 and March 2004, the share trading price for the QQQs fell 65.85%, so any hope that investors would make money faded dramatically. As shown in Chapter 5, on a roughly annual basis a $10,000 investment in dividend achievers would have compounded at a much faster rate than a $10,000 investment in the QQQs.

INVESTING IN STOCKS OF FOREIGN COMPANIES

Of course, dividend stocks are not only found in the US—many foreign companies have a long standing history of dividend achievement and have generated higher-than-average returns for investors. Just as dividend achievers are not restricted to the United States, nor are Mergent's efforts to track the highest dividend paying companies focused solely on the domestic market. Mergent has created an index of American Depository Receipts (ADRs)—the most common form of purchasing a stock in a foreign company for individual U.S. investors. ADRs trade on U.S. stock exchanges and indicate ownership of a certain number of a foreign company's shares. Introduced in the United States in 1927, ADRs are issued and sponsored by a bank or brokerage.

ADRs allow investors to buy shares in companies outside the United States easily but also come with a greater level of risk. Depending on the location of the company, there may be greater political risks attached. Other countries have different corporate governance standards and sometimes more relaxed regulations around financial disclosure. There is also a risk attached to currency and stock market fluctuations in the countries in which the company is based. So as you are effectively buying into a company outside the United States, it is a matter of being aware of the current environment in that country.

Even so, more individual Americans are investing in stocks abroad. A study by the Investment Company Institute and the Securities Industry Association in 2002 found that 18% of people who owned individual stock

FIGURE 8.2   GROWTH IN U.S. INVESTMENT ABROAD

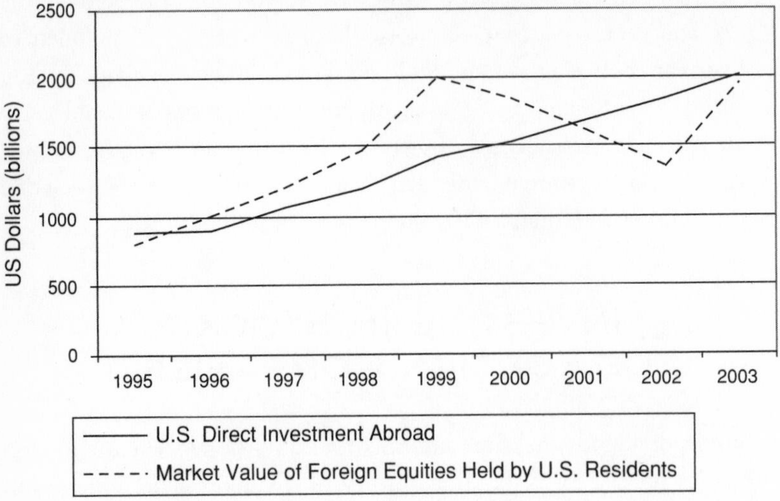

SOURCE: Flow of Funds Accounts of the United States; Federal Reserve, September 16, 2004.

owned shares in foreign companies, compared to 12% in a similar study in 1999.[1] At the same time the amount of money invested in foreign stocks has risen—from $885.5 billion in 1995 to $2013.8 billion in 2003.[2]

The ADR index created by Mergent currently includes some of the world's leading companies. As with the top dividend achievers in the United States, they tend to be companies that sell a lot of product to a lot of people: banks, consumer product companies, pharmaceutical companies and utilities. Mergent's index includes companies such as Novartis AG Basel (Switzerland), ENI S.p.A., Barclays PLC (United Kingdom), Canon, Inc. (Japan), Royal Bank of Canada (Montreal, Quebec), Bank of Nova Scotia (Toronto, Canada), Unilever Plc (United Kingdom), Toronto Dominion Bank, Imperial Oil Ltd. (Canada) and Thomson Corporation.

Here's a list of some of the ADR index's top dividend achievers as of September 2004.

TABLE 8.2   TOP TEN AMERICAN DEPOSITORY RECEIPTS BY DIVIDEND YIELD, NOVEMBER 2004

NAME	COUNTRY	EXCHANGE	TICKER	PRICE DATE	CLOSE PRICE	TOTAL DIVIDEND YEAR*	DIVIDEND YIELD
Volvo AB	Sweden	NMS	VOLVY	30–Nov–04	40.63	3.00	7.38%
AB Electrolux	Sweden	NMS	ELUX	30–Nov–04	44.12	1.70	3.84%
Barclays PLC	United Kingdom	NYSE	BCS	30–Nov–04	41.62	1.56	3.74%
Unilever Plc	United Kingdom	NYSE	UL	30–Nov–04	37.01	1.31	3.54%
Allied Irish Banks Plc	Ireland	NYSE	AIB	30–Nov–04	38.99	1.34	3.45%
Endesa SA	Spain	NYSE	ELE	30–Nov–04	21.59	0.74	3.41%
Governor & Co of the Bank of Ireland	Ireland	NYSE	IRE	30–Nov–04	61.45	2.06	3.35%
Royal Bank of Canada	Canada	NYSE	RY	30–Nov–04	52.63	1.75	3.32%
Bank of Nova Scotia	Canada	NYSE	BNS	30–Nov–04	31.49	1.01	3.20%
Bank of Montreal	Canada	NYSE	BMO	30–Nov–04	46.35	1.48	3.19%

*Total amount of dividends per share paid for the trailing 12 months.
NMS = Nasdaq
SOURCE: Mergent Inc.

FIGURE 8.3   TOTAL RETURN ON $10,000 INVESTMENT IN
THE MERGENT DIVIDEND ACHIEVERS ADR

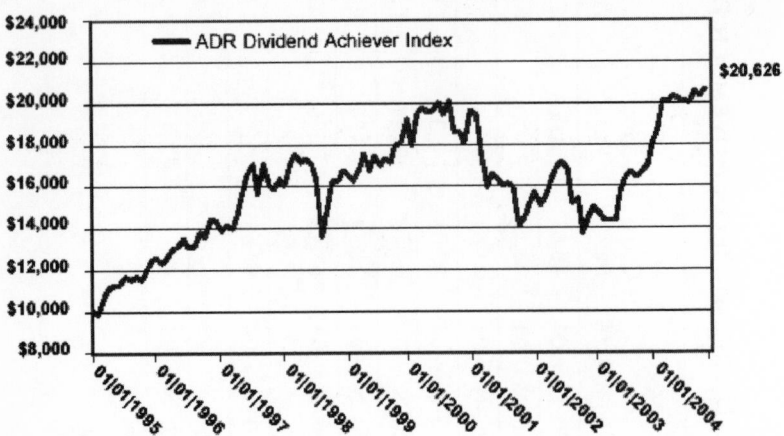

SOURCE: Mergent Inc.

According to Mergent data as of October 2004, an investment in Mergent's ADR index for the 12 months ended September 30, 2004 would have delivered a total return of 25.40%. For the 10 years to this date, the annualized average total return was 8.16%. Even though the ADR index returns were not as great as Mergent's index of large cap stocks over this period, investments in these companies would have yielded greater returns that many other forms of investment. A $10,000 investment in January 1995 would be worth $20,626 at the beginning of 2004 (see Figure 8.3).

CONCLUSION

In summary, assessing a company's dividend payment history is a matter of risk assessment. The longer and more established history a company has of making dividend payments, the less likely it is not to do so in the future.

CHAPTER NINE

Dividend Investment Options

All stock market investments carry a certain level of risk, and choosing your own investments has a certain degree of risk attached. Dividend payers tend to be on the lower-risk side, often sacrificing rapid growth for long-term growth and stability. Thus, for investors looking for a stock that offers quick returns, dividend companies may not be the right choice. If you don't have the time to choose your own dividend investments—or even if you do—you might want to give at least part of the responsibility to a professional.

Dividend investments may only be one in an array of investments—property, growth stocks, art, gems, rare antiques, and so on. You may choose dividends simply because you want or need to diversify your stock investments. Or you may even be too busy to do the research or even buy them yourself, if you fall into this category, you may want give the job to a fund manager—and there are plenty of them. Some funds have performed very well over the last 10 years, especially when the dividends have been reinvested, in some cases returning 10 to 12% despite the downturn in the equity markets in 2000. Many of the major fund managers have dividend investment funds or funds that invest at least partly in dividend stocks. The investment opportunities available fall broadly into three categories: mutual funds, closed-end funds, or exchange-traded funds.

Many Americans got their first taste of the stock market through their employer-sponsored or individual retirement plan. In fact, according to the Investment Company Institute, about 36.4% of Americans had investments in employer-sponsored plans in 2003 That represents 32.7% of U.S. households.[1] Further, an estimated 45.2 million people or 41.4% of U.S. households owned individual retirement accounts (IRAs) as of mid-2003—and this is an increase from the 43.2 million (or 39.5%) which owned them a year earlier in mid-2002.

Many employer-sponsored 401(k), 403(k), or other federal, state, and local retirement plans, as well as IRAs, pay dividends. Additionally, many of the investment or fund managers appointed to run your plan may have invested substantially in high-yielding dividend stocks, so it is useful to know where your investments lie and what to do with them.

A Warning About Fees

If you are investing in a mutual fund or have an employer-sponsored fund, there is a word of caution: nothing comes for free. By this we mean that if you employ or engage anyone to do something for you, there is going to be a catch. If there is an opportunity that genuinely carries no cost to you as an investor, then you shouldn't tell anyone about it because it's a find in a million! There inevitably will be a cost either in the form of up-front entry fees, exit fees, commissions, or a reduced return in some way or another. It's always wise to not only find out what these cost are in detail and establish when these cost are to be paid, but to also build them into the calculation of your return on investment. Many investors have found—especially over the last few years in light of poor performances by many funds—that fees can make your investment not worthwhile at all. You may be better off investing in fixed-income opportunities or even putting your cash in a simple savings account! Some fees can amount to 2% of your investment so if you were getting are return of 5% a year, take away the fees and you could be getting somewhere in the vicinity of 3% (depending on how your investments are structured).

MUTUAL FUNDS

A mutual fund pools money from investors and buys and sells stocks on their behalf. Mutual funds have come a long way since the first U.S. fund was launched in 1893 for Harvard University staff. The number of mutual funds in the United States has exploded over the last two decades, and now there are funds that cater to almost every investment need. In 1980 only a handful of Americans held investments in mutual funds, but holdings of mutual funds skyrocketed in the 1990s and have only fallen in recent years (from 2001 onward) largely as a result of the dramatic downturn in the stock market in 2001. In 1980 the percentage of U.S. households that held ownership in a mutual fund was 5.7% and the number of households was 4.6 million, according to research by the Investment Company Institute and the U.S. Census Bureau. However, the percentage rose to 25% in 1990 (23.4 million households) and nearly doubled again to 49% (51.7 million households) in 2000. It reached a peak in 2001 at 52% (56.3 million households), and in 2003 47.9% of Americans (53.5 million households) had investments in mutual funds. Many people acquired these investments as part of their employee plans, but a greater interest in stock investing accounted for a large proportion of the growth. According to the Investment Company Institute, about 38.4% of Americans have investments that are not related to employer-sponsored plans.

There are a number of funds that focus solely on investing in dividend stoks. These funds were not so popular in the 1990s, but since the returns of growth stocks have plummeted in the last three years particularly, dividend funds have become much more popular in the investment community. Typically, mutual funds offer both dividends and capital gains. Accordingly, funds that cater to investors interested in growth stocks, income and growth stocks or equity income offers an array of risk.

Here's just a point to keep in mind: just because a fund says it's a dividend income fund doesn't mean it invests just in dividend-yielding stocks. Some funds invest mostly in high dividend-yielding stocks but also in other lower-risk investments such as bonds. For example, the Dreman/Claymore Dividend and Income Fund, managed by Dreman Value Management LLC, invests in mostly dividend stocks. In announcing its launch on the NYSE in January 2004, it said "under normal market conditions" the fund would invest "at least 80% of its total assets in dividend-paying or other income-producing securities, and at least 65% of the fund's total assets will consist of investments in dividend-paying common and preferred stocks." This is fairly common so it's wise to always ask about the composition of dividend stocks in the portfolio.

Many fund managers manage different types of dividend funds that carry different levels of risk. For example, Hennessy Funds, a mutual fund company based in Marin County, north of San Francisco, California, has three dividend funds which invest in large, high-quality, high dividend-yielding stocks. Its Cornerstone Value Fund invests in very large companies that have above-average sales and cash flow and buys the 50 highest dividend-yielding stocks. Its Hennessy Total Return Fund invests 75% of its assets in the 10 highest dividend-yielding Dow Jones Industrial Average companies.

Mutual fund shares and stock holdings can form part of 401(k) plan retirement plans or other employee plans, in which dividends are reinvested and the taxation liabilities that would normally be associated with the dividends are deferred. Table 9.1 shows the recent yields of some dividend funds. It's easy to do your own research, and most mutual funds have more than ample information of their web sites, including their fund prospectuses. If you can't get a fund's prospectus, most are more than willing to provide them to you or answer any questions you may have.

CLOSED-END FUNDS

A closed-end fund (CEF) is a publicly traded company that makes investments in particular types of securities on behalf of its shareholders. Its shares are traded on the open exchanges in the same way that stock in a particular company is, and, similarly, they issue dividends (see Table 9.2). Its assets and investments are managed by professionals in the same way

TABLE 9.1   YIELDS OF SELECTED DIVIDEND MUTUAL
FUNDS

FUND	SYMBOL	YIELD, %
AXP Funds Dividend Opportunity Fund	INUTX	3.08
Delaware Investments Dividend and Income Fund Inc	DDF	8.26
Delaware Investments Global Dividend And Income Fund Inc	DGF	8.00
Fidelity Advisor Series I Dividend Growth Fund	FADAX	0.54
Fidelity Dividend Growth Mutual Fund	FTGFX	0.82
Hartford Mutual Funds Inc Dividend and Income Fund	NGDCX	0.17
John Hancock Patriot Global Dividend Fund	PGD	7.21
John Hancock Patriot Preferred Dividend Fund	PPF	6.52
Morgan Stanley Dean Witter Global Dividend Growth Securities	GLBAX	1.21
Morgan Stanley Dividend Growth Securities Income	DIVAX	1.31
Nuveen California Dividend Advantage Muni Fund	NAC	6.55
Smith Barney Income Funds Dividend and Income Fund	SBBLX	1.80
Stratton Monthly Dividend Shares	STMDX	5.51
T Rowe Price Dividend Growth Fund	PRGDX	1.01
Franklin Managed Trust Rising Dividends Fund	FRDPX	0.52

NOTE: Yields as of September 15, 2004.

that assets held by mutual funds are managed and typically have a particular profile.

There are a number of benefits to closed-end funds. Most CEFs are traded at a discount to their net asset value (NAV); in other words, their value or market capitalization is usually less than the value of the assets they hold. This is the result of the number of shares exceeding demand for those shares. One explanation is that the market simply does not value the assets held by the company as highly as the does. According to the

TABLE 9.2 YIELDS OF SOME DIVIDEND CLOSED-END
FUNDS IN THE UNITED STATES

FUND	EXCHANGE	SYMBOL	YIELD, %
BlackRock Dividend Achievers Trust	NYSE	BDV	6.04
Chartwell Dividend and Income Fund	NYSE	CWF	6.04
Dreman Claymore Dividend and Income Fund	NYSE	DCS	7.07
First Trust Value Line Dividend	AMEX	FVD	7.07
Gabelli Dividend and Income Trust	NYSE	GDV	6.66
Neuberger Berman Dividend Advantage	AMEX	NDD	6.66
Nuveen Diversified Dividend & Income	NYSE	JDD	8.31
Nuveen Dividend Advantage Muni 2	AMEX	NXZ	8.31

NOTE: Yields as of September 15, 2004.

Closed-End Fund Association, as of September 2003, 78% of closed-end funds traded at a discount to NAV. About 62% of them traded at a discount of 10% or less, and 31% traded at less than a 5% discount. This is a phenomenon that is not easily explained, but it is one that nevertheless benefits investors. The discount gives investors a slightly better lead in terms of performance and a slightly better yield. Investors also tend to incur lower costs. Unlike mutual funds, which typically have entry and exit fees, the only fees associated with investing in a CEF are the brokerage fees you would normally pay when you buy stocks.

Like mutual funds, there are a number of CEFs and, like mutual funds, their numbers have risen dramatically in recent decades. According to the Closed-End Fund Association, there are 633 CEFs in the United States with total assets worth about $170 billion.[2]

Some CEFs focus on particular industries, and others are more broadly based. Additionally, some funds are based on fixed-income securities, others are based on equities, and some are based on strong dividend stocks. For example, in the last two years, two funds have launched on the NYSE that follow the Mergent dividend investment strategy. The BlackRock Dividend Achievers Trust (NYSE: BDV) and the BlackRock Strategic Dividend Achievers Trust (NYSE: BDT) both invest in different size consistent dividend-paying companies. The BlackRock Dividend Achievers Trust, which opened on the NYSE on December 19, 2003 and raised $720 million, is based on the top 100 dividend achievers by yield. The BlackRock Strategic Dividend Achievers Trust, however, focuses on small- and mid-cap dividend achievers; it opened on the NYSE on March 26, 2004, and raised $382 million. On June 15, 2004, both funds paid 22.5 cents a share.

A NOTE ABOUT TAX TREATMENT OF CLOSED-END FUND DIVIDENDS

Although the regular monthly or quarterly payments of a CEF are called dividends, they are not actually dividends, as defined by the IRS. According to the Closed-End Fund Association, "They are actually distributions that reflect the payment to the closed-end fund's shareholders of long-term capital gains, short-term capital gains, interest income, and/or corporate dividends. To make matters more confusing, interest income, short-term capital gains, and corporate dividends are collectively referred to as ordinary dividends, whereas long-term capital gains are referred to as capital gain dividends. Although any type of fund may distribute capital gains (short- or long-term), interest income and corporate dividend income are typically tied to the specific asset class held by a fund. For example, fixed-income closed-end funds typically make distributions that consist of interest income, while some equity funds typically make distributions that include a significant amount of dividend income." Given the potential confusion that may arise, you should consult your tax advisor about the tax treatment of such payments.

EXCHANGE-TRADED FUNDS

An exchange-traded fund (ETF) is another type of publicly listed investment company that invests in particular types of stocks and whose shares are traded on key stock exchanges. ETFs typically invest in a particular index of stocks and differ from other types of funds in that their shares are sold in large blocks (e.g., 50,000 shares), with investors sometimes selling portions of their holdings on the secondary stock markets. They are generally for large institutional investors and not the type of investment an individual investor tends to buy. However, blocks of ETF shares often are bought by other mutual funds on behalf of individual investors. There are only a few dividend-specific ETFs. One fund offered by PowerShares Capital Management, for example, bases its investments on Mergent's Dividend Achievers 50, an index of the 50 highest-yielding stocks of the Mergent dividend achievers index.

A NOTE ABOUT EX-DIVIDEND DATES

Some investors buy stocks only to find out that they are not yet entitled to share in their portion of the company's profits by receiving a dividend. This may be because the stock was purchased after the ex-dividend date—a date set by the company to establish at what date shareholders are eligible for a dividend and which shareholders are sent financial statements and other information. If you buy a share of a company before its ex-dividend date, you will be entitled to a dividend, but if you buy it on or after the announced ex-dividend date, the seller of the share will get the dividend. Thus, timing can make a difference when you buy or sell a share. If you sell the share just before the ex-dividend date, you may be short-changing yourself. At the same time, if you sell your dividend-yielding shares just after an ex-dividend date is announced, you may not be maximizing the use of your capital.

DIRECT PURCHASE PLANS

Ever since the Securities and Exchange Commission (SEC) paved the way for Direct Purchase Plans and Direct Reinvestment Plans in the mid-1990s, millions of Americans have taken the opportunity to buy stock directly from individual companies and reinvest their dividends without having to use a broker. Direct Purchase Plans (DPPs) also known as Direct Stock Plans, have grown rapidly in popularity since then, allowing individual investors to buy shares for as little as $25 in some cases.

In fact, Direct Purchase Plans have always been a way of getting small investors involved in the stock market. Perhaps the most significant plan dates back to 1954 when the New York Stock Exchange itself introduced a Monthly Investment Plan that allowed individual investors to invest in certain stocks with as little as $44.[3] There were no fees to open an account and no annual dues. As it turns out, the plan's popularity diminished and the exchange ended up closing it in 1976.

By that time, however, a number of companies had launched their own plans and, by the 1980s, a number of companies sold their stock directly in one way or another. But Direct Purchase Plans really took off when in 1994 the SEC granted an exemption to Rule 10b-6 under Section 10(b) of the Exchange Act of 1934 and lifted restrictions on the creation and marketing of this emerging low-cost alternative to share purchasing.

Direct Purchase Plans have continued to grow in popularity ever since. A study by the Investment Company Institute and the Securities Industry Association in 2002 found that of the channels used to purchase or obtain individual stock (outside of employer-sponsored retirement plans), 32% of investors bought stock directly from the company issuing the stock, compared with 23% who purchased stock this way in 1999.[4] Now, around one-third of companies offer a Direct Purchase Plan, with most seeing them as a way of encouraging brand loyalty and many believing they create a more stable shareholder base by discouraging speculators and day traders. An analysis by Mergent of 283 dividend-achieving companies shows that 97 companies (or 34%) offer a direct purchase plan and 186 (or 66%) do not.[5]

Direct Purchase Plans may be for you if you are the sort of investor who is keen on making his or her own choices. The main advantage of investing via a Direct Purchase Plan is that you save brokerage fees. Another is that you can invest small amounts. For example, the Wells Fargo and Co. Direct Purchase Plan, Wells Fargo Direct, permits a minimum investment of $250, or just $25 if you elect to have automatic monthly debits from your account. If you don't own existing Wells Fargo stock, then enrolling in the plan online incurs a one-time account set-up fee of $10. The company also charges small fees for optional cash investments. Such plans are good for investors who do not have large amounts of cash, are specific about which stock they want to buy, and are happy to bypass the services that a broker provides.

As is the case with all investment options, there are drawbacks involved. You may need to buy a certain number of shares or spend a certain dollar amount to be part of a Direct Purchase Plan. There may also be restrictions on the number of shares you can buy and sell. In some cases, some companies' plans are open only to investors in certain states—for example, the states in which the company is based.

Moreover, remember that when you pay a broker a fee, you are buying a service. With a broker, you can buy and sell at a specific price and buy and sell when you want. However, companies that run Direct Purchase Plans usually buy and sell shares in the company at set times of the week or month. At the time of writing, for example, Wells Fargo's plan administrator buys its shares on the Thursday of each week or, if the New York Stock Exchange is not open on Thursday, then the next business day the exchange is open.

Companies typically buy stocks for Direct Purchase Plans directly from their own treasury or through an independent agent in an open market purchase. When shares are purchased this way (or through an alternative negotiated transaction), the purchase price is usually set at the weighted average purchase price per share for all shares purchased for the date on which the investment is made, or even the average over the whole week.

Another disadvantage is that Direct Purchase Plans also come with paperwork, whereas a broker will usually handle most of it for you. Buying through Direct Purchase Plans means reading prospectuses, filling out application forms, drawing and mailing checks, or filling out direct debit forms. Brokers do a lot of this for you. If you have an account in 10 or 20 companies' Direct Purchase Plans, that's 10 or 20 sets of paperwork to manage instead of just one from your broker. This can turn into an even bigger headache when it comes to preparing your tax returns. Additionally, brokers tend to hold your stock certificates for you in safekeeping (although many Direct Purchase Plans provide a service whereby they hold the certificates for you).

It also should be considered that while DPPs allow you to avoid paying fees to stockbrokers, many DPPs themselves have fees attached to buy or sell transactions. Thus, it is a matter of working out whether the financial benefit is clear. It may be that you make more money buying or selling shares at the right time than you save on broker fees by purchasing directly. This is why any form of direct purchase should be based on good and solid research. Companies that offer Direct Purchase Plans are obliged to provide information about them. Most have much of the information you'll need, including details of buy and sell transaction fees, on their respective web sites. Of course, the other benefit of getting into a Direct Purchase Plan is that it is easy to step into the company's Direct Reinvestment Plan when dividends come your way.

DIRECT REINVESTMENT PLANS

If you choose to invest in a mutual fund yourself or via an employer-sponsored plan or decide to invest in dividends directly, you are given the choice of taking your money and running or reinvesting it. The answer, of course, is entirely personal. Do you need the cash now, or not? Are your dividends intended to provide you with income, or are they meant to provide you with a nest egg when you retire? You may even want to pass the investment on to your kids or grandkids. There are many Americans who are happy to sit back and let their investments compound and grow. If you choose to reinvest them the outcomes can be very good. Choosing a dividend investment based on its current yield or its expected annual yield is useful if you calculate your investments on an annual basis.

There are thousands of companies in the United States that have formal dividend reinvestment plans. There are three main benefits from reinvesting your dividends in such plans. First, the taxation liability that a dividend attracts is deferred. You only have to pay tax on growth when you get cold hard cash! So if you take your dividend in the form of cash, the tax man comes knocking. Dividends are taxable as income. The other benefit is that there are no fees or commission attached. For example, if you took your dividend and then decided to reinvest it in another form of investment (be it stocks or another type such as property), there would be a cost involved. So this cost has to be offset against the money you are making. If you plan to reinvest it in, say, a mutual fund, you may find that after taxes and the fees involved, it's not worth it! Another great benefit, of course, is that your investment compounds and grows and grows and keeps on growing.

Following is a list of 300 leading dividend-achieving companies in the United States, their web sites, and whether the company has a reinvestment plan. Note that the information was correct as of December 2004.

Company	Ticker Symbol	Web Site	Dividend Reinvestment Plan?	Direct Purchase Plan?
1st Source Corp.	SRCE	www.1stsource.com	No	No
3M Co.	MMM	www.3m.com	Yes	No
Abbott Laboratories	ABT	www.abbott.com	Yes	No
ABM Industries, Inc.	ABM	www.abm.com	No	No
AFLAC Inc.	AFL	www.aflac.com	Yes	Yes
Air Products & Chemicals	APD	www.airproducts.com	Yes	Yes
Alberto-Culver Co.	ACV	www.alberto.com	No	No
Alfa Corp.	ALFA	www.alfains.com	Yes	No
Allstate Corp.	ALL	www.allstate.com	Yes	Yes
ALLTEL Corp.	AT	www.alltel.com	Yes	No
Altria Group Inc.	MO	www.philipmorris.com	Yes	Yes
Ambac Financial Group, Inc.	ABK	www.ambac.com	No	No
American International Group	AIG	www.aig.com	No	No
American States Water Co.	AWR	www.aswater.com	Yes	Yes
AmSouth Bancorporation	ASO	www.amsouth.com	Yes	Yes
Anchor BanCorp Wisconsin	ABCW	www.anchorbank.com	No	Yes
Anheuser-Busch Cos., Inc.	BUD	www.anheuser-busch.com	Yes	Yes

Company	Symbol	Website		
Applebee's International, Inc.	APPB	www.applebees.com	No	No
AptarGroup Inc.	ATR	www.aptargroup.com	No	No
Aqua America Inc.	WTR	www.suburbanwater.com	Yes	Yes
Archer Daniels Midland Co.	ADM	www.admworld.com	Yes	No
Arrow International, Inc.	ARRO	www.arrowintl.com	No	No
Artesian Resources Corp.	ARTNA	www.artesianwater.com	Yes	No
Associated Banc-Corp.	ASBC	www.associatedbank.com	Yes	Yes
Atmos Energy Corp.	ATO	www.atmosenergy.com	Yes	Yes
Automatic Data Processing	ADP	www.adp.com	No	N/A
Avery Dennison Corp.	AVY	www.averydennison.com	Yes	Yes
Avon Products, Inc.	AVP	www.avon.com	Yes	No
Badger Meter, Inc.	BMI	www.badgermeter.com	Yes	Yes
BancFirst Corp.	BANF	www.bancfirst.com	No	No
BancorpSouth Inc.	BXS	www.bancorpsouth.com	Yes	Yes
Bandag, Inc.	BDG	www.bandag.com	Yes	No
Bank of America Corp.	BAC	www.bankofamerica.com	Yes	Yes
Bank of Hawaii Corp.	BOH	www.boh.com	Yes	Yes
Banta Corporation	BN	www.banta.com	Yes	Yes
Bard (C.R.), Inc.	BCR	www.crbard.com	Yes	Yes

(*Continued*)

Company	Ticker Symbol	Web Site	Dividend Reinvestment Plan?	Direct Purchase Plan?
BB&T Corp.	BBT	www.bbandt.com	Yes	Yes
Beckman Coulter, Inc.	BEC	www.beckmancoulter.com	Yes	No
Becton, Dickinson and Co.	BDX	www.bd.com	Yes	Yes
Bemis, Inc.	BMS	www.bemis.com	Yes	No
Black Hills Corporation	BKH	www.blackhillscorp.com	Yes	No
Bowl America Inc.	BWLA	www.bowl-america.com	No	No
Brady Corp.	BRC	www.bradycorp.com	Yes	No
Briggs & Stratton Corp.	BGG	www.briggsandstratton.com	Yes	No
Brown & Brown, Inc.	BRO	www.bbinsurance.com	No	N/A
Brown-Forman Corp.	BFB	www.brown-forman.com	Yes	Yes
California Water Service	CWT	www.calwater.com	Yes	No
Camden Property Trust	CPT	www.camdenliving.com	Yes	No
Carlisle Companies Inc.	CSL	www.carlisle.com	Yes	No
Caterpillar Inc.	CAT	www.CAT.com	Yes	Yes
Cedar Fair, L.P.	FUN	www.cedarfair.com	Yes	No

Company	Symbol	Website	Col4	Col5
CenturyTel, Inc.	CTL	www.centurytel.com	Yes	No
Charter One Financial, Inc.	CF	www.charterone.com	Yes	No
Chemical Financial Corp.	CHFC	www.chemicalbankmi.com	Yes	Yes
ChevronTexaco Corp.	CVX	www.chevrontexaco.com	Yes	Yes
Chittenden Corp.	CHZ	www.chittendencorp.com	Yes	Yes
Chubb Corp.	CB	www.chubb.com	Yes	No
Cincinnati Financial Corp.	CINF	www.cinfin.com	Yes	No
Cintas Corporation	CTAS	www.cintas.com	No	No
Citigroup Inc.	C	www.citigroup.com	Yes	No
Citizens Banking Corp.	CBCF	www.citizensonline.com	Yes	Yes
Clarcor Inc.	CLC	www.clarcor.com	Yes	Yes
Cleco Corp.	CNL	www.cleco.com	Yes	No
Clorox Co.	CLX	www.clorox.com	Yes	No
Coca-Cola Co	KO	www.coca-cola.com	Yes	No
Colgate-Palmolive Co.	CL	www.colgate.com	Yes	No
Comerica, Inc.	CMA	www.comerica.com	Yes	No
Commerce Bancorp, Inc.	CBH	www.commerceonline.com	Yes	No
Commerce Bancshares, Inc.	CBSH	www.commercebank.com	Yes	No
Commercial Net Lease Realty	NNN	www.cnlreit.com	Yes	No

Company	Ticker Symbol	Web Site	Dividend Reinvestment Plan?	Direct Purchase Plan?
Community Bank System, Inc.	CBU	www.communitybankna.com	Yes	Yes
Community First Bankshares	CFBX	www.communityfirst.com	Yes	M or A
Community Trust Bancorp	CTBI	www.ctbi.com	No	No
Compass Bancshares Inc.	CBSS	www.compassweb.com	Yes	No
ConAgra Foods, Inc.	CAG	www.conagra.com	Yes	Yes
Connecticut Water Service	CTWS	www.ctwater.com	Yes	No
Consolidated Edison, Inc.	ED	www.conedison.com	Yes	No
Corus Bankshares, Inc.	CORS	www.corusbank.com	No	No
Courier Corp.	CRRC	www.courier.com	No	No
Cullen/Frost Bankers, Inc.	CFR	www.frostbank.com	No	No
CVB Financial Corp.	CVBF	www.cbbank.com	No	Yes
Danaher Corp.	DHR	www.danaher.com	No	No
Diebold, Inc.	DBD	www.diebold.com	Yes	No
Donnelley (R.R.) & Sons Co.	RRD	www.rrdonnelley.com	Yes	No
Doral Financial Corp.	DRL	www.doralfinancial.com	No	No

Company	Ticker	Website		M or A
Dover Corp.	DOV	www.dovercorporation.com	Yes	No
Duke Realty Corp.	DRE	www.dukerealty.com	Yes	Yes
EastGroup Properties, Inc.	EGP	www.eastgroup.net	No	No
Eaton Vance Corp.	EV	www.eatonvance.com	No	No
Ecolab, Inc.	ECL	www.ecolab.com	Yes	No
Emerson Electric Co.	EMR	www.gotoemerson.com	Yes	Yes
Energen Corp.	EGN	www.energen.com	Yes	Yes
EnergySouth, Inc.	ENSI	www.energysouth.com	Yes	No
Exxon Mobil Corp.	XOM	www.exxonmobil.com	Yes	Yes
Family Dollar Stores, Inc.	FDO	www.familydollar.com	No	No
Fannie Mae	FNM	www.fanniemae.com	Yes	Yes
Farmer Bros. Co.	FARM	www.farmerbroscousa.com	No	No
Federal Realty Investment	FRT	www.federalrealty.com	Yes	Yes
Federal Signal Corp.	FSS	www.federalsignal.com	Yes	No
Fidelity National Financial	FNF	www.fnf.com	No	No
Fifth Third Bancorp	FITB	www.53.com	Yes	Yes
First Charter Corp.	FCTR	www.firstcharter.com	Yes	Yes
First Commonwealth Fin.	FCF	www.fcbanking.com	Yes	Yes
First Federal Capital Corp.	FTFC	www.firstfed.com	Yes	

Company	Ticker Symbol	Web Site	Dividend Reinvestment Plan?	Direct Purchase Plan?
First Financial Corp.	THFF	www.first-online.com	No	No
First Financial Holdings, Inc.	FFCH	www.firstfinancialholdings.com	Yes	Yes
First Indiana Corp.	FINB	www.firstindiana.com	Yes	No
First Merchants Corp.	FRME	www.firstmerchants.com	Yes	Yes
First Midwest Bancorp, Inc.	FMBI	www.firstmidwest.com	Yes	No
FirstMerit Corp.	FMER	www.firstmerit.com	Yes	No
F.N.B. Corp.	FNB	www.fnbcorporation.com	Yes	Yes
Florida Public Utilities Co.	FPU	www.fpuc.com	Yes	No
Franklin Electric Co., Inc.	FELE	www.franklin-electric.com	No	No
Franklin Resources, Inc.	BEN	www.frk.com	Yes	No
Freddie Mac	FRE	www.freddiemac.com	Yes	Yes
Frisch's Restaurants, Inc.	FRS	www.frischs.com	No	No
Fuller (H.B.) Company	FUL	www.hbfuller.com	Yes	No
Fulton Financial Corp.	FULT	www.fult.com	Yes	No
Gallagher (Arthur J.) & Co.	AJG	www.ajg.com	No	Yes

Company	Ticker	Website		
Gannett Co., Inc.	GCI	www.gannett.com	Yes	No
General Dynamics Corp.	GD	www.generaldynamics.com	No	No
General Electric Co.	GE	www.ge.com	Yes	Yes
General Growth Properties	GGP	www.generalgrowth.com	Yes	Yes
Genuine Parts Co.	GPC	www.genpt.com	Yes	No
Glacier Bancorp, Inc.	GBCI	www.glacierbancorp.com	Yes	Yes
Golden West Financial Corp.	GDW	www.gdw.com	No	No
Gorman-Rupp Co.	GRC	www.gormanrupp.com	Yes	No
Grainger (W.W.) Inc.	GWW	www.grainger.com	No	No
Harley-Davidson, Inc.	HDI	www.harley-davidson.com	Yes	No
Harleysville Group, Inc.	HGIC	www.harleysvillegroup.com	Yes	No
Harleysville National Corp.	HNBC	www.hncbank.com	Yes	No
Haverty Furniture Cos., Inc.	HVT	www.havertys.com	No	No
Health Care Property Inv.	HCP	www.hcpi.com	Yes	Yes
Healthcare Realty Trust, Inc.	HR	www.healthcarerealty.com	Yes	No
Heinz (H.J.) Co.	HNZ	www.heinz.com	Yes	Yes
Helmerich & Payne, Inc.	HP	www.hpinc.com	No	No
Hershey Foods Corp.	HSY	www.hersheys.com	Yes	Yes
Hibernia Corp.	HIB	www.hibernia.com	No	No

COMPANY	TICKER SYMBOL	WEB SITE	DIVIDEND REINVESTMENT PLAN?	DIRECT PURCHASE PLAN?
Hilb Rogal & Hobbs Co.	HRH	www.hrh.com	No	No
Hillenbrand Industries, Inc.	HB	www.hillenbrand.com	Yes	No
HNI Corp.	HNI	www.honi.com	No	No
Holly Corp.	HOC	www.hollycorp.com	No	No
Home Depot, Inc.	HD	www.homedepot.com	Yes	Yes
Hormel Foods Corp.	HRL	www.hormel.com	Yes	No
Hudson United Bancorp	HU	www.hudsonunitedbank.com	Yes	No
Illinois Tool Works, Inc.	ITW	www.itw.com	Yes	No
Independent Bank Corp.	IBCP	www.ibcp.com	Yes	No
Irwin Financial Corp.	IFC	www.irwinfinancial.com	Yes	No
Jack Henry & Associates	JKHY	www.jackhenry.com	Yes	No
Jefferson-Pilot Corp.	JP	www.jpfinancial.com	Yes	No
Johnson & Johnson	JNJ	www.jnj.com	Yes	No
Johnson Controls Inc.	JCI	www.johnsoncontrols.com	Yes	No
KeyCorp	KEY	www.key.com	Yes	No

Company	Ticker	Website		
Kimberly-Clark Corp.	KMB	www.kimberly-clark.com	Yes	No
Kimco Realty Corp.	KIM	www.kimcorealty.com	Yes	Yes
Lancaster Colony Corp.	LANC	www.lancastercolony.com	Yes	No
La-Z-Boy Inc.	LZB	www.la-z-boy.com	Yes	No
Legg Mason, Inc.	LM	www.leggmason.com	No	No
Leggett & Platt, Inc.	LEG	www.leggett.com	No	No
Lilly (Eli) & Co.	LLY	www.lilly.com	Yes	No
Lincoln National Corp.	LNC	www.lfg.com	Yes	Yes
Linear Technology Corp.	LLTC	www.linear.com	No	No
Lowe's Cos., Inc.	LOW	www.lowes.com	Yes	Yes
M & T Bank Corp.	MTB	www.mandtbank.com	Yes	No
Marsh & McLennan Cos.	MMC	www.mmc.com	Yes	No
Marshall & Ilsley Corp.	MI	www.micorp.com	Yes	No
Masco Corp.	MAS	www.masco.com	Yes	No
May Department Stores	MAY	www.maycompany.com	Yes	No
MBIA Inc.	MBI	www.mbia.com	No	No
MBNA Corp.	KRB	www.mbna.com	No	No
McCormick & Co., Inc.	MKC	www.mccormick.com	Yes	No
McDonald's Corp.	MCD	www.mcdonalds.com	Yes	Yes

(Continued)

COMPANY	TICKER SYMBOL	WEB SITE	DIVIDEND REINVESTMENT PLAN?	DIRECT PURCHASE PLAN?
McGrath RentCorp	MGRC	www.mgrc.com	No	N/A
McGraw-Hill Cos., Inc.	MHP	www.mcgraw-hill.com	Yes	No
MDU Resources Group	MDU	www.mdu.com	Yes	Yes
Medtronic, Inc.	MDT	www.medtronic.com	Yes	Yes
Mercantile Bankshares	MRBK	www.mercantile.com	Yes	No
Merck & Co., Inc.	MRK	www.merck.com	Yes	Yes
Mercury General Corp.	MCY	www.mercuryinsurance.com	No	N/A
Meredith Corp.	MDP	www.meredith.com	No	No
Meridian Bioscience Inc.	VIVO	www.meridianbioscience.com	Yes	No
MGE Energy Inc.	MGEE	www.mge.com	Yes	Yes
Middlesex Water Co.	MSEX	www.middlesexwater.com	Yes	No
Midland Co.	MLAN	www.midlandcompany.com	Yes	No
Mine Safety Appliances Co.	MSA	www.msanet.com	No	No
Myers Industries Inc.	MYE	www.myersind.com	Yes	No
NACCO Industries Inc.	NC	www.naccoind.com	No	No

Company	Symbol	Website		M or A
National City Corp.	NCC	www.nationalcity.com	Yes	No
National Commerce Fin.	NCF	www.ncbcorp.com	Yes	M or A
National Fuel Gas Co.	NFG	www.nationalfuelgas.com	Yes	Yes
National Penn Bancshares	NPBC	www.nationalpennbancshares.com	Yes	No
National Security Group	NSEC	www.nationalsecuritygroup.com	No	N/A
NICOR Inc.	GAS	www.nicor.com	Yes	No
Nordson Corp.	NDSN	www.nordson.com	Yes	No
Northern Trust Corp.	NTRS	www.northerntrust.com	No	No
Nucor Corp.	NUE	www.nucor.com	Yes	Yes
Nuveen Investments Inc.	JNC	www.nuveen.com	No	No
Old National Bancorp	ONB	www.oldnational.com	Yes	Yes
Old Republic International	ORI	www.oldrepublic.com	Yes	No
Otter Tail Corp.	OTTR	www.ottertail.com	Yes	No
Pacific Capital Bancorp	PCBC	www.pcbancorp.com	No	No
Park National Corp.	PRK	www.parknationalcorp.com	Yes	No
Parker-Hannifin Corp.	PH	www.parker.com	Yes	No
Paychex Inc.	PAYX	www.paychex.com	Yes	Yes
Pennichuck Corp.	PNNW	www.pennichuck.com	Yes	no
Pentair, Inc.	PNR	www.pentair.com	Yes	No

(Continued)

COMPANY	TICKER SYMBOL	WEB SITE	DIVIDEND REINVESTMENT PLAN?	DIRECT PURCHASE PLAN?
People's Bank	PBCT	www.peoples.com	Yes	Yes
Peoples Energy Corp.	PGL	www.peoplesenergy.com	Yes	Yes
PepsiCo Inc.	PEP	www.pepsico.com	Yes	No
Pfizer Inc.	PFE	www.pfizer.com	Yes	Yes
Piedmont Natural Gas Co.	PNY	www.piedmontng.com	Yes	Yes
Pier 1 Imports Inc.	PIR	www.pier1.com	Yes	Yes
Pinnacle West Capital Corp.	PNW	www.pinnaclewest.com	Yes	Yes
Pitney Bowes, Inc.	PBI	www.pb.com	Yes	No
Popular Inc.	BPOP	www.popularinc.com	Yes	Yes
PPG Industries, Inc.	PPG	www.ppg.com	Yes	Yes
Praxair, Inc.	PX	www.praxair.com	Yes	No
Procter & Gamble Co.	PG	www.pg.com	Yes	Yes
Progress Energy, Inc.	PGN	www.progress-energy.com	Yes	Yes
Progressive Corp.	PGR	www.progressive.com	No	No
Protective Life Corp.	PL	www.protective.com	Yes	N/A

Company	Ticker	Website		
Quaker Chemical Corp.	KWR	www.quakerchem.com	Yes	No
Questar Corp.	STR	www.questar.com	Yes	Yes
Quixote Corp.	QUIX	www.quixotecorp.com	No	No
Raven Industries, Inc.	RAVN	www.ravenind.com	Yes	No
Regions Financial Corp.	RF	www.regions.com	Yes	Yes
Republic Bancorp, Inc.	RBNC	www.republicbancorp.com	Yes	No
RLI Corp.	RLI	www.rlicorp.com	Yes	No
Rohm & Haas Co.	ROH	www.rohmhaas.com	Yes	No
Roper Industries, Inc.	ROP	www.roperind.com	No	N/A
Rouse Co.	RSE	www.therousecompany.com	Yes	M or A
RPM International Inc.	RPM	www.rpminc.com	Yes	No
S & T Bancorp, Inc.	STBA	www.stbank.com	Yes	Yes
Sara Lee Corp.	SLE	www.saralee.com	Yes	Yes
SBC Communications	SBC	www.sbc.com	Yes	Yes
SEI Investments Co.	SEIC	www.seic.com	No	N/A
ServiceMaster Co.	SVM	www.servicemaster.com	Yes	N/A
Sherwin-Williams Co.	SHW	www.sherwin.com	Yes	No
Sigma-Aldrich Corp.	SIAL	www.sigma-aldrich.com	No	No
Simmons First National	SFNC	www.simmonsfirst.com	No	N/A

COMPANY	TICKER SYMBOL	WEB SITE	DIVIDEND REINVESTMENT PLAN?	DIRECT PURCHASE PLAN?
SJW Corp.	SJW	www.sjwater.com	No	No
SLM Corp.	SLM	www.salliemae.com	Yes	N/A
Smith (A.O.) Corp.	AOS	www.aosmith.com	Yes	N/A
Sonoco Products Co.	SON	www.sonoco.com	Yes	Yes
SouthTrust Corp.	SOTR	www.southtrust.com	Yes	M or A
Stanley Works	SWK	www.stanleyworks.com	Yes	N/A
State Auto Financial Corp.	STFC	www.stauto.com	Yes	No
State Street Corp.	STT	www.statestreet.com	Yes	No
Stepan Co.	SCL	www.stepan.com	Yes	No
Sterling Bancshares, Inc.	SBIB	www.banksterling.com	No	No
Sterling Financial Corp.	SLFI	www.sterlingfi.com	Yes	Yes
Stryker Corp.	SYK	www.stryker.com	No	N/A
SunTrust Banks, Inc.	STI	www.suntrust.com	Yes	No
Superior Industries Intern'l	SUP	www.supind.com	Yes	No
Supervalu Inc.	SVU	www.supervalu.com	Yes	No

Company	Symbol	Website		
Susquehanna Bancshares	SUSQ	www.susqbanc.com	Yes	Yes
SWS Group, Inc.	SWS	www.southwestsecurities.com	No	N/A
Synovus Financial Corp.	SNV	www.synovus.com	Yes	Yes
Sysco Corp.	SYY	www.sysco.com	Yes	No
T Rowe Price Group Inc.	TROW	www.troweprice.com	No	No
Tanger Factory Outlet	SKT	www.tangeroutlet.com	Yes	No
Target Corp.	TGT	www.targetcorp.com	Yes	Yes
TCF Financial Corp.	TCB	www.tcfexpress.com	Yes	No
Teleflex Incorporated	TFX	www.teleflex.com	Yes	No
Telephone and Data Sys.	TDS	www.teldta.com	Yes	No
Tennant Co.	TNC	www.tennantco.com	Yes	Yes
TEPPCO Partners, L.P.	TPP	www.teppco.com	No	No
The St Paul Travelers Co.	STA	www.stpaul.com		No
Tootsie Roll Industries Inc.	TR	www.tootsie.com	No	No
Transatlantic Holdings, Inc.	TRH	www.transre.com	No	No
Trustmark Corp.	TRMK	www.trustmark.com	Yes	No
UGI Corp.	UGI	www.ugicorp.com	Yes	No
United Bankshares, Inc.	UBSI	www.ubsi-wv.com	Yes	No
United Dominion Realty	UDR	www.udrt.com	Yes	No

(Continued)

Company	Ticker Symbol	Web Site	Dividend Reinvestment Plan?	Direct Purchase Plan?
United Mobile Homes, Inc.	UMH	www.umh.com	Yes	No
United Technologies Corp.	UTX	www.utc.com	Yes	No
Universal Corp.	UVV	www.universalcorp.com	Yes	No
Universal Health Realty Inc.	UHT	www.uhrit.com	Yes	No
Unizan Financial Corp.	UNIZ	www.unizan.com	Yes	Yes
Valley National Bancorp	VLY	www.valleynationalbank.com	Yes	Yes
Valspar Corp.	VAL	www.valspar.com	Yes	Yes
Vectren Corp.	VVC	www.vectren.com	Yes	No
VF Corp.	VFC	www.vfc.com	Yes	No
Vulcan Materials Co.	VMC	www.vulcanmaterials.com	Yes	Yes
Walgreen Co.	WAG	www.walgreens.com	Yes	Yes
Wal-Mart Stores, Inc.	WMT	www.wal-mart.com	Yes	Yes
Washington Federal Inc.	WFSL	www.washingtonfederal.com	No	No
Washington Mutual Inc.	WM	www.wamu.com	Yes	Yes
Washington REIT	WRE	www.writ.com	Yes	Yes

Webster Financial Corp.	WBS	www.websteronline.com	Yes	No
Weingarten Realty Inv.	WRI	www.weingarten.com	Yes	Yes
Wells Fargo & Co.	WFC	www.wellsfargo.com	Yes	Yes
Wesbanco, Inc.	WSBC	www.wesbanco.com	Yes	No
Wesco Financial Corp.	WSC	www.wescofinancial.com	No	No
West Pharmaceutical Svcs.	WST	www.westpharma.com	Yes	No
WestAmerica Bancorp	WABC	www.westamerica.com	Yes	No
Weyco Group, Inc.	WEYS	www.weycogroup.com	No	No
WGL Holdings, Inc.	WGL	www.wglholdings.com	Yes	Yes
Whitney Holding Corp.	WTNY	www.whitneybank.com	Yes	No
Wiley (John) & Sons Inc.	JWA	www.wiley.com	No	N/A
Wilmington Trust Corp.	WL	www.wilmingtontrust.com	Yes	Yes
Wolverine World Wide	WWW	www.wolverineworldwide.com	No	No
WPS Resources Corp.	WPS	www.wpsr.com	Yes	Yes
Wrigley (William) Jr. Co.	WWY	www.wrigley.com	Yes	No

SOURCE: Company Websites and Investor Relations Departments. Mergent Inc.
N/A = Information Not Available
M or A = Company Recently Merged or Acquired by Another Company

CHAPTER TEN

Real Estate Investment Trusts

Real estate investment trusts (REITs) are unique in the dividend world and require special mention. Unlike most dividend-paying companies, REITs are required by law to issue dividends. A REIT is a trust that pools investors' funds to buy and/or take rent from real estate, whether it is commercial, industrial, or residential. REITs tend to focus on a particular industry, as is the case with Healthcare Realty Trust, which focuses on the health care industry, particularly outpatient and medical office properties, or on a geographic region, as is the case with Washington Real Estate Investment Trust, which invests in different property types but only in the Washington, D.C. area.

There are a number of major benefits for investors in REITs. One is that the trusts are professionally managed—in the same way that mutual funds are. Additionally, investors get a chance to get a stake in property markets that they may not otherwise be able to buy into themselves. Under the United States Tax Code Act that created them, REITs are not generally subject to the normal company tax rates provided they distribute at least 90% of their income to shareholders as dividends. Incidentally, because REITs have not been subject to the same corporate tax rates as other companies, the tax cuts in 2003 designed to eliminate the double taxation on most dividends has no impact for REITs. Investors who receive dividends from REITS will still pay the normal income tax rates. REITs are among the highest dividend-paying companies in the market. According to the National Association of Real Estate Investment Trusts, REITs currently yield around 5.4%, compared to the average yield of 1.6% for stocks in the S&P 500 (as of January 30, 2004). A quick search of almost any stock screening tool will reveal that REITs dominate the top dividend performers. Seven of the 10 top yielding companies in Mergent's dividend achiever index of companies (those that have increased their dividend consecutively every quarter for the longest time) are REITs.

Another major benefit is that REITs are effectively inflation-combating investments. Few people consider that their money is actively devaluing every day. If, say, inflation averages at about 2% a year, you can immediately wipe off 2% of any return you get. With inflation at 2% a year, for example, if you left your money under your bed, it will, of course, diminish in value. If you have it in a savings account where you earn 2% a year, you will not lose money but you will not gain money. If you buy into another form of fixed-income investment, such as a bond, you would only make money if you made more than 2%. Alternatively, if you invested in a REIT that was providing a 7% return, you are getting ahead of the devaluing effect of inflation. But there's another hidden benefit as well. Inflation tends to drive up prices of property. Because REITs typically make most of their income from rents, when inflation rises they theoretically should make even greater profits from higher rents. So, in this respect, they are perfect for beating inflation.

Of course, a drawback of investing in REITs is that if the property markets falter, RENTs tend to feel the impact, often generating lower profits. The choice of REIT in which you may wish to invest depends on your investment goals. If you are looking for a short-term investment, then you may choose a higher-yielding REIT that may not necessarily be a long-term consistent dividend achiever. However, for long-term investors, there are plenty of REITs that aim to increase their dividends consistently every quarter—through bull and bear markets—over long periods of time.

Table 10.1 shows the top yielding mid-cap REITs in the market as of July 31, 2004. Table 10.2 shows the top yielding small-cap REITs, as of July 31, 2004.

TABLE 10.1 MID-CAP REAL ESTATE INVESTMENT TRUSTS

TICKER SYMBOL	NAME	DIVIDEND YIELD %	10-YEAR DIVIDEND GROWTH RATE %	EPS (TTM*) $	PE RATIO (TTM*)	SHARES OUT-STANDING	CLOSING PRICE $	MARKET CAPITA-LIZATION $
HR	Healthcare RealtyTrust Inc	7.03	16.19	1.63	22.16	47,670,000	36.12	1,721,840,400
HCP	Health Care Property Investors	6.69	6.05	0.99	25.21	132,700,000	24.96	3,312,192,000
DRE	Duke Realty Corp	6.05	11.25	1.03	29.92	142,210,000	30.76	4,374,379,600
UDR	United Dominion Realty Trust	6.03	5.08	0.05	387.8	127,900,000	19.39	2,479,981,000
CPT	Camden Property Trust	5.64	24.67	0.73	61.64	39,810,000	45.00	1,791,450,000
KIM	Kimco Realty Corp	4.74	9.96	2.05	23.46	111,210,000	48.10	5,349,201,000
FRT	Federal Realty Investment Trust	4.64	2.33	1.17	36.07	51,780,000	42.20	2,185,116,000
GGP	General Growth Properties Inc	4.08	16.23	1.23	23.89	218,600,000	30.08	6,384,068,340
RSE	Rouse Co	3.85	10.48	1.51	32.32	102,720,000	48.80	5,012,736,000
WRI	Weingarten Realty Investors	5.39	4.97	1.18	26.1	85,610,000	30.80	2,636,788,000

*Trading Twelve Months (TTM) refers to 12 months to July 31, 2004.

TABLE 10.2 SMALL-CAP REAL ESTATE INVESTMENT TRUSTS

TICKER SYMBOL	NAME	DIVIDEND YIELD %	10-YEAR DIVIDEND GROWTH RATE %	EPS (TTM) $	PE RATIO (TTM)	SHARES OUTSTANDING	CLOSING PRICE $	MARKET CAPITALIZATION $
NNN	Commercial Net Lease Realty Inc	7.53	1.53	1.15	14.78	51,850,000	17.00	881,450,000
UHT	Universal Health Realty Income Trust	6.96	1.68	2.33	12.21	11,736,000	28.44	333,771,840
UMH	United Mobile Homes Inc	6.60	10.78	1.18	12.07	8,700,000	14.24	123,888,000
SKT	Tanger Factory Outlet Centers Inc	6.31	16.47	1.17	33.89	13,690,000	39.65	542,808,500
EGP	EastGroup Properties Inc	5.92	6.28	0.74	43.82	20,950,000	32.43	679,408,500
WRE	Washington Real Estate Investment Trust	5.62	5.15	1.12	24.95	41,764,000	27.94	1,166,886,160
MGRC	McGrath Rent Corp	2.72	14.87	1.92	16.87	12,140,000	32.39	393,214,600

CHAPTER ELEVEN

Selected Dividend Achievers

A t this stage of the book we have explained the ins and outs of dividend investing and hopefully convinced you that not only are dividend-paying companies an essential part of your portfolio, but that if they were a bigger part of your portfolio you would probably make better returns over the long term than if you invested in growth stocks. If you are convinced that the best way to go about it is to sit back and let a dividend fund manager do the work for you, then this chapter is little more than interesting reading. However, if you're actively going to search and find the best dividend-paying companies you can, then this chapter will help you on the right path to dividend returns.

Although mention of the stocks in the following pages does not constitute a recommendation (it's always best to consult professional advisers who know your situation), they are some of the better known dividend companies. We've sorted them into three categories: the top 10 companies by dividend yield, the top 14 by well-known brand names, and the top 10 by consecutive years of dividend increases.

As you will see, there are some definite dividend achievers here. American States Water Co, Diebold, and Proctor & Gamble, as of mid-2004, had increased their dividends every quarter for an astonishing 50 years. That means for 50 years these companies' boards of directors have voted to increase dividends. That means they were confident that their companies were in a position to do so. And that means that they are all solid companies financially. Further, even though, as we discussed earlier, there are some pitfalls in picking companies based on high yield alone, there are some definite high yielders in this section. Commercial Net Lease Realty Inc and Healthcare Realty Trust Inc both have healthy and attractive yields above 7%.

TOP 10 DIVIDEND ACHIEVERS BY YIELD

RANK	COMPANY	YIELD, %*
1	Commercial Net Lease Realty Inc	7.65
2	Healthcare Realty Trust Inc	7.09
3	Universal Health Realty Inc Trust	6.96
4	TEPPCO Partners LP	6.74
5	Health Care Property Investors	6.69
6	United Mobile Homes Inc	6.67
7	Tanger Factory Outlet Centers	6.31
8	Duke Realty Corp	6.05
9	Cedar Fair LP	6.04
10	United Dominion Realty Trust	6.03

*As of July 31, 2004.

COMMERCIAL NET LEASE REALTY INC.

Symbol: NNN
Exchange: NYSE
Address: 450 South Orange Avenue, Orlando, FL 32801
Telephone: 407-265-7348
Web site: www.cnlreit.com
Investor contact: 407-265-7348

Commercial Net Lease Realty is a Florida-based real REIT that owns and manages mostly single-tenant retail, office, and industrial properties. The company and its subsidiaries generally lease long term, and many of its lessees include large household name businesses, such as Best Buy, Barnes & Noble, and Office Max. In 2003 the average term of the company's leases was 11 years. As of July 2004, it owned 348 properties in 38 states; it also had extensive holdings in real estate properties through its investment interests. It also provides 1,031 replacement properties, provides geographic information systems capabilities, and runs active developer partnership programs. Commercial Net Lease Realty actively acquires properties that are located on strategic and highly visible corners on highways and successful shopping malls.

Traded on the New York Stock Exchange under the ticker symbol NNN, the company prides itself on its dividend-issuing history, and as of July 2004 it had increased its dividend every quarter for 15 consecutive years. It boasts on its web site that this makes it one of 221 companies to do so among the 10,000 public companies in the United States. For the six months ended June 30, 2004, revenues were up 36% to $63.8 million, while net income from continuing operations was up 29% to $22.2 million. Much of this was attributable to higher rental income in a buoyant real estate market. Among the factors contributing to these increases have been higher needs for rental space from some major retailers, such as Home Dept, that have enjoyed healthy sales as a result of high consumer spending on home improvement. See Tables 11.1 through 11.3, for details on the company's performance.

TABLE 11.1   INTERIM EARNINGS, $ PER SHARE

	MARCH	JUNE	SEPTEMBER	DECEMBER
2001	0.38	0.34	0.00	0.19
2002	0.29	0.27	0.23	0.25
2003	0.21	0.28	0.30	0.29
2004	0.28	0.20	...	...

TABLE 11.2   INTERIM QUARTERLY DIVIDENDS, $ PER SHARE

AMOUNT	DECLARED	EX-DIVIDEND	RECORD DATE	PAID
0.32	10/15/2003	10/29/2003	10/31/2003	11/15/2003
0.32	1/16/2004	1/28/2004	1/30/2004	2/13/2004
0.32	4/14/2004	4/28/2004	4/30/2004	5/14/2004
0.325	7/14/2004	7/28/2004	7/30/2004	8/13/2004

Indicated dividend: $1.30 (company has a dividend reinvestment plan).

TABLE 11.3   OTHER DIVIDEND INFORMATION

	12/31/ 2003	12/31/ 2002	12/31/ 2001	12/31/ 2000	12/31/ 1999	12/31/ 1998
Earnings per share, $	1.08	1.04	0.91	1.27	1.16	1.10
PE ratio	16.94– 13.31	15.71– 12.50	15.66– 11.26	8.91– 7.63	11.96– 8.19	16.36– 11.48
Average yield, %	7.70	8.50	9.97	11.94	10.38	7.92
Dividend payout, $	118.52	122.12	138.46	98.03	106.90	111.82
Dividends per share, $	1.28	1.27	1.26	1.25	1.24	1.23
Return on equity, %	7.32	8.75	5.13	9.71	9.02	8.45
Return on assets, %	4.42	5.04	2.88	5.02	4.71	4.73

Healthcare Realty Trust Inc.

Symbol: HR
Exchange: NYSE
Address: 3310 West End Avenue, Nashville, TN 37203
Telephone: 615-269-8175
Web site: www.healthcarerealty.com
Investor contact: 781-575-3400

Healthcare Realty Trust is a REIT that focuses on owning, acquiring, managing and developing real estate properties and mortgages in the U.S. health care industry, particularly properties that contain outpatient services and medical offices. It also aims to position itself differently from other health care REITs by providing a range of related services to clients, including equity funding, project development, design and construction, and property management. Traded on the New York Stock Exchange under the ticker symbol HR, as of June 30, 2004, it held around $1.8 billion of investments in 237 properties and mortgages, covering approximately 12.7 million square feet. With properties in 32 states, it owns medical and outpatient office properties in key cities such as Las Vegas, San Antonio, and Memphis.

Founded in 1992 and based in Nashville, the company announced its 44th consecutive common stock dividend increase in the quarter ended June 30, 2004. As of December 31, 2003, it held $1,525,710,000 worth of assets. For the six months ended June 30, revenues rose 14% to $106.9 million. Net income from continuing operations fell 3% following the acquisition of 29 properties. See Tables 11.4 through 11.6 for details on the company's performance.

TABLE 11.4   INTERIM EARNINGS, $ PER SHARE

	MARCH	JUNE	SEPTEMBER	DECEMBER
2001	0.47	0.44	0.45	0.45
2002	0.44	0.50	0.44	0.17
2003	0.45	0.42	0.42	0.37
2004	0.42	0.37	...	...

TABLE 11.5   INTERIM QUARTERLY DIVIDENDS, $ PER SHARE

AMOUNT	DECLARED	EX-DIVIDEND	RECORD DATE	PAID
0.625	10/28/2003	11/12/2003	11/14/2003	12/4/2003
0.63	1/27/2004	2/11/2004	2/13/2004	3/4/2004
0.635	4/27/2004	5/12/2004	5/14/2004	6/3/2004
0.64	7/27/2004	8/12/2004	8/16/2004	9/2/2004

Indicated dividend: $2.56 (company has a dividend reinvestment plan).

TABLE 11.6   OTHER DIVIDEND INFORMATION

	12/31/2003	12/31/2002	12/31/2001	12/31/2000	12/31/1999	12/31/1998	12/31/1997
Earnings per share, $	1.66	1.55	1.81	1.82	1.99	1.63	1.68
PE ratio	21.96–14.71	20.74–17.60	15.61–11.81	11.78–8.59	11.46–7.38	18.37–13.04	17.78–15.18
Average yield, %	8.06	7.94	9.14	12.25	10.90	7.86	7.17
Dividend payout, $	148.80	154.19	127.62	122.53	108.04	126.99	118.45
Dividends per share, %	2.470	2.390	2.310	2.230	2.150	2.070	1.990
Return on equity, %	7.67	7.72	7.89	7.82	8.45	3.98	8.29
Return on assets, %	4.54	4.71	5.13	4.97	5.35	2.51	6.39

UNIVERSAL HEALTH REALTY INC TRUST

Symbol: UHT
Exchange: NYSE
Address: Universal Corporate Center, King of Prussia,
    PA 19406-0958
Telephone: 610-265-0688
Web site: www.uhrit.com
Investor contact: 610-265-0688

Universal Health Realty Income Trust is another health care-based REIT that focuses on a broad range of heath care facilities including acute care hospitals, medical offices, rehabilitation hospitals, behavioral health care facilities, subacute care facilities, and child care centers. Established in 1986 and based in Pennsylvania, as of March 2004 the company had 44 property investments in 15 states. These included four acute care facilities, one behavioral health care facility, two rehabilitation hospitals, 32 medical office buildings, four child care centers, and one subacute facility. Six of the company's hospital facilities and three medical office buildings are leased to subsidiaries of Universal Health Services Inc, one of the country's largest hospital operations companies.

Although not as large as some other health care REITs, Universal Health Realty Income Trust has one of the highest dividend yields. Its dividend history dates back 16 years. For the six-month period ended June 30, 2004, net income was $11.5 million. Its most recent declared dividend was $0.50 per share payable on June 30, 2004, to shareholders of record as of June 16, 2004. See Tables 11.7 through 11.9 for details on the company's performance.

TABLE 11.7   INTERIM EARNINGS, $ PER SHARE

	MARCH	JUNE	SEPTEMBER	DECEMBER
2001	0.46	0.44	0.42	0.42
2002	0.53	0.44	0.43	0.44
2003	0.48	0.45	0.45	0.69
2004	0.43	0.52	···	···

TABLE 11.8   INTERIM QUARTERLY DIVIDENDS, $ PER SHARE

AMOUNT	DECLARED	EX-DIVIDEND	RECORD DATE	PAID
0.49	9/4/2003	9/12/2003	9/16/2003	9/30/2003
0.495	12/2/2003	12/15/2003	12/17/2003	12/31/2003
0.495	3/10/2004	3/17/2004	3/19/2004	3/31/2004
0.50	6/3/2004	6/14/2004	6/16/2004	6/30/2004

Indicated dividend: $2.00 (company has a dividend reinvestment plan).

TABLE 11.9   OTHER DIVIDEND INFORMATION

	12/31/ 2003	12/31/ 2002	12/31/ 2001	12/31/ 2000	12/31/ 1999	12/31/ 1998
Earnings per share, $	2.07	1.84	1.74	1.81	1.56	1.76
PE ratio	14.76– 12.22	15.49– 12.33	14.77– 10.88	10.98– 7.91	13.14– 9.38	12.78– 10.26
Average yield, %	7.02	7.55	8.40	10.76	10.30	8.68
Dividend payout, $	94.69	104.35	107.76	101.66	116.03	99.72
Dividends per share, $	1.960	1.920	1.875	1.84	1.810	1.755
Return on equity, %	16.05	14.53	12.23	16.38	14.02	14.15
Return on assets, %	12.57	11.68	9.77	8.85	7.81	8.46

TEPPCO PARTNERS LP

Symbol: TPP
Exchange: NYSE
Address: 2929 Allen Parkway, Houston, TX 77252-2521
Telephone: 713-759-3636
Web site: www.teppco.com
Investor contact: 800-659-0059

TEPPCO owns and operates one of the largest petroleum product and liquefied petroleum gas pipeline networks in the United States. Based in Houston and trading on the New York Stock Exchange under the ticker symbol TPP, it has a number of subsidiaries through which it has investments in the downstream, upstream, and midstream segments of the petroleum industry. The downstream segment includes transportation and storage of refined products, liquefied petroleum gases, and petrochemicals. The upstream segment includes gathering, transportation, marketing, and storage of crude oil, and distribution of lubrication oils and specialty chemicals. The midstream segment includes natural gas gathering services, fractionation of natural gas liquids (NGLs), and transportation of NGLs.

The company has a history dating back to the 1940s but has diversified considerably in the 1990s and since. As of mid-2004 it had increased its dividend for 11 consecutive years. In July 2004, it announced a second quarter dividend of $0.6625 per unit. For the six months ended June 30, 2004, its revenues rose 25% to $2.67 billion, while net income applicable to LP and Class B unit holders rose 12% to $55.6 million. See Tables 11.10 through 11.12 for details on the company's performance.

TABLE 11.10   INTERIM EARNINGS, $ PER SHARE

	MARCH	JUNE	SEPTEMBER	DECEMBER
2001	0.55	0.89	0.35	0.39
2002	0.46	0.39	0.48	0.46
2003	0.43	0.43	0.36	0.30
2004	0.46	0.43	...	...

TABLE 11.11   INTERIM QUARTERLY DIVIDENDS, $ PER SHARE

AMOUNT	DECLARED	EX-DIVIDEND	RECORD DATE	PAID
0.65	10/17/2003	10/29/2003	10/31/2003	11/7/2003
0.65	1/16/2004	1/28/2004	1/30/2004	2/6/2004
0.663	4/16/2004	4/28/2004	4/30/2004	5/7/2004
0.663	7/16/2004	7/28/2004	7/30/2004	8/6/2004

Indicated dividend: $2.65 (company has a dividend reinvestment plan).

TABLE 11.12   OTHER DIVIDEND INFORMATION

	12/31/2003	12/31/2002	12/31/2001	12/31/2000	12/31/1999	12/31/1998	12/31/1997
Earnings per share, $	1.52	1.79	2.18	1.89	1.91	1.61	1.95
PE ratio	27.07–18.26	18.44–14.58	16.47–11.35	14.09–10.22	14.63–9.42	18.94–15.06	14.29–10.32
Average yield, %	7.26	7.80	7.32	8.72	7.79	6.35	6.56
Dividend payout, $	164.47	131.28	98.62	105.82	96.86	108.70	79.49
Dividends per share, %	2.500	2.350	2.150	2.000	1.850	1.750	1.550
Return on equity, %	11.69	13.22	20.09	24.56	31.39	23.48	20.23
Return on assets, %	4.41	4.25	5.28	4.77	6.93	5.83	9.10

HEALTH CARE PROPERTY INVESTORS

Symbol: HCP
Exchange: NYSE
Address: 4675 MacArthur Court, Newport Beach, CA 92660
Telephone: 949-221-0600
Web site: www.hcpi.com
Investor contact: 949-221-0600

Health Care Property Investors is a real estate investment trust that invests in health care-related facilities throughout the United States, including long-term care facilities, congregate care and assisted living facilities, acute care and rehabilitation hospitals, medical office buildings, and physician group practice clinics. Trading on the New York Stock Exchange under the ticker symbol HCP, its investment portfolio as at December 31, 2003, included 554 facilities in 44 states covering 34.2 million square feet. These included 173 long-term care facilities, 124 retirement and assisted living facilities, 196 medical office buildings, 31 hospitals, and 30 other health care facilities. It also has a number of key joint ventures and mortgage loans. In the 2003 financial year it acquired 11 properties but sold 27.

Established in 1985 and based in Long Beach, California, the company has an 18-year history of consecutive dividend increases. For the six months ended June 30, 2004, revenues rose 15% to $204.8 million. Net income from continuing operations rose 52% to $67.9 million. See Tables 11.13 through 11.15 for details on the company's performance.

TABLE 11.13   INTERIM EARNINGS, $ PER SHARE

	MARCH	JUNE	SEPTEMBER	DECEMBER
2001	0.195	0.27	0.16	0.265
2002	0.21	0.295	0.265	0.195
2003	0.18	0.185	0.26	0.315
2004	0.23	0.28	...	...

TABLE 11.14   INTERIM QUARTERLY DIVIDENDS, $ PER SHARE

AMOUNT	DECLARED	EX-DIVIDEND	RECORD DATE	PAID
0.418	1/22/2004	2/2/2004	2/4/2004	2/19/2004
100%	1/22/2004	3/2/2004	2/4/2004	3/1/2004
0.418	4/26/2004	5/4/2004	5/6/2004	5/21/2004
0.418	7/23/2004	8/2/2004	8/4/2004	8/19/2004

Indicated dividend: $1.67 (company has a dividend reinvestment plan).

TABLE 11.15   OTHER DIVIDEND INFORMATION

	12/31/ 2003	12/31/ 2002	12/31/ 2001	12/31/ 2000	12/31/ 1999	12/31/ 1998
Earnings per share, $	0.94	0.965	0.89	1.065	1.125	1.27
PE ratio	27.27– 17.74	23.24– 18.76	21.92– 16.61	14.06– 11.12	14.64– 9.75	15.45– 11.37
Average yield, %	8.01	8.00	8.87	10.77	10.09	7.57
Dividend payout, $	176.60	168.91	174.16	138.03	123.56	103.15
Dividends per share, $	1.660	1.630	1.550	1.470	1.390	1.310
Return on equity, %	10.76	10.71	9.72	11.66	8.02	14.64
Return on assets, %	5.11	4.99	4.98	5.57	3.90	6.43

UNITED MOBILE HOMES INC

Symbol: UMH
Exchange: AMEX
Address: Juniper Business Plaza, Freehold, NJ 07728
Telephone: 732-577-9997
Web site: www.umh.com
Investor contact: 732-577-9997

United Mobile Homes is a REIT, is engaged in the ownership and oper-
ation of manufactured home communities located in mostly eastern
states, including New Jersey, New York, Ohio, Pennsylvania, and
Tennessee. Its primary business is leasing manufactured home spaces on a
month-to-month basis to private manufactured home owners. However,
it also leases manufactured homes to residents and, through its wholly-
owned taxable REIT subsidiary, sells homes to residents and prospective
residents of its communities. As of December 31 2003, United Mobile
Homes owned 26 manufactured home communities including 6,129
sites, making it the 25th largest company of its type in the United States.
It also has a portfolio of REIT securities valued in mid-2004 at more than
$30 million and generating over $2 million in annual income.

Formed in 1968 by Eugene W. Landy, a pioneer in the REIT industry, the company is based in New Jersey. The company operates as part of
a group of three public companies (all REITs) that includes United Mobile
Homes, Inc., Monmouth Capital Corporation, and Monmouth Real
Estate Investment Corporation (the affiliated companies). It trades on the
AMEX exchange under the ticker symbol UMH. With a 13-year history
of consecutive dividend increases, in April 2004 it raised its dividend to
$0.94 per share. For the six months ended June 30, 2004, revenues rose 9%
to $17.5 million and net income rose 31% to $4.9 million. See Tables
11.16 through 11.18 for details on the company's performance.

TABLE 11.16   INTERIM EARNINGS, $ PER SHARE

	MARCH	JUNE	SEPTEMBER	DECEMBER
2001	0.19	0.21	0.23	0.11
2002	0.24	0.20	0.19	0.22
2003	0.23	0.25	0.29	0.25
2004	0.39	0.20	···	···

TABLE 11.17   INTERIM QUARTERLY DIVIDENDS, $ PER SHARE

AMOUNT	DECLARED	EX-DIVIDEND	RECORD DATE	PAID
0.233	1/14/2004	2/12/2004	2/17/2004	3/15/2004
0.235	4/1/2004	5/13/2004	5/17/2004	6/15/2004
0.238	7/1/2004	8/12/2004	8/16/2004	9/15/2004

Indicated dividend: $0.952 (company has a dividend reinvestment plan).

TABLE 11.18   OTHER DIVIDEND INFORMATION

	12/31/ 2003	12/31/ 2002	12/31/ 2001	12/31/ 2000	12/31/ 1999	12/31/ 1998
Earnings per share, $	1.02	0.85	0.74	0.71	0.63	0.60
PE ratio	17.16–12.61	16.18–13.88	16.76–13.01	13.91–9.95	17.06–12.70	20.83–16.15
Average yield, %	5.98	6.76	7.33	8.90	8.12	6.76
Dividend payout, $	88.73	101.76	108.45	106.69	119.05	122.92
Dividends per share, $	0.905	0.865	0.803	0.758	0.750	0.738
Return on equity, %	12.63	10.75	9.74	11.23	11.46	11.61
Return on assets, %	5.23	3.59	3.39	4.07	4.18	5.39

TANGER FACTORY OUTLET CENTERS

Symbol: SKT
Exchange: NYSE
Address: 3200 Northline Avenue, Greensboro, NC 27408
Telephone: 336-292-3010
Web site: www.tangeroutlet.com
Investor contact: 336-292-3010

Tanger Factory Outlet Centers is a real estate investment trust that focuses on factory outlet center properties. A pioneer in the area when it was established in 1981 as a small real estate company focusing on factory outlets, it now acquires, manages, operates, and leases factory outlet centers in 23 states. As of December 2003, Tanger had ownership interests in or management responsibilities for 40 centers with a total gross leasable area of approximately 9.3 million square feet. It centers were approximately 96% occupied, included over 2,000 stores, and represented over 400 store brands. Its factory outlet centers and other assets are all branded under the Tanger Factory Outlet name; all are held by and all operations are conducted by the related entity Tanger Properties Limited Partnership.

Public since May 1993, it trades on the New York Stock Exchange under the ticker symbol SKT and is based in Greensboro, North Carolina. Tanger has a 10-year history of consecutive dividend increases and for the second quarter ended June 30, 2004, declared a dividend of $0.6250 per share. For the six months ended June 30, 2004, total revenues rose 65% to $94.4 million. Net income from continuing operations fell 29% to $2.9 million although a number of key properties were acquired in this period. See Tables 11.19 through 11.21 for details on the company's performance.

TABLE 11.19   INTERIM EARNINGS, $ PER SHARE

	MARCH	JUNE	SEPTEMBER	DECEMBER
2001	0.06	0.12	0.17	0.35
2002	0.12	0.13	0.20	0.35
2003	0.19	0.26	0.33	0.39
2004	0.08	0.15	...	...

TABLE 11.20   INTERIM QUARTERLY DIVIDENDS, $ PER SHARE

AMOUNT	DECLARED	EX-DIVIDEND	RECORD DATE	PAID
0.615	10/9/2003	10/29/2003	10/31/2003	11/14/2003
0.615	1/15/2004	1/28/2004	1/30/2004	2/16/2004
0.625	4/15/2004	4/28/2004	4/30/2004	5/14/2004
0.625	7/15/2004	7/28/2004	7/30/2004	8/16/2004

Indicated dividend: $2.50 (company has a dividend reinvestment plan).

TABLE 11.21   OTHER DIVIDEND INFORMATION

	12/31/ 2003	12/31/ 2002	12/31/ 2001	12/31/ 2000	12/31/ 1999	12/31/ 1998	12/31/ 1997
Earnings per share, $	1.17	0.80	0.70	0.31	1.77	1.28	1.54
PE ratio	36.21– 24.66	39.00– 26.06	33.30– 28.30	80.24– 59.68	14.94– 10.63	24.80– 14.79	20.09– 15.42
Average yield, %	7.16	9.02	11.27	11.19	10.49	8.55	7.87
Dividend payout, $	210.04	305.94	348.21	783.06	136.44	183.59	140.91
Dividends per share, %	2.458	2.448	2.438	2.427	2.415	2.350	2.170
Return on equity, %	7.68	N.A.	N.A.	N.A.	N.A.	N.A.	N.A.
Return on assets, %	1.30	N.A.	N.A.	N.A.	N.A.	N.A.	N.M.

N.A. = data not available.

DUKE REALTY CORP

Symbol: DRE
Exchange: NYSE
Address: 600 East 96th Street, Indianapolis, IN 46240
Telephone: 317-808-6000
Web site: www.dukerealty.com
Investor contact: 317-808-6005

Duke Realty is the largest publicly traded office and industrial real estate company in the United States, managing primarily industrial and office properties in 13 major markets throughout the Midwest and Southeast. Founded in 1972 and based in Indianapolis, as of December 2003, 47% of its net effective rental income was industrial, 52% office, and just 1% retail. Its property portfolio embraces 4,000 tenants in 109 million square feet of property that produces nearly $800 million in annual rental revenue. Duke also provides, on a fee basis, leasing, property and asset management, development, construction, build-to-suit, and other tenant-related services; its in-house construction company is one of the largest in the country. The company also owns or controls nearly 3,800 acres of unencumbered land ready for development.

Traded on the New York Stock Exchange under the ticker symbol DRE, the company went public in 1993. Its dividend history goes back 11 years and in July 2004 it declared a quarterly common stock dividend of $0.465 per share. For the six months ended June 30, 2004, total revenues rose 17% to $56.1 million. Net income from continuing operations applicable to common stock fell 5% to $62.9 million. See Tables 11.22 through 11.24 for details on the company's performance.

TABLE 11.22   INTERIM EARNINGS, $ PER SHARE

	MARCH	JUNE	SEPTEMBER	DECEMBER
2001	0.45	0.38	0.58	0.34
2002	0.33	0.34	0.29	0.19
2003	0.26	0.25	0.28	0.29
2004	0.21	0.24	···	···

TABLE 11.23   INTERIM QUARTERLY DIVIDENDS, $ PER SHARE

AMOUNT	DECLARED	EX-DIVIDEND	RECORD DATE	PAID
0.46	7/30/2003	8/12/2003	8/14/2003	8/29/2003
0.46	10/30/2003	11/12/2003	11/14/2003	11/28/2003
0.46	1/28/2004	2/10/2004	2/12/2004	2/27/2004
0.465	7/28/2004	8/11/2004	8/13/2004	8/31/2004

Indicated dividend: $1.86 (company has a dividend reinvestment plan).

TABLE 11.24   OTHER DIVIDEND INFORMATION

	12/31/ 2003	12/31/ 2002	12/31/ 2001	12/31/ 2000	12/31/ 1999	12/31/ 1998
Earnings per share, $	1.08	1.15	1.75	1.66	1.32	1.12
PE ratio	29.40–22.69	25.17–19.50	14.84–12.57	15.51–10.77	18.13–12.74	22.27–17.69
Average yield, %	6.53	7.15	7.36	7.45	6.85	5.56
Dividend payout, $	169.44	157.39	100.57	98.80	110.61	114.29
Dividends per share, $	1.83	1.81	1.76	1.64	1.46	1.28
Return on equity, %	6.93	7.68	10.14	9.66	6.83	7.05
Return on assets, %	3.32	3.76	5.30	4.80	3.32	3.88

Cedar Fair LP

Symbol: FUN
Exchange: NYSE
Address: One Cedar Point Drive, Sandusky, OH 44870-5259
Telephone: 419-626-0830
Web site: www.cedarfair.com
Investor contact: 419-627-2233

Cedar Fair is a limited partnership managed by Cedar Fair Management Company, which primarily owns and operates amusement parks and water parks across the United States. Its seven amusement parks are Cedar Point, located on Lake Erie between Cleveland and Toledo; Knott's Berry Farm in Buena Park, California, near Los Angeles; Dorney Park and Wildwater Kingdom near Allentown, Pennsylvania; Geauga Lake, located near Cleveland; Valleyfair near Minneapolis/St. Paul; Worlds of Fun, located in Kansas City, Missouri; and Michigan's Adventure near Muskegon, Michigan. The Cedar Fair parks boast 5 of the top 11 steel rollercoasters in the world. Its five water parks are near San Diego and in Palm Springs, California, and are adjacent to the Cedar Point, Knott's Berry Farm, and Worlds of Fun amusement parks. The company also owns and operates four hotel facilities.

Traded on the New York Stock Exchange under the ticker symbol FUN, it is based in Sandusky, Ohio. It incorporated in 1983, reincorporated in 1987, and went public in April 1987. With a dividend history going back 16 years, in September 2004 it declared a quarterly distribution of $0.45 per share. For the six months ended June 27, 2004, the company reported a 1% rise in total revenues to $168.2 million. However, is also reported a 12% rise in net loss to $16.7 million. See Tables 11.25 through 11.27 for details on the company's performance.

TABLE 11.25   INTERIM EARNINGS, $ PER SHARE

	MARCH	JUNE	SEPTEMBER	DECEMBER
2001	(0.60)	0.13	2.10	(0.50)
2002	(0.63)	0.40	2.01	(0.39)
2003	(0.62)	0.33	2.16	(0.20)
2004	(0.59)	0.25	…	…

TABLE 11.26   INTERIM QUARTERLY DIVIDENDS, $ PER SHARE

AMOUNT	DECLARED	EX-DIVIDEND	RECORD DATE	PAID
0.44	9/26/2003	10/1/2003	10/3/2003	11/17/2003
0.44	12/12/2003	1/2/2004	1/6/2004	2/17/2004
0.45	3/8/2004	4/1/2004	4/5/2004	5/17/2004
0.45	6/24/2004	7/1/2004	7/6/2004	8/16/2004

Indicated dividend: $1.80 (company has a dividend reinvestment plan).

TABLE 11.27   OTHER DIVIDEND INFORMATION

	12/31/ 2003	12/31/ 2002	12/31/ 2001	12/31/ 2000	12/31/ 1999	12/31/ 1998
Earnings per share, $	1.67	1.39	1.13	1.50	1.63	1.58
PE ratio	18.58– 13.62	17.83– 14.60	22.11– 15.96	13.83– 11.71	15.95– 11.35	18.67– 13.92
Average yield, %	6.51	7.10	7.50	8.05	6.07	4.88
Dividend payout, $	104.19	118.71	139.82	100.17	85.12	81.33
Dividends per share, $	1.74	1.65	1.58	1.50	1.39	1.29
Return on equity, %	27.81	23.39	18.78	23.54	24.51	24.40
Return on assets, %	10.48	8.69	7.15	10.18	12.10	13.22

UNITED DOMINION REALTY TRUST

Symbol: UDR
Exchange: NYSE
Address: 1745 Shea Center Drive, Highlands Ranch, CO 80129
Telephone: 720-283-6120
Web site: www.udrt.com
Investor contact: 804-780-2691

United Dominion Realty Trust is a real estate investment trust that owns, develops, acquires, renovates, and manages middle-market apartment communities nationwide. As of December 31, 2003, its apartment portfolio included 264 communities located in 55 markets in 19 states, with a total of 76,244 completed apartment homes. United Dominion has historically acquired apartments, but in 1996 it acquired another apartment company and began building communities. As of September 2004, the company reported 1,311 homes under development. Traded on the New York Stock Exchange under the ticker symbol UDR, the company focuses on the broad middle-market segment of the apartment that generally consists of young professionals, blue-collar families, single-parent households, older singles, immigrants, nonrelated parties, and families renting while waiting to purchase a home.

Founded in 1972 and based in Colorado, the company is one of the largest multifamily REITs in the United States. United Dominion Realty Trust has raised its dividend over last 28 years and has provided a total annualized return to shareholders of 17%. It revenues rose 8% to $311.2 million in the six months ended June 30, 2004, and net income from continuing operations rose $2.9 million to $13.9 million on the back of increased rental incomes. See Tables 11.28 through 11.30 for details on the company's performance.

TABLE 11.28   INTERIM EARNINGS, $ PER SHARE

	MARCH	JUNE	SEPTEMBER	DECEMBER
2001	(0.03)	0.20	0.07	0.03
2002	0.07	0.07	0.03	0.04
2003	0.05	0.01	(0.06)	0.05
2004	0.05	0.06	…	…

TABLE 11.29   INTERIM QUARTERLY DIVIDENDS, $ PER SHARE

AMOUNT	DECLARED	EX-DIVIDEND	RECORD DATE	PAID
0.285	9/25/2003	10/15/2003	10/17/2003	10/31/2003
0.285	12/5/2003	1/14/2004	1/16/2004	2/2/2004
0.293	3/18/2004	4/14/2004	4/16/2004	4/30/2004
0.293	5/11/2004	7/14/2004	7/16/2004	8/2/2004

Indicated dividend: $1.17 (company has a dividend reinvestment plan).

TABLE 11.30   OTHER DIVIDEND INFORMATION

	12/31/ 2003	12/31/ 2002	12/31/ 2001	12/31/ 2000	12/31/ 1999	12/31/ 1998
Earnings per share, $	0.05	0.21	0.27	0.41	0.54	0.49
PE ratio	387.4– 304.4	79.52– 66.43	54.52– 39.81	28.66– 23.02	22.11– 17.25	30.10– 20.54
Average yield, %	6.53	7.18	8.10	10.22	9.86	8.11
Dividend payout, $	N.A.	525.00	399.07	260.37	195.83	212.24
Dividends per share, $	1.132	1.103	1.078	1.068	1.058	1.040
Return on equity, %	4.44	5.00	6.26	6.22	7.07	5.27
Return on assets, %	1.46	1.53	1.95	2.19	2.51	1.93

TOP 14 HOUSEHOLD NAME DIVIDEND ACHIEVERS

RANK	COMPANY	TICKER SYMBOL
1	ALLTEL Corp	AT
2	Altria Group Inc	MO
3	Anheuser-Busch Companies Inc	BUD
4	Caterpillar Inc	CAT
5	Citigroup Inc	C
6	Coca-Cola Co (The)	KO
7	Exxon Mobil Corp	XOM
8	General Electric Co	GE
9	Harley-Davidson Inc	HDI
10	Hershey Foods Corp	HSY
11	Home Depot Inc	HD
12	McDonald's Corp	MCD
13	Merck & Co Inc	MRK
14	Wal-Mart Stores Inc	WMT

ALLTEL CORP

Symbol: AT
Exchange: NYSE
Address: One Allied Drive, Little Rock, AR 72202
Telephone: 501-905-8000
Web site: www.alltel.com
Investor contact: 501-905-8991

ALLTEL is the country's sixth largest local telephone company and the seventh largest wireless company, providing telecommunications services to business and residential customers in 26 states. It provides wireless and wireline local and long-distance services, as well as network access and Internet services, via a subsidiary. It has a number of subsidiaries, including ALLTEL Publishing, which publishes more than 338 directories in 35 states annually and distributes more than 8 million directory copies a year. Another subsidiary, ALLTEL Communications Products, and ALLTEL Telecom (formerly Convergys), provides billing, customer service and other outsourcing services such as data outsourcing and HR management. ALLTEL has grown quickly over the last 10 years, with its communications customer base growing from 2.5 million in 1996 to 12.8 million customers as of mid-2004. Its revenues over the same period increased from $2.4 billion to $8 billion. Based in Little Rock, Arkansas, and traded on the New York Stock Exchange under the ticker symbol AT, it mainly services the East, South, and Midwest.

ALLTEL has a history of dividend increases going back 43 years as of mid-2004. In July 2004 it announced a quarterly dividend of $0.37 on the company's common stock; its current annual payment is $1.43 per share. For the six months ended June 2004, ALLTEL reported revenues of $4 billion, 2% higher than the previous period. It also reported net income from continuing operations for the period of $452.3 million. See Tables 11.31 through 11.33 for details on the company's performance.

TABLE 11.31   INTERIM EARNINGS, $ PER SHARE

	MARCH	JUNE	SEPTEMBER	DECEMBER
2001	1.19	0.70	0.71	0.74
2002	0.68	0.69	0.76	0.83
2003	0.73	0.72	0.78	0.82
2004	0.61	0.85	…	…

TABLE 11.32   INTERIM QUARTERLY DIVIDENDS, $ PER SHARE

AMOUNT	DECLARED	EX-DIVIDEND	RECORD DATE	PAID
0.37	10/23/2003	12/4/2003	12/8/2003	1/3/2004
0.37	1/22/2004	2/20/2004	2/24/2004	4/3/2004
0.37	4/22/2004	6/9/2004	6/11/2004	7/3/2004
0.37	7/22/2004	9/8/2004	9/10/2004	10/3/2004

Indicated dividend: $1.48 (company has a dividend reinvestment plan).

TABLE 11.33   OTHER DIVIDEND INFORMATION

	12/31/ 2003	12/31/ 2002	12/31/ 2001	12/31/ 2000	12/31/ 1999	12/31/ 1998
Earnings per share, $	3.05	2.96	3.34	6.20	2.47	1.89
PE ratio	18.38– 13.49	21.14– 12.48	20.43– 15.12	13.34– 7.73	36.99– 23.10	32.34– 20.83
Average yield, %	2.99	2.74	2.25	2.05	1.72	2.58
Dividend payout, $	45.90	45.95	39.52	20.65	49.39	61.38
Dividends per share, $	2.99	2.74	2.25	2.05	1.72	2.58
Return on equity, %	13.58	15.41	18.82	38.57	18.63	16.07
Return on assets, %	5.72	5.64	8.31	16.13	7.27	5.61

ALTRIA GROUP INC

Symbol: MO
Exchange: NYSE
Address: 120 Park Avenue, New York, NY 10017
Telephone: 917-663-5000
Web site: http://www.altria.com
Investor contact: 917-663-3460

Altria Group, through its wholly-owned subsidiaries Philip Morris USA Inc. and Philip Morris International Inc. and its 84.6% majority-owned subsidiary Kraft Foods Inc., is engaged in the manufacture and sale of various consumer products, including cigarettes, packaged grocery products, snacks, beverages, cheese, and convenience meals. Formerly Philip Morris Companies Inc, its major premium brands (now held by Philip Morris USA) include Marlboro, Virginia Slims, and Parliament. Its principal discount brand is Basic. Philip Morris Capital Corporation, another wholly-owned subsidiary, is primarily engaged in leasing activities. Altria Group is also the largest shareholder in the world's second-largest brewer, SABMiller plc, with a 36% interest. Traded on the New York Stock Exchange under the ticker symbol MO, but only in existence since 1985, the company's roots go back 150 years.

Although Altria Group has been embroiled in ongoing tobacco-related litigation for years, it retains its place as a leading U.S. company—and continues to be highly profitable. For the six months ended June 30, 2004, it reported sales of $44.85 billion—12% higher than the previous period. Net income was $4.82 billion, up 4%. The company also has a consistently strong record of dividend increases, with quarterly increases going back 38 years. More recently, in August 2004, it increased its regular quarterly dividend by 7.4%, to $0.73 per common share, or an annualized rate of $2.92 per common share. See Tables 11.34 through 11.36 for details on the company's performance.

TABLE 11.34   INTERIM EARNINGS, $ PER SHARE

	MARCH	JUNE	SEPTEMBER	DECEMBER
2001	0.80	1.03	1.06	0.99
2002	1.09	1.21	2.06	0.85
2003	1.07	1.20	1.22	1.03
2004	1.07	1.27	...	...

TABLE 11.35   INTERIM QUARTERLY DIVIDENDS, $ PER SHARE

AMOUNT	DECLARED	EX-DIVIDEND	RECORD DATE	PAID
0.68	12/10/2003	12/18/2003	12/22/2003	1/9/2004
0.68	2/25/2004	3/11/2004	3/15/2004	4/12/2004
0.68	5/26/2004	6/14/2004	6/15/2004	7/9/2004
0.73	8/25/2004	9/13/2004	9/15/2004	10/12/2004

Indicated dividend: $2.92 (company has a dividend reinvestment plan).

TABLE 11.36   OTHER DIVIDEND INFORMATION

	12/31/ 2003	12/31/ 2002	12/31/ 2001	12/31/ 2000	12/31/ 1999	12/31/ 1998
Earnings per share, $	4.52	5.21	3.88	3.75	3.19	2.20
PE ratio	12.15–6.22	11.08–6.94	13.65–10.34	12.07–5.03	17.28–6.92	26.51–15.99
Average yield, %	6.29	4.99	4.59	7.14	4.94	3.70
Dividend payout, $	57.52	45.68	55.93	52.53	56.43	74.55
Dividends per share, $	2.60	2.38	2.17	1.97	1.80	1.64
Return on equity, %	36.83	57.41	43.66	56.71	50.15	33.17
Return on assets, %	9.60	12.77	10.08	10.76	12.50	8.97

ANHEUSER-BUSCH COMPANIES INC

Symbol: BUD
Exchange: NYSE
Address: One Busch Place, St. Louis, MO 63118
Telephone: 314-577-2000
Web site: www.anheuser_busch.com
Investor contact: 314-577-9629

Anheuser-Busch is the parent holding company of Anheuser-Busch, Inc., the world's largest brewer of beer. Its beer is sold under well-known brand names including Budweiser, Michelob, Busch, and Natural Light, with worldwide sales of beer brands reaching 129 million barrels in 2003. Gross sales in 2003 exceeded $16 billion. Anheuser-Busch also runs theme park operations via a subsidiary, Busch Entertainment Corporation, which owned nine theme parks as of December 2003. As of September 2004 the company actually had 13 subsidiaries running various aspects of the company's empire. Among its other activities are packaging, malt and rice production, international beer, nonbeer beverages, real estate development, marketing communications, and transportation services. The company is a major manufacturer of aluminum cans. Recently it made a big assault on the rapidly growing Chinese market.

Established in 1852 and based in St. Louis, Missouri, the company trades on the New York Stock Exchange under the symbol and short name of one of its famous brands, BUD. It has increased its dividends for 29 years as of mid-2004. In July 2004 it announced another increase—a quarterly dividend of $0.245, an increase from the previous quarter's $0.22. For the six months ended June 2004, its net sales were $7.49 billion, up 6%. Net income was $1.22 billion, up 9%. See Tables 11.37 through 11.39 for details on the company's performance.

TABLE 11.37   INTERIM EARNINGS, $ PER SHARE

	MARCH	JUNE	SEPTEMBER	DECEMBER
2001	0.43	0.58	0.62	0.26
2002	0.51	0.66	0.71	0.32
2003	0.57	0.75	0.80	0.36
2004	0.67	0.83	...	...

TABLE 11.38   INTERIM QUARTERLY DIVIDENDS, $ PER SHARE

AMOUNT	DECLARED	EX-DIVIDEND	RECORD DATE	PAID
0.22	10/22/2003	11/6/2003	11/10/2003	12/9/2003
0.22	1/14/2004	2/5/2004	2/9/2004	3/9/2004
0.22	4/28/2004	5/6/2004	5/10/2004	6/9/2004
0.245	7/28/2004	8/5/2004	8/9/2004	9/9/2004

Indicated dividend: $0.98 (company has a dividend reinvestment plan).

TABLE 11.39   OTHER DIVIDEND INFORMATION

	12/31/2003	12/31/2002	12/31/2001	12/31/2000	12/31/1999	12/31/1998
Earnings per share, $	2.48	2.20	1.89	1.69	1.47	1.27
PE ratio	21.65–18.52	24.99–20.00	24.61–20.37	29.47–16.29	27.85–22.15	26.98–17.14
Average yield, %	1.65	1.49	1.62	1.62	1.59	2.11
Dividend payout, $	33.47	34.09	36.51	37.28	39.46	42.69
Dividends per share, $	0.83	0.75	0.69	0.63	0.58	0.54
Return on equity, %	76.55	63.36	42.41	37.58	35.76	29.25
Return on assets, %	14.13	13.70	12.42	11.86	11.09	9.88

CATERPILLAR INC

Symbol: CAT
Exchange: NYSE
Address: 100 NE Adams Street, Peoria, IL 61629-7310
Telephone: 309-675-1000
Web site: www.cat.com
Investor contact: 309-675-4549

Caterpillar is a leading manufacturer of construction and mining equipment, diesel and natural gas engines, and industrial gas turbines. It operates three principal lines of business: a machinery division, an engine division, and a financial products division. The machinery division designs, manufactures, and markets construction, mining, agricultural, and forestry machinery. The engine division designs, manufactures, and markets engines for Caterpillar machinery; electric power generation systems; on-highway trucks and locomotives; and marine, petroleum, construction, industrial, agricultural, and other applications. Its engines range from 5 to over 22,000 horsepower, and turbines range from 1,600 to 19,500 horsepower. The financial products division consists primarily of Caterpillar Financial Services Corporation, Caterpillar Insurance Holdings Inc., and subsidiaries.

Based in Peoria, Illinois, it has offices all over the world and manufacturing operations in 50 locations across the United States and 65 other locations in 23 countries. Established in 1890, it now trades on the New York Stock Exchange under the ticker symbol CAT. As of mid-2004, it had increased its dividend every quarter for 10 years and in June 2004 announced an $0.04 per share dividend increase to $0.41 per share (or $1.64 on an annualized basis). For the six months ended June 30, 2004, revenues were $14.03 billion, up 30%, and net income was $964 million. In 2003, Caterpillar posted sales and revenues of $22.76 billion and a profit of $1.1 billion. Approximately half of all sales were to customers outside the United States. See Tables 11.40 through 11.42 for details on the company's performance.

TABLE 11.40   INTERIM EARNINGS, $ PER SHARE

	MARCH	JUNE	SEPTEMBER	DECEMBER
2001	0.47	0.78	0.59	0.48
2002	0.23	0.58	0.61	0.88
2003	0.37	1.15	0.62	0.99
2004	1.16	1.55	...	...

TABLE 11.41   INTERIM QUARTERLY DIVIDENDS, $ PER SHARE

AMOUNT	DECLARED	EX-DIVIDEND	RECORD DATE	PAID
0.37	10/8/2003	10/16/2003	10/20/2003	11/20/2003
0.37	12/10/2003	1/15/2004	1/20/2004	2/20/2004
0.37	4/14/2004	4/22/2004	4/26/2004	5/20/2004
0.41	6/9/2004	7/16/2004	7/20/2004	8/20/2004

Indicated dividend: $1.64 (company has a dividend reinvestment plan).

TABLE 11.42   OTHER DIVIDEND INFORMATION

	12/31/ 2003	12/31/ 2002	12/31/ 2001	12/31/ 2000	12/31/ 1999	12/31/ 1998
Earnings per share, $	3.13	2.30	2.32	3.02	2.63	4.11
PE ratio	27.08– 13.43	26.00– 14.72	24.22– 17.28	17.65– 9.87	24.90– 16.33	14.77– 9.81
Average yield, %	2.34	2.91	2.84	3.44	2.31	2.18
Dividend payout, $	45.37	60.87	59.48	44.04	47.53	26.76
Dividends per share, $	1.42	1.40	1.38	1.33	1.25	1.10
Return on equity, %	10.35	5.06	2.64	6.52	7.06	19.96
Return on assets, %	1.72	0.84	0.48	1.28	1.45	4.08

CITIGROUP INC

Symbol: C
Exchange: NYSE
Address: 399 Park Avenue, New York, NY 10043
Telephone: 212-559-1000
Web site: www.citigroup.com
Investor contact: 212-559-9446

Citigroup is one of the world's largest banking groups and provides a wide array of financial services to consumers and corporations through its many divisions. For reporting purposes Citigroup is organized into five groups: Citigroup Global Consumer Group, Global Corporate and Investment Banking Group, Citigroup Global Investment Management, Citigroup International, and Smith Barney. Dating back to 1812, the group has more than 200 million customer accounts in more than 100 countries. It focuses on nine key product lines: credit cards, consumer finance, retail banking, capital markets and banking, global transaction services, life insurance and annuities, private banking, asset management, and private client services. Other major brand names under Citigroup's trademark red umbrella include CitiCards, CitiFinancial, CitiMortgage, CitiInsurance, Primerica, Diners Club, Citigroup Asset Management, The Citigroup Private Bank, and CitiCapital.

Based in New York City, it trades under the ticker symbol C on the New York Stock Exchange. As of mid-2004, Citigroup had a 17-year history of consecutive dividend increases every quarter. In July 2004, it announced a dividend of $0.40 per share. It also reported net income for the three months ended June 30, 2004 of $1.14 billion. However, its results were hit by a $4.95 billion after-tax charge for the WorldCom class action settlement and increased litigation reserves related to 2003 regulatory settlements. For the six months ended June 30, 2004, net income was $6.4 billion. See Tables 11.43 through 11.45 for details on the company's performance.

TABLE 11.43   INTERIM EARNINGS, $ PER SHARE

	MARCH	JUNE	SEPTEMBER	DECEMBER
2001	0.70	0.71	0.61	0.73
2002	0.94	0.78	0.72	0.15
2003	0.79	0.83	0.90	0.90
2004	1.01	0.22	...	...

TABLE 11.44   INTERIM QUARTERLY DIVIDENDS, $ PER SHARE

AMOUNT	DECLARED	EX-DIVIDEND	RECORD DATE	PAID
0.35	10/21/2003	10/30/2003	11/3/2003	11/26/2003
0.40	1/20/2004	1/29/2004	2/2/2004	2/27/2004
0.40	4/20/2004	4/29/2004	5/3/2004	5/28/2004
0.40	7/20/2004	7/29/2004	8/2/2004	8/27/2004

Indicated dividend: $1.60 (company has a dividend reinvestment plan).

TABLE 11.45   OTHER DIVIDEND INFORMATION

	12/31/ 2003	12/31/ 2002	12/31/ 2001	12/31/ 2000	12/31/ 1999	12/31/ 1998
Earnings per share, $	3.42	2.59	2.75	2.62	2.15	1.22
PE ratio	14.33– 9.19	20.08– 10.32	20.47– 13.22	22.28– 13.76	20.32– 11.54	30.04– 13.07
Average yield, %	2.63	1.75	1.23	1.08	1.18	1.02
Dividend payout, $	32.16	27.03	21.82	19.85	18.88	22.84
Dividends per share, $	1.10	0.70	0.60	0.52	0.41	0.28
Return on equity, %	18.21	15.51	17.58	20.42	20.11	13.60
Return on assets, %	1.41	1.23	1.36	1.50	1.39	0.87

COCA-COLA CO (THE)

Symbol: KO
Exchange: NYSE
Address: One Coca-Cola Plaza, Atlanta, GA 30313
Telephone: 404-676-2121
Web site: www.coca-cola.com
Investor contact: 404-676-5766

The Coca-Cola Company is arguably the world's leading and most famous bottled beverage maker, although its has diversified considerably since it first sold it famous drink in 1886. It now engages in the manufacturing, distributing, and marketing of a wide range of nonalcoholic beverage concentrates and syrups (more than 400 beverages, in fact). Its principal brands, include: Coca-Cola, Coca-Cola Classic, Diet Coke, Vanilla Coke, Cherry Coke, Fanta, Sprite, Mr. Pibb, Mello Yellow, Barq's, Powerade, Fresca, and Dasani. The company's drinks can be bought in almost all countries in the world, with more than 70% of the company's income coming from outside the United States.

Traded on the New York Stock Exchange under the ticker symbol KO, Coca-Cola has established a strong record of consistent dividend increases going back 42 years as of February 2004. In February, it announced a 14% increase of its quarterly dividend from $0.22 to $0.25 per common share, which equates to an annual dividend of $1.00 per share, up from $0.88 per share in 2003. For the six months ended June 30, 2004, it reported revenues of $11.04 billion, up 8%. Net income was $2.71 billion, an increase of 23%. See Tables 11.46 through 11.48 for details on the company's performance.

TABLE 11.46   INTERIM EARNINGS, $ PER SHARE

	MARCH	JUNE	SEPTEMBER	DECEMBER
2001	0.35	0.45	0.43	0.37
2002	0.32	0.52	0.47	0.29
2003	0.34	0.55	0.50	0.38
2004	0.46	0.65	...	...

TABLE 11.47   INTERIM QUARTERLY DIVIDENDS, $ PER SHARE

AMOUNT	DECLARED	EX-DIVIDEND	RECORD DATE	PAID
0.22	10/16/2003	1/26/2003	12/1/2003	12/15/2003
0.25	2/19/2004	3/11/2004	3/15/2004	4/1/2004
0.25	4/21/2004	6/14/2004	6/15/2004	7/1/2004
0.25	7/22/2004	9/13/2004	9/15/2004	10/1/2004

Indicated dividend: $1.00 (company has a dividend reinvestment plan).

TABLE 11.48   OTHER DIVIDEND INFORMATION

	12/31/ 2003	12/31/ 2002	12/31/ 2001	12/31/ 2000	12/31/ 1999	12/31/ 1998
Earnings per share, $	1.77	1.60	1.60	0.88	0.98	1.42
PE ratio	28.67– 20.94	36.03– 27.17	38.01– 26.78	75.99– 49.01	72.07– 48.53	61.93– 39.57
Average yield, %	2.00	1.61	1.48	1.23	1.03	0.83
Dividend payout, $	49.72	50.00	45.00	77.27	65.31	42.25
Dividends per share, $	0.88	0.80	0.72	0.68	0.64	0.60
Return on equity, %	30.85	33.69	35.01	23.37	25.55	42.04
Return on assets, %	15.90	16.23	17.75	10.45	11.24	18.45

Exxon Mobil Corp

Symbol: XOM
Exchange: NYSE
Address: 5959 Las Colinas Boulevard, Irving, TX 75039-2298
Telephone: 972-444-1000
Web site: www.exxonmobil.com
Investor contact: 212-444-1900

Exxon Mobil is one of the world's leading energy companies and is involved in exploration for crude oil and natural gas and the production and distribution of petroleum and petroleum products. Formed by the combination of two large companies in their own right, Exxon and Mobil, in 1998, the company is now a major manufacturer and marketer of basic petrochemicals, including olefins, aromatics, polyethylene and polypropylene plastics, and a wide variety of specialty products. Operating in more than 200 countries throughout the world, it has four key business areas: upstream exploration and production, downstream refining and marketing, chemicals production, and technology solutions.

Based in Texas, and traded on the New York Stock Exchange under the ticker symbol XOM, it also has significant investments in electric power generation facilities. Exxon and Mobil had a common history in the first place. In 1882 John D. Rockefeller organized his petroleum interests under the Standard Oil Trust, in which Standard Oil Co. of New Jersey and Standard Oil Co. of New York were incorporated. These two companies later became Exxon and Mobil, respectively. When considered as one entity, the company has a history of consecutive quarterly dividend increases going back 21 years. Its latest dividend was $0.27 per share, announced in July 2004. For the six months ended June 2004, its revenues were $138.30 billion, up 14%, and net income was $11.23 billion, up 5%. See Tables 11.49 through 11.51 for details on the company's performance.

TABLE 11.49   INTERIM EARNINGS, $ PER SHARE

	MARCH	JUNE	SEPTEMBER	DECEMBER
2001	0.71	0.63	0.46	0.38
2002	0.30	0.38	0.39	0.54
2003	0.97	0.62	0.55	1.01
2004	0.83	0.88	...	...

TABLE 11.50   INTERIM QUARTERLY DIVIDENDS, $ PER SHARE

AMOUNT	DECLARED	EX-DIVIDEND	RECORD DATE	PAID
0.25	10/29/2003	11/7/2003	11/12/2003	12/10/2003
0.25	1/28/2004	2/9/2004	2/11/2004	3/10/2004
0.27	4/28/2004	5/11/2004	5/13/2004	6/10/2004
0.27	7/28/2004	8/11/2004	8/13/2004	9/10/2004

Indicated dividend: $1.08 (company has a dividend reinvestment plan).

TABLE 11.51   OTHER DIVIDEND INFORMATION

	12/31/ 2003	12/31/ 2002	12/31/ 2001	12/31/ 2000	12/31/ 1999	12/31/ 1998
Earnings per share, $	3.15	1.61	2.18	2.28	1.13	1.31
PE ratio	13.02– 10.10	27.57– 18.80	21.00– 16.44	20.73– 15.60	38.42– 28.81	29.38– 22.27
Average yield, %	2.71	2.44	2.20	2.13	2.18	2.37
Dividend payout, $	31.11	57.14	41.74	38.68	74.22	62.84
Dividends per share, $	0.98	0.92	0.91	0.88	0.84	0.82
Return on equity, %	23.31	14.76	20.65	22.60	12.46	14.72

GENERAL ELECTRIC CO

Symbol: GE
Exchange: NYSE
Address: 3135 Easton Turnpike, Fairfield, CT 06828-0001
Telephone: 203-373-2211
Web site: www.ge.com
Investor contact: 203-373-2816

General Electric is one of the world's most pioneering companies. Its founder, Thomas Alva Edison, was the man credited with developing the electric light bulb as we know it today. In 1876 electrical exhibits at the Centennial Exposition in Philadelphia marked the beginning of a new era in energy. Just four years later, in 1890, Edison had organized his various businesses into the Edison General Electric Company. Now, General Electric is a highly diversified company developing, manufacturing, and marketing a wide variety of products for the generation, transmission, distribution, control, and utilization of electricity. It is organized into 11 segments: Advanced Materials, Commercial Finance, Consumer Finance, Consumer and Industrial, Energy, Equipment and Other Services, Healthcare, Infrastructure, Insurance, NBC Universal, and Transportation. Products include electrical distribution, power generation, and power delivery products; nuclear power support services and fuel assemblies; jet engines, chemicals and engineered materials; industrial automation products; major household appliances; lighting products; medical diagnostic imaging equipment; motors; and locomotives; the list seems to go on and on. Company dividend payments are as fundamental as the company itself. Its consecutive dividend payment history goes back 28 years. For the six months ended June 30, 2004, it reported revenues of $70.39 billion and net income of $7.16 billion. See Tables 11.52 through 11.54 for details on the company's performance.

TABLE 11.52   INTERIM EARNINGS, $ PER SHARE

	MARCH	JUNE	SEPTEMBER	DECEMBER
2001	0.30	0.39	0.33	0.39
2002	0.35	0.44	0.41	0.31
2003	0.32	0.38	0.40	0.45
2004	0.32	0.38	⋯	⋯

TABLE 11.53   INTERIM QUARTERLY DIVIDENDS, $ PER SHARE

AMOUNT	DECLARED	EX-DIVIDEND	RECORD DATE	PAID
0.19	9/12/2003	9/25/2003	9/29/2003	10/27/2003
0.20	12/12/2003	12/29/2003	12/31/2003	1/26/2004
0.20	2/13/2004	2/26/2004	3/1/2004	4/26/2004
0.20	6/11/2004	6/24/2004	6/28/2004	7/26/2004

Indicated dividend: $0.80 (company has a dividend reinvestment plan).

TABLE 11.54   OTHER DIVIDEND INFORMATION

	12/31/ 2003	12/31/ 2002	12/31/ 2001	12/31/ 2000	12/31/ 1999	12/31/ 1998
Earnings per share, $	1.55	1.51	1.41	1.27	1.07	0.93
PE ratio	20.72– 14.30	27.52– 14.57	37.87– 21.54	47.24– 32.84	49.55– 29.80	36.81– 25.56
Average yield, %	2.71	2.31	1.47	1.05	1.21	1.42
Dividend payout, $	49.03	47.68	45.39	43.04	43.49	42.86
Dividends per share, $	0.88	0.80	0.72	0.68	0.64	0.60
Return on equity, %	19.69	23.75	25.77	25.22	25.18	23.91
Return on Assets %	2.41	2.63	2.85	2.91	2.64	2.61

HARLEY-DAVIDSON INC

Symbol: HDI
Exchange: NYSE
Address: 3700 West Juneau Avenue, Milwaukee, WI 53208
Telephone: 414-342-4680
Web site: www.harley-davidson.com
Investor contact: 877-437-8625

Harley-Davidson began in 1901 when William S. Harley, at 21 years of age, created a blueprint drawing of an engine designed to fit into a bicycle. More than 100 years later the company is still producing some of the most famous motorcycles and parts in the world. It manufactures five families of motorcycles: Touring, Dyna Glide, Softail, VRSC, and Sportster. Its Buell Motorcycle Company subsidiary produces sport motorcycles, including four big-twin XB models and the single-cylinder Buell Blast.

Over the years, Harley-Davidson has turned itself into much more than just a motorcycle company. Harley-Davidson, Inc. (HDI) is the parent company for the group of companies doing business as Harley-Davidson Motor Company, Buell Motorcycle Company, and Harley-Davidson Financial Services. Harley-Davidson Financial Services Inc and its subsidiaries provide financing and servicing of wholesale inventory receivables and retail loans, primarily for the purchase of motorcycles, but also offer property/casualty insurance and extended service contracts through certain unaffiliated carriers. Harley-Davidson has also turned itself into a solid performing company. It boasts that as of mid-2004 it had produced 18 consecutive years of record revenues and earnings. Based in Milwaukee, Wisconsin, and traded on the New York Stock Exchange under the ticker symbol HDI, Harley-Davidson had raised its dividend every quarter for ten consecutive years as of mid-2004. For the six months ended June 2004, the company reported sales of $2.66 billion and net income of $451.8 million. See Tables 11.55 through 11.57 for details on the company's performance.

TABLE 11.55   INTERIM EARNINGS, $ PER SHARE

	MARCH	JUNE	SEPTEMBER	DECEMBER
2001	0.30	0.38	0.36	0.39
2002	0.39	0.47	0.54	0.50
2003	0.61	0.66	0.62	0.61
2004	0.68	0.83	...	...

TABLE 11.56   INTERIM QUARTERLY DIVIDENDS, $ PER SHARE

AMOUNT	DECLARED	EX-DIVIDEND	RECORD DATE	PAID
0.08	12/5/2003	12/11/2003	12/15/2003	12/29/2003
0.08	2/10/2004	3/9/2004	3/11/2004	3/25/2004
0.10	4/24/2004	6/1/2004	6/3/2004	6/24/2004
0.10	8/4/2004	9/13/2004	9/15/2004	9/29/2004

Indicated dividend: $0.40 (company has a dividend reinvestment plan).

TABLE 11.57   OTHER DIVIDEND INFORMATION

	12/31/ 2003	12/31/ 2002	12/31/ 2001	12/31/ 2000	12/31/ 1999	12/31/ 1998	12/31/ 1997
Earnings per share, $	2.50	1.90	1.43	1.13	0.865	0.69	0.565
PE ratio	20.98– 14.38	30.00– 22.54	38.92– 24.61	44.25– 26.22	37.03– 26.84	34.33– 18.21	27.27– 14.99
Average yield, %	0.52	0.20	0.25	0.24	0.31	0.55	0.42
Dividend payout, $	9.20	5.26	8.04	8.63	10.12	13.77	8.85
Dividends per share, %	0.230	0.100	0.115	0.098	0.088	0.095	0.050
Return on equity, %	25.73	25.98	24.92	24.74	23.01	20.73	21.06
Return on assets, %	15.46	15.03	14.04	14.27	12.65	11.12	10.89

Hershey Foods Corp

Symbol: HSY
Exchange: NYSE
Address: 100 Crystal A Drive, Hershey, PA 17033
Telephone: 717-534-6799
Web site: www.hersheys.com
Investor contact: 800-539-0261

Hershey Foods is a leading confectionery and grocery products manufacturer, producing more than 50 brands and selling them in more than 90 countries. It also manufactures and distributes a range of related products, including baking ingredients, chocolate drink mixes, peanut butter, dessert toppings, and a range of beverages. Its leading brands include Hershey's, Reese's, Mr. Goodbar, Jolly Rancher, Kit Kat, Milk Duds, Whoppers, York, Twizzlers, Super Bubble, Ice Breakers, Breath Savers, and Carefree. The company's origins date back to 1894 in Lancaster, Pennsylvania, when Milton Hershey produced sweet chocolate as a coating for his caramels. The Hershey Chocolate Company was later formed. Still based in Pennsylvania, Hershey Foods Corporation now has 13,700 employees and net sales in excess of $4 billion. As of mid-2004 it had raised its dividend every quarter for 29 consecutive years, and in July 2004 it announced a quarterly dividend increase of 11.4%. For the six months ended July 4, 2004, it reported a 6% increase in revenue from the previous period's $1.91 billion. Net income was $254.4 million. See Tables 11.58 through 11.60 for details on the company's performance.

TABLE 11.58   INTERIM EARNINGS, $ PER SHARE

	MARCH	JUNE	SEPTEMBER	DECEMBER
2001	0.285	0.19	0.44	(0.165)
2002	0.315	0.23	0.445	0.475
2003	0.365	0.27	0.575	0.55
2004	0.41	0.56	···	···

TABLE 11.59   INTERIM QUARTERLY DIVIDENDS, $ PER SHARE

AMOUNT	DECLARED	EX-DIVIDEND	RECORD DATE	PAID
0.198	2/17/2004	2/23/2004	2/25/2004	3/15/2004
100%	4/22/2004	6/16/2004	5/25/2004	6/15/2004
0.198	4/28/2004	5/21/2004	5/25/2004	6/15/2004
0.22	7/28/2004	8/23/2004	8/25/2004	9/15/2004

Indicated dividend: $0.88 (company has a dividend reinvestment plan).

TABLE 11.60   OTHER DIVIDEND INFORMATION

	12/31/ 2003	12/31/ 2002	12/31/ 2001	12/31/ 2000	12/31/ 1999	12/31/ 1998
Earnings per share, $	1.76	1.465	0.75	1.21	1.63	1.17
PE ratio	22.30– 17.41	27.13– 19.58	46.21– 38.00	27.12– 15.60	19.63– 14.21	32.51– 25.56
Average yield, %	2.05	1.86	1.85	2.20	1.82	1.36
Dividend payout, $	41.05	43.00	77.67	44.63	30.67	39.32
Dividends per share, $	0.723	0.630	0.583	0.540	0.500	0.460
Return on equity, %	36.98	29.42	19.73	28.47	64.09	32.71
Return on Assets %	13.21	11.60	6.97	9.70	21.04	10.01

HOME DEPOT INC

Symbol: HD
Exchange: NYSE
Address: 2455 Paces Ferry Road N.W., Atlanta, GA 30339-4024
Telephone: 770-433-8211
Web site: www.homedepot.com
Investor contact: 770-384-4388

Home Depot is one of the country's largest home improvement retailers and it has done well from the boom in home renovations and improvements in recent years, claiming to be the fastest growing retailer in history and now having reached $20 billion in sales in a quarter. More than 22 million people visit one of Home Depot's more than 1,700 stores in the United States, Canada, Mexico, and Puerto Rico each week. Catering to both individuals and professionals who serve the home improvement, construction, and building maintenance markets, it also operates 54 Expo Design Center stores that sell products and services primarily for home decorating and remodeling projects. Under the Home Depot name are also 11 Home Depot Landscape Supply stores, 5 Home Depot Supply stores, and 2 Home Depot Floor Store outlets.

Founded in 1978, the Atlanta-based company has publicly traded on the New York Stock Exchange under the ticker symbol HD since 1981. It has consistently raised its dividend for the past 16 years and in August 2004 announced its 69th consecutive quarterly cash dividend—$0.085 cents per share. It also reported record second quarter fiscal 2004 net earnings of $1.5 billion, up 25 percent, from second quarter fiscal 2003. Sales for the period increased $2 billion, or 1%, to $20 billion. See Tables 11.61 through 11.63 for details on the company's performance.

TABLE 11.61   INTERIM EARNINGS, $ PER SHARE

	APRIL	JULY	OCTOBER	JANUARY
2001	0.27	0.39	0.33	0.30
2002	0.36	0.50	0.40	0.30
2003	0.39	0.56	0.50	0.43
2004	0.49	0.70	...	...

TABLE 11.62   INTERIM QUARTERLY DIVIDENDS, $ PER SHARE

AMOUNT	DECLARED	EX-DIVIDEND	RECORD DATE	PAID
0.07	11/20/2003	12/2/2003	12/4/2003	12/18/2003
0.07	2/26/2004	3/9/2004	3/11/2004	3/22/2004
0.085	5/26/2004	6/8/2004	6/10/2004	6/24/2004
0.085	8/6/2004	8/31/2004	9/2/2004	9/16/2004

Indicated dividend: $0.34 (company has a dividend reinvestment plan).

TABLE 11.63   OTHER DIVIDEND INFORMATION

	02/01/ 2004	02/02/ 2003	02/03/ 2002	01/28/ 2001	01/30/ 2000	01/31/ 1999	02/01/ 1998
Earnings per share, $	1.88	1.56	1.29	1.10	1.00	0.71	0.5167
PE ratio	19.96– 11.01	33.38– 13.16	41.43– 25.43	61.82– 31.70	68.56– 36.29	57.81– 29.02	39.15– 21.50
Average yield, %	0.83	0.60	0.37	0.31	0.25	0.27	0.40
Dividend payout, $	13.83	13.46	13.18	14.55	11.33	10.80	12.26
Dividends per share, %	0.260	0.210	0.170	0.160	0.113	0.077	0.063
Return on equity, %	19.21	18.50	16.83	17.20	18.80	18.47	16.34
Return on assets, %	12.50	12.21	11.53	12.07	13.58	11.99	10.33

McDonald's Corp

Symbol: MCD
Exchange: NYSE
Address: McDonald's Plaza, Oak Brook, IL 60523
Telephone: 630-623-3000
Web site: www.mcdonalds.com
Investor contact: 630-623-7428

McDonald's is most famous for its hamburgers, but the company has come a long way since Ray Kroc opened his first McDonald's restaurant in 1955 in Des Plaines, Illinois. The company now has more than 30,000 restaurants in 119 countries and serves 47 million customers each day. As December 2003, McDonald's had around 18,000 restaurants operated by franchisees, more than 8,000 restaurants operated by the company itself, and about 4,000 operated by affiliates. It also has diversified into other businesses, although it has scaled back a little in recent years. It also operates Boston Market and Chipotle Mexican Grill in the United States and has a minority ownership interest in Pret A Manger. In 2003, however, it sold its Donatos Pizzeria business.

Based in Illinois and traded on the New York Stock Exchange under the ticker symbol MCD, it has raised its dividend every quarter consecutively for 27 years as of mid-2004. In September 2004 it announced a 38% increase on its annual dividend from $0.40 per share to $0.55 per share—totaling nearly $690 million in distributions. As such, over the past two years, McDonald's has more than doubled the dividend from $0.235 per share in 2002 to $0.55 per share in 2004. For the six months ended June 30, 2004, total revenues increased 13% to $9.13 billion and net income 32% to $1.1 billion. See Tables 11.64 through 11.66 for details on the company's performance.

TABLE 11.64   INTERIM EARNINGS, $ PER SHARE

	MARCH	JUNE	SEPTEMBER	DECEMBER
2001	0.29	0.34	0.42	0.20
2002	0.27	0.39	0.38	(0.27)
2003	0.29	0.37	0.43	0.09
2004	0.40	0.47	…	…

TABLE 11.65   INTERIM QUARTERLY DIVIDENDS, $ PER SHARE

AMOUNT	DECLARED	EX-DIVIDEND	RECORD DATE	PAID
0.215A	9/12/2000	11/13/2000	11/15/2000	12/1/2000
0.225A	10/29/2001	11/13/2001	11/15/2001	12/3/2001
0.235A	10/22/2002	11/13/2002	11/15/2002	12/2/2002
0.40A	9/24/2003	11/12/2003	11/14/2003	12/1/2003

Indicated dividend: $0.40 (company has a dividend reinvestment plan).

TABLE 11.66   OTHER DIVIDEND INFORMATION

	12/31/ 2003	12/31/ 2002	12/31/ 2001	12/31/ 2000	12/31/ 1999	12/31/ 1998
Earnings per share, $	1.18	0.77	1.25	1.46	1.39	1.10
PE ratio	22.51– 10.49	39.81– 20.10	27.75– 20.00	29.32– 18.36	34.80– 27.09	35.60– 20.63
Average yield, %	1.98	0.97	0.79	0.64	0.46	0.57
Dividend payout, $	33.90	30.52	18.00	14.73	14.03	16.02
Dividends per share, $	0.400	0.235	0.225	0.215	0.195	0.176
Return on equity, %	13.66	11.22	18.72	24.92	22.93	17.95
Return on Assets %	6.41	4.81	7.88	10.58	10.53	8.59

MERCK & CO INC

Symbol: MRK
Exchange: NYSE
Address: One Merck Drive, Whitehouse Station, NJ 08889-0100
Telephone: 908-423-1000
Web site: www.merck.com
Investor contact: 908-423-5881

Merck & Co. is a multinational pharmaceutical company that develops and distributes a wide range of pharmaceutical agents and vaccines in a number of therapeutic areas. With more than 60,000 employees, it has an active research program and has joined the race for an effective treatment for HIV and SARS. It has achieved strong sales results over the last year with Fosamax for osteoporosis, Cozaar/Hyzaar for high blood pressure, Vioxx and Arcoxia for arthritis and pain (although Vioxx has been re-called), and Proscar for benign prostate enlargement. Merck has 11 research facilities in the United States, Europe, and Japan; the primary therapeutic areas on which it focuses its research are arthritis, asthma, cancer, cardiovascular disease, diabetes, gastroenterology, immunology, infectious diseases, neurology, obesity, ophthalmology, osteoporosis, and prostate disease. As a manufacturer, Merck sells its products primarily to wholesalers and retail outlets such as hospitals, clinics, government agencies, and managed health care providers. It manufactures in 32 facilities and sells its products in more than 150 countries.

Based in New Jersey and traded on the New York Stock Exchange under the ticker symbol MRK, it has increased its dividend every quarter for 20 years. In July 2004 it announced a quarterly dividend of $0.38 per share for the fourth quarter of 2004. Full-year dividends paid per share will be $1.49, a 3% increase over dividends paid in 2003. For the six months ended June 30, 2004, net sales were $11.65 billion, up 5%, and net income from continuing operations was $3.39 billion, up 2%. See Tables 11.67 through 11.69 for details on the company's performance.

TABLE 11.67   INTERIM EARNINGS, $ PER SHARE

	MARCH	JUNE	SEPTEMBER	DECEMBER
2001	0.71	0.78	0.84	0.81
2002	0.71	0.77	0.83	0.8.
2003	0.76	0.83	0.83	0.50
2004	0.73	0.79	...	...

TABLE 11.68   INTERIM QUARTERLY DIVIDENDS, $ PER SHARE

AMOUNT	DECLARED	EX-DIVIDEND	RECORD DATE	PAID
0.37	11/25/2003	12/3/2003	12/5/2003	1/2/2004
0.37	2/24/2004	3/3/2004	3/5/2004	4/1/2004
0.37	5/25/2004	6/2/2004	6/4/2004	7/1/2004
0.38	7/27/2004	9/1/2004	9/3/2004	10/1/2004

Indicated dividend: $1.52 (company has a dividend reinvestment plan).

TABLE 11.69   OTHER DIVIDEND INFORMATION

	12/31/ 2003	12/31/ 2002	12/31/ 2001	12/31/ 2000	12/31/ 1999	12/31/ 1998
Earnings per share, $	2.92	3.14	3.14	2.90	2.45	2.15
PE ratio	21.66– 13.90	20.50– 12.44	29.62– 18.21	32.72– 18.60	35.26– 24.87	36.93– 23.98
Average yield, %	2.72	2.61	1.92	1.64	1.50	1.47
Dividend payout, $	49.66	44.90	43.63	41.72	44.90	43.95
Dividends per share, $	1.450	1.410	1.370	1.210	1.100	0.945
Return on equity, %	48.39	46.37	53.92	56.31	55.99	71.59
Return on Assets %	18.57	17.74	19.66	20.93	20.81	28.77

WAL-MART STORES INC

Symbol: WMT
Exchange: NYSE
Address: 702 S.W. Eighth Street, Bentonville, AR 72716
Telephone: 479-273-4000
Web site: www.wal-mart.com
Investor contact: 479-273-8446

Founded by Sam Walton in Newport, Arkansas, the Wal-Mart's origins date back to 1945. But it was in the 1950s that the retailing empire that later became Wal-Mart began to take off. Now Wal-Mart claims 100 million customers every week across the United States as well as in its international businesses in Canada, Mexico, Puerto Rico, China, Brazil, Germany, Japan, the United Kingdom and South Korea. As of January 2004, it operated 1,478 discount department stores, 1,471 Supercenters, 538 Sam's Clubs, and 64 Neighborhood Markets in the United States. Its merchandise is widely diverse and includes food, household items, general merchandise, and pharmaceuticals, as well as services such as dry cleaning, portrait studios, photo finishing, hair salons, and optical services. It also runs an extensive membership warehouse club and a foundation.

Based in Arkansas, Wal-Mart trades on the New York and Pacific stock exchanges under the symbol WMT. In March 1974, Wal-Mart declared its first cash dividend of $0.05 per share and for the last 22 years it has increased its dividend every quarter. Most recently, in March 2004 it declared a quarterly dividend of $0.13 per share. It also announced an increase its annual dividend to $0.52 per share, a 44% increase from the $0.36 per share paid the previous fiscal year. For the second quarter ended July 31, 2004, net sales were $69.7 billion, an increase of 11.3% over the second quarter of fiscal 2003, and income from continuing operations was $2.7 billion, an increase of 16.1%. See Tables 11.70 through 11.72 for details on the company's performance.

TABLE 11.70   INTERIM EARNINGS, $ PER SHARE

	APRIL	JULY	OCTOBER	JANUARY
2001–02	0.30	0.36	0.33	0.50
2002–03	0.37	0.46	0.41	0.57
2003–04	0.41	0.52	0.46	0.64
2004–05	0.50	0.62	...	...

TABLE 11.71   INTERIM QUARTERLY DIVIDENDS, $ PER SHARE

AMOUNT	DECLARED	EX-DIVIDEND	RECORD DATE	PAID
0.13	3/2/2004	8/18/2004	8/20/2004	9/7/2004
0.13	3/2/2004	12/15/2004	12/17/2004	1/3/2005
0.13	3/2/2004	5/19/2004	5/21/2004	6/7/2004
0.13	3/2/2004	3/17/2004	3/19/2004	4/5/2004

Indicated dividend: $0.52 (company has a dividend reinvestment plan).

TABLE 11.72   OTHER DIVIDEND INFORMATION

	01/31/ 2004	01/31/ 2003	01/31/ 2002	01/31/ 2001	01/31/ 2000	01/31/ 1999	01/31/ 1998
Earnings per share, $	2.03	1.81	1.49	1.40	1.25	0.99	0.78
PE ratio	29.60– 23.02	35.22– 24.64	40.26– 29.53	45.40– 30.89	55.80– 32.15	43.43– 20.61	26.76– 14.90
Average yield, %	0.66	0.55	0.53	0.45	0.40	0.50	0.80
Dividend payout, $	17.73	16.57	18.79	17.14	16.00	15.66	17.31
Dividends per share, %	0.360	0.300	0.280	0.240	0.200	0.155	0.135
Return on equity, %	20.31	20.44	19.00	20.08	21.58	20.98	19.06
Return on assets, %	8.45	8.49	7.99	8.06	7.92	8.86	7.77

Top 10 Dividend Achievers by Consecutive Years of Dividend Increases

Rank	Years	Company	Ticker Symbol
Tie 1	50	American States Water Co.	AWR
Tie 1	50	Diebold Inc	DBD
Tie 1	50	Procter & Gamble Co	PG
2	48	Dover Corp	DOV
Tie 3	47	Emerson Electric Co	EMR
Tie 3	47	Genuine Parts Co	GPC
Tie 3	47	Parker-Hannifin Corp	PH
Tie 4	45	3M Co	MMM
Tie 4	45	Masco Corp	MAS
Tie 4	45	WPS Resources Corp	WPS

AMERICAN STATES WATER CO

Symbol: AWR
Exchange: NYSE
Address: 630 East Foothill Blvd., San Dimas, CA 91773-1212
Telephone: 909-394-3600
Web site: www.aswater.com
Investor contact: 909-394-3633

American States Water is a utility that generates and distributes water and electricity through its subsidiaries Southern California Water Company and American States Utility Services Inc. Through these, it provides water to 1 out of every 30 Californians in 75 communities in 10 counties in Northern, Coastal, and Southern California. In 2000, it acquired Chaparral City Water Company, an Arizona public company that serves approximately 11,000 customers in the Arizona town of Fountain Hills and parts of the city of Scottsdale. It also contracts with a number of municipalities and private companies in both California and Arizona to provide services to an additional 97,000 customers. It provides options for lease or purchase of tailored service contracts ranging from meter reading, customer service, system maintenance, and full operations.

Founded in 1929, the company trades on the New York Stock Exchange under the trading symbol AWR. It has a strong record of dividend achievement, paying dividends every year since 1931 and increasing its annual dividends consistently since 1953. More recently, in July, the company announced a quarterly dividend of $0.221 per share. In June, for the second quarter of 2004, it announced total operating revenues of $59.3 million, an increase of $7.5 million from revenues of $51.8 million in the second quarter of 2003. See Tables 11.73 through 11.75 for details on the company's performance.

TABLE 11.73 INTERIM EARNINGS, $ PER SHARE

	MARCH	JUNE	SEPTEMBER	DECEMBER
2001	0.71	0.78	0.84	0.81
2002	0.71	0.77	0.83	0.8.
2003	0.76	0.83	0.83	0.50
2004	0.73	0.79	...	...

TABLE 11.74 INTERIM QUARTERLY DIVIDENDS, $ PER SHARE

AMOUNT	DECLARED	EX-DIVIDEND	RECORD DATE	PAID
0.221	10/28/2003	11/5/2003	11/8/2003	12/1/2003
0.221	2/3/2004	2/5/2004	2/9/2004	3/1/2004
0.221	4/30/2004	5/6/2004	5/10/2004	6/1/2004
0.221	7/27/2004	8/5/2004	8/9/2004	9/1/2004

Indicated dividend: 0.884 (company has a dividend reinvestment plan).

TABLE 11.75 OTHER DIVIDEND INFORMATION

	12/31/ 2003	12/31/ 2002	12/31/ 2001	12/31/ 2000	12/31/ 1999	12/31/ 1998
Earnings per share, $	0.78	1.34	1.33	1.27	1.19	1.08
PE ratio	36.81–27.95	21.53–15.68	18.99–14.52	19.44–13.35	22.21–12.47	17.98–13.43
Average yield, %	3.56	3.54	3.86	4.20	4.20	5.03
Dividend payout, $	113.33	65.02	65.00	67.28	71.48	77.78
Dividends per share, $	0.88	0.87	0.867	0.857	0.853	0.840
Return on equity, %	8.75	15.61	17.77	17.09	18.35	15.85

DIEBOLD INC

Symbol: DBD
Exchange: NYSE
Address: 5995 Mayfair Road, North Canton, OH 44720-8077
Telephone: 330-490-4000
Web site: www.diebold.com
Investor contact: 330-490-5900

Diebold is a highly diversified manufacturer of security systems, card-based systems, security systems, voting systems, currency processing systems, and security software. Its products and related support, consulting, and maintenance services are widely used throughout the financial, education, government, health, retail, and gaming sectors. Diebold has offices or representatives in more than 88 countries. Diebold's security systems help banks maintain financial security, and its election voting systems help uphold the integrity of the election process. In the financial services sector, for example, it is one of the world leaders in banking automatic teller machines. The company's international sales and service arm distributes its products and services directly, through wholly-owned subsidiaries or joint ventures throughout Europe, the Middle East, Africa, Latin America, and most Asian-Pacific countries.

Founded in 1859 in Cincinnati as a company that made bank vaults and safes, it trades on the New York Stock Exchange under the ticker symbol DBD and in 2003 reported revenue of $2.11 billion. The Ohio-based company has more than 13,000 employees and has increased its dividends for an almost staggering 50 years. It did not pay dividends between 1950 and 1953, but since then dividends have been raised every year. In August 2004, Diebold announced a third quarter dividend of $0.185 per share. In July it reported record second quarter revenue of $552 million, 14.8% higher than the second quarter of 2003, and net income of $43.7. See Tables 11.76 through 11.78 for details on the company's performance.

TABLE 11.76 INTERIM EARNINGS, $ PER SHARE

	MARCH	JUNE	SEPTEMBER	DECEMBER
2001	0.11	0.39	0.20	0.23
2002	0.37	0.55	0.61	0.30
2003	0.36	0.57	0.66	0.81
2004	0.40	0.60	...	...

TABLE 11.77 INTERIM QUARTERLY DIVIDENDS, $ PER SHARE

AMOUNT	DECLARED	EX-DIVIDEND	RECORD DATE	PAID
0.17	10/9/2003	11/12/2003	11/14/2003	12/5/2003
0.185	2/11/2004	2/17/2004	2/19/2004	3/11/2004
0.185	4/22/2004	5/12/2004	5/14/2004	6/4/2004
0.185	8/5/2004	8/11/2004	8/13/2004	9/3/2004

Indicated dividend: $0.74 (company has a dividend reinvestment plan).

TABLE 11.78 OTHER DIVIDEND INFORMATION

	12/31/ 2003	12/31/ 2002	12/31/ 2001	12/31/ 2000	12/31/ 1999	12/31/ 1998
Earnings per share, $	2.40	1.83	0.93	1.92	1.85	1.10
PE ratio	23.93– 14.14	23.17– 16.94	44.09– 27.91	18.00– 11.26	21.55– 11.08	49.66– 18.30
Average yield, %	1.52	1.76	1.93	2.24	2.22	1.59
Dividend payout, $	28.33	36.07	68.82	32.29	32.43	50.91
Dividends per share, $	0.68	0.66	0.64	0.62	0.60	0.56
Return on equity, %	15.22	14.06	7.41	14.6	15.26	10.89
Return on Assets %	9.20	8.14	4.05	8.64	9.92	7.58

PROCTER & GAMBLE CO

Symbol: PG
Exchange: NYSE
Address: 1 Procter & Gamble Plaza, Cincinnati, OH 45202
Telephone: 513-983-1100
Web site: www.pg.com
Investor contact: 1-800-764-7483

Procter & Gamble manufactures and markets a wide range of consumer products, from fabric and home care products such as laundry detergents, dish washing soaps, fabric enhancers, and surface cleaners, to beauty care products. Its other key product lines include baby and family care (diapers, wipes, tissue, and towels), health care (oral care, personal health care, pharmaceuticals, and pet health and nutrition), and snacks and beverages (coffee, snacks, commercial services, and juices). Procter & Gamble is an advertising agency's dream, with nearly 200 brands marketed in various parts of the world, including Always, Ariel, Safeguard, Charmin, Herbal Essences, Crest, Downy, Folgers, Iams, Olay, Pampers, Pantene, Pringles, and Tide.

Starting as a soap and candle making company in 1837, and officially incorporating in 1890, Procter & Gamble now sell its products in 140 countries. It trades on the New York Stock Exchange under the ticker symbol PG and has paid dividends every year since 1890. It, too, has a long-standing history of consecutive dividend increases, increasing them every year for 50 years as of mid-2004. More recently, in July 2004, it declared a quarterly dividend of $0.25 per share. For the same quarter, the company's net sales were $12.96 billion, up 19% from the previous quarter. It also reported that for the fiscal year, sales also grew 19% to $51.41 billion, crossing the $50 billion threshold for the first time in company history. See Tables 11.79 through 11.81 for details on the company's performance.

TABLE 11.79   INTERIM EARNINGS, $ PER SHARE

	SEPTEMBER	DECEMBER	MARCH	JUNE
2000–01	0.41	0.42	0.315	(0.11)
2001–02	0.395	0.465	0.37	0.315
2002–03	0.52	0.53	0.455	0.34
2003–04	0.63	0.65	0.545	0.50

TABLE 11.80   INTERIM QUARTERLY DIVIDENDS, $ PER SHARE

AMOUNT	DECLARED	EX-DIVIDEND	RECORD DATE	PAID
0.228	1/13/2004	1/21/2004	1/23/2004	2/17/2004
100%	3/9/2004	6/21/2004	5/21/2004	6/18/2004
0.25	3/9/2004	4/21/2004	4/23/2004	5/14/2004
0.25	7/13/2004	7/21/2004	7/23/2004	8/16/2004

Indicated dividend: $0.74 (company has a dividend reinvestment plan).

TABLE 11.81   OTHER DIVIDEND INFORMATION

	06/30/ 2003	06/30/ 2002	06/30/ 2001	06/30/ 2000	06/30/ 1999
Earnings per share, $	1.845	1.545	1.035	1.235	1.295
PE ratio	25.20– 20.18	30.55– 20.86	37.92– 26.36	47.67– 21.48	39.74– 25.87
Average yield, %	1.87	1.89	2.10	1.47	1.30
Dividend payout, $	0.820	0.760	0.700	0.640	0.570
Dividends per share, $	32.04	31.75	24.33	28.83	31.21
Return on equity, %	15.61	17.77	17.09	18.35	15.85
Return on Assets %	11.87	10.67	8.50	10.36	11.72

DOVER CORP

Symbol: DOV
Exchange: NYSE
Address: 280 Park Avenue, New York, NY 10017
Telephone: 212-922-1640
Web site: www.dovercorporation.com
Investor contact: 212-922-1640

Dover is an industrial manufacturing corporation consisting of 52 operating companies that make highly specialized industrial products and manufacturing equipment. Divided into four business segments—Diversified, Industries, Resources, and Technologies—its companies' products include packaging and printing machinery, heat transfer equipment, food refrigeration equipment, and display cases. Its technologies include automated assembly and testing equipment and electronic components for electrical manufacturing. Its products are used widely in a broad range of industries, including the defense, aerospace, automotive, transportation, commercial food service and packaging, finance, and construction industries, to name a few. Dover is highly focused on acquisition, bringing companies with proprietary engineered products that are leaders in their field and financial criteria into its empire. It also aims to acquire companies that are expected to generate solid cash flow.

This acquisitive strategy has contributed to a history of consecutive quarterly dividend increases going back 48 years. Its most recent dividend increase was an increase of $0.01 per share, from $0.15 to $0.16 per share, for the period ended August 31, 2004. Incorporated in 1947 in Delaware and public since 1995, Dover trades on the New York Stock Exchange under the ticker symbol DOV. In April 2004, the company reported $83.8 million in earnings from continuing operations for the first quarter ended March 31, 2004, a rise of 45% from $57.7 million in the corresponding period last year. See Tables 11.82 through 11.84 for details on the company's performance.

TABLE 11.82   INTERIM EARNINGS, $ PER SHARE

	MARCH	JUNE	SEPTEMBER	DECEMBER
2001	0.39	0.70	0.01	(0.28)
2002	0.22	0.31	0.28	0.23
2003	0.29	0.36	0.37	0.38
2004	0.41	0.53	...	...

TABLE 11.83   INTERIM QUARTERLY DIVIDENDS, $ PER SHARE

AMOUNT	DECLARED	EX-DIVIDEND	RECORD DATE	PAID
0.15	11/6/2003	11/25/2003	11/28/2003	12/12/2003
0.15	2/12/2004	2/25/2004	2/27/2004	3/15/2004
0.15	5/6/2004	5/26/2004	5/28/2004	6/15/2004
0.16	8/5/2004	8/27/2004	8/31/2004	9/15/2004

Indicated dividend: $0.64 (company has a dividend reinvestment plan).

TABLE 11.84   OTHER DIVIDEND INFORMATION

	12/31/ 2003	12/31/ 2002	12/31/ 2001	12/31/ 2000	12/31/ 1999	12/31/ 1998
Earnings per share, $	1.40	1.04	0.82	2.61	1.92	1.45
PE ratio	28.63–16.68	41.64–22.99	52.83–35.09	20.62–13.79	24.61–15.36	27.46–17.89
Average yield, %	1.76	1.63	1.39	1.07	1.14	1.17
Dividend payout, $	40.71	51.92	63.41	18.39	22.92	27.59
Dividends per share, $	0.57	0.54	0.52	0.48	0.44	0.40
Return on equity, %	10.40	8.82	6.62	21.84	19.87	17.08
Return on assets, %	5.56	4.76	3.63	10.90	9.80	9.00

EMERSON ELECTRIC CO

Symbol: EMR
Exchange: NYSE
Address: 8000 West Florissant Avenue, St. Louis, MO 63136
Telephone: 314-553-2000
Web site: www.gotoemerson.com
Investor contact: 314-553-2197

Emerson Electric is a diversified manufacturer of electrical motors, equipment, components, and appliances, making equipment from air conditioning systems and process control systems to kitchen food disposers, ceiling fans, plumbing, and hand tools. Founded in 1890 as a manufacturer of electric motors and fans, its products are now highly sophisticated, including climate control systems that can sense the environment and powerful backup electrical power systems. Industrial automation products include industrial valves, electrical equipment, and specialty heating, lighting, testing, and ultrasonic welding and cleaning products for use in industrial settings. It operates 60 divisions through five market segments: industrial automation; process control; heating, ventilation, and air conditioning; electronics and telecommunications; and appliances and tools.

Based in St. Louis, Emerson has become a global company, with more than 290 manufacturing locations and employing 106,700 people worldwide. Approximately 45% of its sales are international. In 2003 it brought in $14 billion in revenue, and in August 2004 it announced net sales for the quarter ended June 30, 2004, of $4.036 billion, an increase of 13% from $3.573 billion in the third quarter of fiscal 2003. Traded on the New York Stock Exchange under the ticker symbol EMR, Emerson has increased its dividend every quarter consecutively for 47 years (as of mid-2004). In August 2004 it announced a quarterly cash dividend of $0.40 per share. In 2003 its annualized dividend was $1.57, up from $1.55 in 2002. See Tables 11.85 through 11.87 for details on the company's performance.

TABLE 11.85   INTERIM EARNINGS, $ PER SHARE

	DECEMBER	MARCH	JUNE	SEPTEMBER
000–01	0.83	0.83	0.77	(0.03)
2001–02	0.61	0.65	0.68	0.58
2002–03	0.52	0.56	0.66	0.67
2003–04	0.58	0.75	0.81	...

TABLE 11.86   INTERIM QUARTERLY DIVIDENDS, $ PER SHARE

AMOUNT	DECLARED	EX-DIVIDEND	RECORD DATE	PAID
0.40	11/4/2003	11/12/2003	11/14/2003	12/10/2003
0.40	2/3/2004	2/11/2004	2/13/2004	3/10/2004
0.40	5/4/2004	5/12/2004	5/14/2004	6/10/2004
0.40	8/3/2004	8/11/2004	8/13/2004	9/10/2004

Indicated dividend: $0.74 (company has a dividend reinvestment plan).

TABLE 11.87   OTHER DIVIDEND INFORMATION

	12/31/ 2003	12/31/ 2002	12/31/ 2001	12/31/ 2000	12/31/ 1999
Earnings per share, $	2.41	2.52	2.40	3.30	3.00
PE ratio	23.56– 17.60	26.00– 17.14	32.84– 19.08	21.27– 12.46	23.65– 17.27
Average yield, %	3.11	2.88	2.34	2.47	2.09
Dividend payout, $	65.15	61.51	63.75	43.33	43.33
Dividends per share, $	1.57	1.55	1.53	1.43	1.30
Return on equity, %	16.05	22.49	16.88	22.22	21.25
Return on Assets %	6.83	8.88	6.86	9.38	9.64

Genuine Parts Co

Symbol: GPC
Exchange: NYSE
Address: 2999 Circle 75 Parkway, Atlanta, GA 30339
Telephone: 770-953-1700
Web site: www.genpt.com
Investor contact: 770-953-1700

Genuine Parts is a distributor of automotive replacement parts and accessory items to independent and company-owned NAPA auto parts stores in the United States, Canada, and Mexico. Divided into four lines, it has an Automotive Parts Group (the largest), which distributes auto replacement parts, accessories, and service items through 5,800 NAPA stores throughout the United States and 650 wholesalers in Canada; an Industrial Parts Group, which distributes more than 3 million industrial replacement parts such as bearings, mechanical power transmissions, hydraulics, and hose and rubber parts to 150,000 industrial companies throughout north America; an Electrical/Electronic Materials Group, which manufactures and supplies a range of electrical materials from insulation to conductive materials; and an Office Products Group, which sells more than 30,000 types of business and office products through well-known retail outlets.

Founded in 1928 and based in Atlanta, the company has consistently increased its dividend for 47 years (as of mid-2004), and in February 2004 it increased its cash dividend to an annual rate of $1.20 per share. In July it announced a rise in sales and net profits, with sales of $2.3 billion for the second quarter of 2004 (an increase of 7% compared to the second quarter of 2003). Net income was $101.1 million, a 12% rise compared to $90.1 million for the second quarter of 2003. See Tables 11.88 through 11.90 for details on the company's performance.

TABLE 11.88   INTERIM EARNINGS, $ PER SHARE

	MARCH	JUNE	SEPTEMBER	DECEMBER
2001	0.52	0.55	0.51	0.13
2002	0.50	0.55	0.54	0.51
2003	0.51	0.52	0.51	0.49
2004	0.57	0.58	...	...

TABLE 11.89   INTERIM QUARTERLY DIVIDENDS, $ PER SHARE

AMOUNT	DECLARED	EX-DIVIDEND	RECORD DATE	PAID
0.295	11/17/2003	12/3/2003	12/5/2003	1/2/2004
0.30	2/16/2004	3/3/2004	3/5/2004	4/1/2004
0.30	4/19/2004	6/9/2004	6/11/2004	7/1/2004
0.30	8/16/2004	9/8/2004	9/10/2004	10/1/2004

Indicated dividend: $1.20 (company has a dividend reinvestment plan).

TABLE 11.90   OTHER DIVIDEND INFORMATION

	12/31/ 2003	12/31/ 2002	12/31/ 2001	12/31/ 2000	12/31/ 1999	12/31/ 1998
Earnings per share, $	2.03	2.10	1.71	2.20	2.11	1.98
PE ratio	16.58– 13.51	18.13– 13.16	21.89– 14.19	12.02– 8.47	16.94– 10.96	19.26– 14.84
Average yield, %	3.72	3.47	3.74	4.91	3.46	2.92
Dividend payout, $	57.88	55.00	66.08	49.32	48.82	50.00
Dividends per share, $	1.17	1.15	1.13	1.08	1.03	0.99
Return on equity, %	15.29	17.25	12.67	17.04	17.34	17.33
Return on assets, %	8.59	9.14	7.06	9.30	9.61	9.88

PARKER-HANNIFIN CORP

Symbol: PH
Exchange: NYSE
Address: 6035 Parkland Blvd., Cleveland, OH 44124-4141
Telephone: 216-896-3000
Web site: www.parker.com
Investor contact: 216-896-2240

Parker-Hannifin is a manufacturer of motion-control products, including fluid power systems, electromechanical controls, and related components. The company operates two key business segments: its industrial segment includes several units that manufacture motion-control and fluid power system components for builders and users of various types of manufacturing, packaging, processing, transportation, agricultural, construction, and military vehicles and equipment. The aerospace segment produces hydraulic, fuel and pneumatic systems, and components for domestic commercial, military, and general aviation aircraft, naval vessels, land-based weapons systems, satellites, and space vehicles.

Originally founded in 1918, the company made a name making pneumatic/hydraulic components, and in 1927 it provided high-pressure connection leads for aviator Charles Lindbergh's historic first Atlantic crossing. Now, servicing a number of industries, including the transportation, manufacturing, automotive, mining, oil and gas, and defense and aerospace industries to name a few, Parker-Hannifin has 254 plants and employs more than 48,000 people in 44 countries. Its annual sales recently topped $7 billion. Traded on the New York Stock Exchange under the ticker symbol PH, it has consistently raised its dividend every quarter for 47 years (as of mid-2004). In July 2004, it declared a regular quarterly cash dividend of $0.19 per share. It also announced a 76% increase in net income for the full year ended June 2004 of $345.8 million, and sales of $7.11 billion, up 11%. See Tables 11.91 through 11.93 for details on the company's performance.

TABLE 11.91   INTERIM EARNINGS, $ PER SHARE

	SEPTEMBER	DECEMBER	MARCH	JUNE
2000-01	1.09	0.68	0.80	0.42
2001-02	0.52	0.25	0.45	(0.10)
2002-03	0.52	0.32	0.42	0.42
2003-04	0.48	0.47	0.90	1.05

TABLE 11.92   INTERIM QUARTERLY DIVIDENDS, $ PER SHARE

AMOUNT	DECLARED	EX-DIVIDEND	RECORD DATE	PAID
0.19	10/22/2003	11/18/2003	11/20/2003	12/5/2003
0.19	1/29/2004	2/17/2004	2/19/2004	3/5/2004
0.19	4/22/2004	5/18/2004	5/20/2004	6/4/2004
0.19	7/23/2004	8/18/2004	8/20/2004	9/3/2004

Indicated dividend: $0.76 (company has a dividend reinvestment plan).

TABLE 11.93   OTHER DIVIDEND INFORMATION

	06/30/ 2003	06/30/ 2002	06/30/ 2001	06/30/ 2000	06/30/ 1999
Earnings per share, $	1.68	1.12	2.99	3.31	2.83
PE ratio	29.05– 20.63	48.78– 28.26	16.73– 10.68	15.75– 10.25	17.82– 9.61
Average yield, %	1.77	1.59	1.72	1.55	1.77
Dividend payout, $	44.05	64.29	23.41	20.54	22.61
Dividends per share, $	0.740	0.720	0.700	0.680	0.640
Return on equity, %	7.79	5.04	13.61	15.94	16.75
Return on Assets %	3.28	2.26	6.45	7.93	8.38

3M Co

Symbol: MMM
Exchange: NYSE
Address: 3M Center, St. Paul, MN 55144-1000
Telephone: 651-733-1110
Web site: www.3m.com
Investor contact: 651-733-8206

3M is a technology company with stakes in the health care, pharmaceuticals, consumer and office, safety, security and protection services, display and graphics, electronics, telecommunications and electrical, and transportation sectors. Founded in 1902 in Two Harbors, Minnesota, the company started out trying to make better sandpaper products. It quickly diversified into other product areas, aiming to create better ways of doing things. The world's first waterproof sandpaper was developed by 3M in the early 1920s. More than a century later, 3M is an international company with offices more than 60 countries, with more than 67,000 employees, and with annual sales of more than $18 billion. International sales represent about 58% of total revenue.

With a strong history and culture of innovation and an active research and development program, 3M has seven business segments: Consumer and Office Business; Display and Graphics; Electro and Communications; Health Care; Industrial Business; Safety, Security, and Protection Services; and Transportation. The company has a long history of dividend payments and dividend increases. It paid it first dividend in 1916—of $0.06 a share. As of mid-2004, it had increased its dividend every quarter for 45 years, and in August it announced a quarterly dividend of $0.36. In July it announced second quarter 2004 net income of $773 million, compared to $619 million, in the second quarter of 2003. Worldwide sales in the second quarter were $5.01 billion. See Tables 11.94 through 11.96 for details on the company's performance.

TABLE 11.94 INTERIM EARNINGS, $ PER SHARE

	MARCH	JUNE	SEPTEMBER	DECEMBER
2001	0.565	0.255	0.495	0.475
2002	0.57	0.59	0.69	0.645
2003	0.635	0.78	0.83	0.775
2004	0.9	0.97	...	...

TABLE 11.95 INTERIM QUARTERLY DIVIDENDS, $ PER SHARE

AMOUNT	DECLARED	EX-DIVIDEND	RECORD DATE	PAID
0.33	11/10/2003	11/19/2003	11/21/2003	12/12/2003
0.36	2/9/2004	2/18/2004	2/20/2004	3/12/2004
0.36	5/11/2004	5/19/2004	5/21/2004	6/12/2004
0.36	8/9/2004	8/18/2004	8/20/2004	9/12/2004

Indicated dividend: $1.44 (company has a dividend reinvestment plan).

TABLE 11.96 OTHER DIVIDEND INFORMATION

	12/31/ 2003	12/31/ 2002	12/31/ 2001	12/31/ 2000	12/31/ 1999	12/31/ 1998
Earnings per share, $	3.02	2.49	1.79	2.32	2.17	1.48
PE ratio	28.23– 20.03	26.25– 20.7	35.06– 24.30	26.28– 17.03	23.69– 16.10	32.81– 22.90
Average yield, %	1.92	2.04	2.16	2.52	2.56	2.64
Dividend payout, $	43.71	49.7	67.04	50	51.61	74.07
Dividends per share, $	1.32	1.24	1.2	1.16	1.12	1.1
Return on equity, %	30.48	32.94	23.5	28.43	28.03	20.43
Return on assets, %	13.65	12.88	9.79	12.79	12.69	8.57

MASCO CORP

Symbol: MAS
Exchange: NYSE
Address: 21001 Van Born Road, Taylor, MI 48180
Telephone: 313-274-7400
Web site: www.masco.com
Investor contact: 313-274-7400

Masco Corporation is a leader in the manufacture of home consumer, building, and renovation products, with brand-name cabinetry products, plumbing products, fireplaces, guttering, bath and kitchen accessories, garage doors, shelving, and windows. With names such as Kraftmaid, Merillat, Mill's Pride, Quality Cabinets, Delta, Peerless, Newport Brass, Behr, Premium Plus, Masterchem, Franklin Brass, Ginger, and Bath Unlimited, Masco has five business segments: Cabinets and Related Products, Plumbing Products, Installation and Other Services, Decorative Architectural Products, and Other Specialty Products. It also provides installation services to home builders in the United States and in Canada through a number of subsidiaries. It sells through hardware stores, home centers, builders, and distributors throughout North America as well as through a number of outlets in Europe, including Belgium, Denmark, Germany, Holland, Italy, Spain, and the United Kingdom.

Founded in Detroit in 1924 and now based in Taylor, Michigan, in 2003 it reported worldwide sales of over $10.9 billion. Masco's history of consecutive quarterly dividend increases dates back 45 years, and in September it declared another increased quarterly dividend—$0.18 per share. Trading on the New York Stock Exchange since 1936 under the ticker symbol MAS, in August 2004 it reported net sales from continuing operations for the second quarter ended June 30, 2004, of $3.1 billion, an increase of 16% from $2.6 billion in the corresponding period in 2003. See Tables 11.97 through 11.99 for details on the company's performance.

TABLE 11.97   INTERIM EARNINGS, $ PER SHARE

	MARCH	JUNE	SEPTEMBER	DECEMBER
2001	0.25	0.30	(0.39)	0.26
2002	0.31	0.43	0.24	0.35
2003	0.32	0.46	0.53	0.20
2004	0.52	0.65	…	…

TABLE 11.98   INTERIM QUARTERLY DIVIDENDS, $ PER SHARE

AMOUNT	DECLARED	EX-DIVIDEND	RECORD DATE	PAID
0.16	9/17/2003	10/8/2003	10/10/2003	11/10/2003
0.16	12/10/2003	1/7/2004	1/9/2004	2/9/2004
0.16	3/18/2004	4/6/2004	4/9/2004	5/10/2004
0.16	6/25/2004	7/7/2004	7/9/2004	8/9/2004

Indicated dividend: $0.64 (company has a dividend reinvestment plan).

TABLE 11.99   OTHER DIVIDEND INFORMATION

	12/31/ 2003	12/31/ 2002	12/31/ 2001	12/31/ 2000	12/31/ 1999	12/31/ 1998
Earnings per share, $	1.51	1.33	0.42	1.31	1.28	1.39
PE ratio	18.75– 11.14	21.86– 13.29	63.07– 42.86	19.61– 11.31	26.17– 17.97	23.38– 15.20
Average yield, %	2.50	2.24	2.24	2.46	1.55	1.55
Dividend payout, $	38.41	40.98	125.00	37.40	35.16	30.94
Dividends per share, $	0.580	0.545	0.525	0.490	0.450	0.430
Return on equity, %	13.56	12.88	4.82	17.27	18.16	17.44
Return on assets, %	6.09	5.66	2.16	7.64	8.58	9.21

WPS Resources Corp

Symbol: WPS
Exchange: NYSE
Address: 700 North Adams Street, Green Bay, WI 54307-9001
Telephone: 920-433-4901
Web site: www.wpsr.com
Investor contact: 920-433-1857

WPS Resources operates as a holding company with both regulated utility and nonregulated business units serving an 11,000-square-mile service territory in northeastern Wisconsin and an adjacent portion of the Upper Peninsula of Michigan. Its principal wholly-owned subsidiaries are: Wisconsin Public Service Corporation (WPSC), a regulated electric and gas utility in Wisconsin and Michigan; Upper Peninsula Power Company, a regulated electric utility in Michigan; and WPS Energy Service Inc and WPS Power Development Inc, both nonregulated subsidiaries. As of mid-2004, WPSC served 407,768 electric and 295,816 natural gas customers and Upper Peninsula Power served 51,207 electric power customers. Electric operations accounted for 69% and gas operations accounted for 31% of 2002 revenues.

WPS Resources has its origins dating back to 1883 when Wisconsin Public Service Corporation was founded. The Upper Peninsula Power Company was founded the following year, WPS Energy Services Inc in 1994, and WPS Power Development Inc in 1995. Paying its first dividend in 1953, it has now increased its dividend for consecutive quarters for 45 years. In July 2004, it announced declared a dividend of $0.555 per share. For the six months ended June 30, 2004, revenues were $2.42 billion, up 7%, and net income from continuing operations was $55.5 million, up 28%. See Tables 11.100 through 11.102 for details on the company's performance.

TABLE 11.100 INTERIM EARNINGS, $ PER SHARE

	MARCH	JUNE	SEPTEMBER	DECEMBER
2001	0.89	0.41	0.76	0.68
2002	0.89	0.68	0.95	0.90
2003	0.92	0.08	1.04	1.20
2004	1.22	0.26	...	...

TABLE 11.101 INTERIM QUARTERLY DIVIDENDS, $ PER SHARE

AMOUNT	DECLARED	EX-DIVIDEND	RECORD DATE	PAID
0.545	9/11/2003	11/25/2003	11/28/2003	12/20/2003
0.545	2/12/2004	2/25/2004	2/27/2004	3/20/2004
0.545	4/1/2004	5/26/2004	5/28/2004	6/19/2004
0.555	7/8/2004	8/27/2004	8/31/2004	9/20/2004

Indicated dividend: $2.22 (company has a dividend reinvestment plan).

TABLE 11.102 OTHER DIVIDEND INFORMATION

	12/31/ 2003	12/31/ 2002	12/31/ 2001	12/31/ 2000	12/31/ 1999	12/31/ 1998
Earnings per share, $	3.24	3.42	2.74	2.53	2.24	1.76
PE ratio	14.44– 11.46	12.41– 9.22	13.34– 11.61	15.29– 9.02	15.85– 10.99	21.16– 17.19
Average yield, %	5.27	5.55	6.08	6.89	6.74	5.88
Dividend payout, $	66.67	61.99	75.91	80.63	89.29	111.36
Dividends per share, $	2.160	2.120	2.080	2.040	2.000	1.960
Return on equity, %	10.49	13.49	10.52	11.80	10.67	8.76

Dividend Actions of Dividend-Achieving Companies

DIVIDEND ACTIONS OF DIVIDEND-ACHIEVING COMPANIES

NAME	TICKER SYMBOL	DECLARED	RECORD DATE	EX-DIVIDEND DATE	DATE PAYABLE	AMOUNT, $	QUARTERLY/ SEMI/ ANNUAL	DIVIDEND ACTION
1st Source Corp	SRCE	29–Jul–04	09–Aug–04	05–Aug–04	08/16/2004	0.11	Q	Increased
3M Co	MMM	09–Aug–04	20–Aug–04	18–Aug–04	09/12/2004	0.36	Q	
Abbott Laboratories	ABT	10–Sep–04	15–Oct–04	13–Oct–04	11/15/2004	0.26	Q	
ABM Industries Inc	ABM	08–Sep–04	11–Oct–04	06–Oct–04	11/01/2004	0.1	Q	
AFLAC Inc	AFL	27–Jul–04	13–Aug–04	11–Aug–04	09/01/2004	0.095	Q	
Air Products & Chemicals Inc	APD	16–Sep–04	01–Oct–04	29–Sep–04	11/08/2004	0.29	Q	
Alberto–Culver Co	ACV	22–Apr–04	03–May–04	29–Apr–04	05/20/2004	0.1	Q	
Alfa Corp	ALFA	26–Jul–04	13–Aug–04	11–Aug–04	09/01/2004	0.0875	Q	
Allstate Corp	ALL	13–Jul–04	31–Aug–04	27–Aug–04	10/01/2004	0.28	Q	
ALLTEL Corp	AT	22–Jul–04	10–Sep–04	08–Sep–04	10/03/2004	0.37	Q	
Altria Group Inc	MO	25–Aug–04	15–Sep–04	13–Sep–04	10/12/2004	0.73	Q	Increased
Ambac Financial Group Inc	ABK	05–May–04	17–May–04	13–May–04	06/02/2004	0.11	Q	
American International Group Inc	AIG	15–Sep–04	03–Dec–04	01–Dec–04	12/17/2004	0.075	Q	

DIVIDEND ACTIONS OF DIVIDEND-ACHIEVING COMPANIES (*Continued*)

NAME	TICKER SYMBOL	DECLARED	RECORD DATE	EX-DIVIDEND DATE	DATE PAYABLE	AMOUNT, $	QUARTERLY/ SEMI-ANNUAL	DIVIDEND ACTION
American States Water Co	AWR	27–Jul–04	09–Aug–04	05–Aug–04	09/01/2004	0.221	Q	
AmSouth Bancorporation	ASO	15–Jul–04	17–Sep–04	15–Sep–04	10/01/2004	0.24	Q	
Anchor BanCorp Wisconsin Inc	ABCW	20–Jul–04	30–Jul–04	28–Jul–04	08/13/2004	0.125	Q	Increased
Anheuser-Busch Cos Inc	BUD	28–Jul–04	09–Aug–04	05–Aug–04	09/09/2004	0.245	Q	Increased
Applebee's International Inc	APPB	13–May–04	28–May–04	16–Jun–04	06/15/2004	1.5	A	
AptarGroup Inc	ATR	16–Jul–04	27–Jul–04	23–Jul–04	08/17/2004	0.15	Q	Increased
Aqua America Inc	WTR	03–Aug–04	15–Nov–04	10–Nov–04	12/01/2004	0.13	Q	Increased
Archer Daniels Midland Co	ADM	05–Aug–04	20–Aug–04	18–Aug–04	09/10/2004	0.075	Q	
Arrow International Inc	ARRO	16–Aug–04	30–Aug–04	26–Aug–04	09/13/2004	0.09	Q	
Artesian Resources Corp	ARTNA	28–Jul–04	09–Aug–04	05–Aug–04	08/20/2004	0.2075	Q	

Company	Symbol							
Associated Banc-Corp	ASBC	28–Jul–04	06–Aug–04	04–Aug–04	08/16/2004	0.25	Q	
Atmos Energy Corp	ATO	10–Aug–04	25–Aug–04	23–Aug–04	09/10/2004	0.305	Q	
Automatic Data Processing Inc	ADP	11–Aug–04	10–Sep–04	08–Sep–04	10/01/2004	0.14	Q	
Avery Dennison Corp	AVY	22–Jul–04	01–Sep–04	30–Aug–04	09/15/2004	0.37	Q	
Avon Products Inc	AVP	05–Aug–04	18–Aug–04	16–Aug–04	09/01/2004	0.14	Q	
Badger Meter Inc	BMI	14–May–04	01–Jun–04	27–May–04	06/15/2004	0.27	Q	
BancFirst Corp	BANF	26–Aug–04	30–Sep–04	28–Sep–04	10/15/2004	0.28	Q	Increased
BancorpSouth Inc	BXS	21–Jul–04	15–Sep–04	13–Sep–04	10/01/2004	0.18	Q	
Bandag Inc	BDG	17–Aug–04	17–Sep–04	15–Sep–04	10/18/2004	0.325	Q	
Bank of America Corp	BAC	23–Jun–04	03–Sep–04	01–Sep–04	09/24/2004	0.45	Q	Increased
Bank of Hawaii Corp (DE)	BOH	23–Jan–04	01–Mar–04	26–Feb–04	03/12/2004	0.3	Q	
Banta Corporation	BN	27–Jul–04	15–Oct–04	13–Oct–04	11/01/2004	0.17	Q	
Bard (CR) Inc	BCR	14–Jul–04	26–Jul–04	22–Jul–04	08/06/2004	0.12	Q	Increased
BB&T Corp	BBT	24–Aug–04	15–Oct–04	13–Oct–04	11/01/2004	0.35	Q	
Beckman Coulter Inc	BEC	26–Jul–04	13–Aug–04	11–Aug–04	09/02/2004	0.13	Q	Increased
Becton Dickinson and Co	BDX	27–Jul–04	09–Sep–04	07–Sep–04	09/30/2004	0.15	Q	

DIVIDEND ACTIONS OF DIVIDEND-ACHIEVING COMPANIES *(Continued)*

NAME	TICKER SYMBOL	DECLARED	RECORD DATE	EX-DIVIDEND DATE	DATE PAYABLE	AMOUNT, $	QUARTERLY/ SEMI-ANNUAL	DIVIDEND ACTION
Bemis Inc	BMS	29–Jul–04	18–Aug–04	16–Aug–04	09/01/2004	0.16	Q	
Black Hills Corporation	BKH	28–Jul–04	16–Aug–04	12–Aug–04	09/01/2004	0.31	Q	
Black Hills Corporation	BKH	28–Jul–04	16–Aug–04	12–Aug–04	09/01/2004	0.31	Q	
Bowl America Inc	BWLA	23–Sep–04	20–Oct–04	18–Oct–04	11/10/2004	0.135	Q	
Brady Corp	BRC	15–Sep–04	11–Oct–04	06–Oct–04	11/01/2004	0.22	Q	Increased
Briggs & Stratton Corp	BGG	04–Aug–04	25–Aug–04	23–Aug–04	10/01/2004	0.34	Q	Increased
Brown & Brown Inc	BRO	21–Jul–04	04–Aug–04	02–Aug–04	08/18/2004	0.07	Q	
Brown–Forman Corp	BFB	22–Jul–04	07–Sep–04	02–Sep–04	10/01/2004	0.2125	Q	
California Water Service Group	CWT	28–Jul–04	09–Aug–04	05–Aug–04	08/20/2004	0.2825	Q	
Camden Property Trust	CPT	16–Sep–04	30–Sep–04	28–Sep–04	10/15/2004	0.635	Q	
Carlisle Companies Inc	CSL	02–Aug–04	19–Aug–04	17–Aug–04	09/01/2004	0.23	Q	Increased
Caterpillar Inc	CAT	09–Jun–04	20–Jul–04	16–Jul–04	08/20/2004	0.41	Q	Increased

Company	Ticker					Amount	Type	Note
Cedar Fair LP	FUN	23–Sep–04	05–Oct–04	01–Oct–04	11/15/2004	0.45	Q	
CenturyTel Inc	CTL	24–Aug–04	07–Sep–04	02–Sep–04	09/17/2004	0.0575	Q	
Charter One Financial Inc	CF	21–Jul–04	06–Aug–04	04–Aug–04	08/20/2004	0.29	Q	
Charter One Financial Inc	CF	21–Jul–04	06–Aug–04	04–Aug–04	08/20/2004	0.29	Q	
Chemical Financial Corp	CHFC	19–Jul–04	03–Sep–04	01–Sep–04	09/17/2004	0.265	Q	
ChevronTexaco Corp	CVX	28–Jul–04	19–Aug–04	17–Aug–04	09/10/2004	0.8	Q	Increased
Chittenden Corp	CHZ	22–Jul–04	30–Jul–04	28–Jul–04	08/13/2004	0.22	Q	
Chubb Corp	CB	09–Sep–04	24–Sep–04	22–Sep–04	10/12/2004	0.39	Q	
Cincinnati Financial Corp	CINF	13–Aug–04	24–Sep–04	22–Sep–04	10/15/2004	0.275	Q	
Cintas Corporation	CTAS	27–Jan–04	10–Feb–04	06–Feb–04	03/16/2004	0.29	A	Increased
Citigroup Inc	C	20–Jul–04	02–Aug–04	29–Jul–04	08/27/2004	0.4	Q	
Citizens Banking Corp	CBCF	15–Jul–04	26–Jul–04	22–Jul–04	08/04/2004	0.285	Q	
Clarcor Inc	CLC	20–Sep–04	19–Oct–04	15–Oct–04	10/29/2004	0.1275	Q	Increased
Cleco Corp (New)	CNL	23–Jul–04	02–Aug–04	29–Jul–04	08/15/2004	0.225	Q	
Clorox Co	CLX	15–Sep–04	29–Oct–04	27–Oct–04	11/15/2004	0.27	Q	
Coca-Cola Co	KO	22–Jul–04	15–Sep–04	13–Sep–04	10/01/2004	0.25	Q	

DIVIDEND ACTIONS OF DIVIDEND-ACHIEVING COMPANIES *(Continued)*

Name	Ticker Symbol	Declared	Record Date	Ex-Dividend Date	Date Payable	Amount, $	Quarterly/ Semi/ Annual	Dividend Action
Colgate-Palmolive Co	CL	08-Jul-04	26-Jul-04	22-Jul-04	08/16/2004	0.24	Q	
Comerica Inc	CMA	27-Jul-04	15-Sep-04	13-Sep-04	10/01/2004	0.52	Q	
Commerce Bancorp Inc	CBH	21-Sep-04	04-Oct-04	30-Sep-04	10/20/2004	0.19	Q	
Commerce Bancshares Inc	CBSH	23-Jul-04	13-Sep-04	09-Sep-04	09/27/2004	0.23	Q	
Commercial Net Lease Realty Inc	NNN	14-Jul-04	30-Jul-04	28-Jul-04	08/13/2004	0.325	Q	Increased
Community Bank System Inc	CBU	19-Aug-04	15-Sep-04	13-Sep-04	10/11/2004	0.18	Q	Increased
Community First Bankshares Inc	CFBX	20-Aug-04	01-Sep-04	30-Aug-04	09/15/2004	0.24	Q	
Community Trust Bancorp Inc	CTBI	27-Jul-04	15-Sep-04	13-Sep-04	10/01/2004	0.23	Q	
Compass Bancshares Inc	CBSS	17-Aug-04	15-Sep-04	13-Sep-04	10/01/2004	0.3125	Q	
ConAgra Foods Inc	CAG	23-Sep-04	01-Nov-04	28-Oct-04	12/01/2004	0.2725	Q	Increased
Connecticut Water Service Inc	CTWS	11-Aug-04	01-Sep-04	30-Aug-04	09/15/2004	0.21	Q	Increased

Company	Ticker					Amount		
Consolidated Edison Inc	ED	22–Jul–04	11–Aug–04	09–Aug–04	09/15/2004	0.565	Q	
Corus Bankshares Inc	CORS	04–Aug–04	27–Sep–04	23–Sep–04	10/08/2004	0.3125	Q	
Courier Corp	CRRC	15–Jul–04	06–Aug–04	04–Aug–04	08/27/2004	0.0875	Q	
Cullen/Frost Bankers Inc	CFR	29–Jul–04	01–Sep–04	30–Aug–04	09/15/2004	0.265	Q	
CVB Financial Corp	CVBF	15–Sep–04	29–Sep–04	27–Sep–04	10/14/2004	0.13	Q	Increased
Danaher Corp	DHR	17–Sep–04	24–Sep–04	22–Sep–04	10/29/2004	0.015	Q	
Diebold Inc	DBD	05–Aug–04	13–Aug–04	11–Aug–04	09/03/2004	0.185	Q	
Donnelley (RR) & Sons Co	RRD	30–Sep–04	08–Nov–04	04–Nov–04	12/01/2004	0.26	Q	
Doral Financial Corp	DRL	14–Jul–04	27–Aug–04	25–Aug–04	09/10/2004	0.15	Q	
Dover Corp	DOV	05–Aug–04	31–Aug–04	27–Aug–04	09/15/2004	0.16	Q	Increased
Duke-Weeks Realty Corp	DRE	28–Jul–04	13–Aug–04	11–Aug–04	08/31/2004	0.465	Q	Increased
EastGroup Properties Inc	EGP	02–Sep–04	17–Sep–04	15–Sep–04	09/30/2004	0.48	Q	
Eaton Vance Corp	EV	07–Jul–04	30–Jul–04	28–Jul–04	08/09/2004	0.15	Q	Increased
Ecolab Inc	ECL	13–Aug–04	21–Sep–04	17–Sep–04	10/15/2004	0.08	Q	
Emerson Electric Co	EMR	03–Aug–04	13–Aug–04	11–Aug–04	09/10/2004	0.4	Q	
Energen Corp	EGN	22–Jul–04	13–Aug–04	11–Aug–04	09/01/2004	0.1925	Q	Increased
EnergySouth Inc	ENSI	30–Jul–04	15–Sep–04	13–Sep–04	10/01/2004	0.2	Q	

DIVIDEND ACTIONS OF DIVIDEND-ACHIEVING COMPANIES *(Continued)*

NAME	TICKER SYMBOL	DECLARED	RECORD DATE	EX-DIVIDEND DATE	DATE PAYABLE	AMOUNT, $	QUARTERLY/ SEMI/ ANNUAL	DIVIDEND ACTION
Exxon Mobil Corp	XOM	28–Jul–04	13–Aug–04	11–Aug–04	09/10/2004	0.27	Q	
Family Dollar Stores Inc	FDO	17–Aug–04	15–Sep–04	13–Sep–04	10/15/2004	0.085	Q	
Fannie Mae	FNM	20–Jul–04	30–Jul–04	28–Jul–04	08/25/2004	0.52	Q	
Farmer Bros Co	FARM	17–Aug–04	22–Oct–04	20–Oct–04	11/08/2004	0.1	Q	Increased
Federal Realty Investment Trust	FRT	07–Sep–04	24–Sep–04	22–Sep–04	10/15/2004	0.505	Q	Increased
Federal Signal Corp	FSS	22–Jul–04	15–Sep–04	13–Sep–04	10/04/2004	0.1	Q	
Fidelity National Financial Inc	FNF	07–Sep–04	17–Nov–04	15–Nov–04	12/01/2004	0.25	Q	Increased
Fifth Third Bancorp	FITB	21–Sep–04	30–Sep–04	28–Sep–04	10/14/2004	0.32	Q	
First Charter Corp	FCTR	29–Jul–04	24–Sep–04	22–Sep–04	10/18/2004	0.19	Q	Increased
First Commonwealth Financial Corp	FCF	21–Sep–04	30–Sep–04	28–Sep–04	10/15/2004	0.16	Q	
First Federal Capital Corp	FTFC	29–Jul–04	19–Aug–04	17–Aug–04	09/09/2004	0.15	Q	
First Financial Corp	THFF	19–May–04	16–Jun–04	14–Jun–04	07/01/2004	0.39	S	Increased

Company	Ticker					Amount		Notes
First Financial Holdings Inc	FFCH	23-Jul-04	06-Aug-04	04-Aug-04	08/20/2004	0.22	Q	
First Indiana Corp	FINB	21-Jul-04	07-Sep-04	02-Sep-04	09/16/2004	0.165	Q	
First Merchants Corp	FRME	10-Aug-04	06-Sep-04	01-Sep-04	09/20/2004	0.23	Q	
First Midwest Bancorp Inc	FMBI	19-Aug-04	24-Sep-04	22-Sep-04	10/19/2004	0.22	Q	
FirstMerit Corp	FMER	19-Aug-04	30-Aug-04	26-Aug-04	09/20/2004	0.27	Q	Increased
Florida Public Utilities Co	FPU	25-Aug-04	10-Sep-04	08-Sep-04	10/01/2004	0.15	Q	
FNB Corp	FNB	18-Aug-04	01-Sep-04	30-Aug-04	09/15/2004	0.23	Q	
Franklin Electric Co Inc	FELE	23-Jul-04	05-Aug-04	03-Aug-04	08/19/2004	0.08	Q	
Franklin Resources Inc	BEN	24-Sep-04	04-Oct-04	30-Sep-04	10/15/2004	0.085	Q	
Freddie Mac	FRE	10-Sep-04	20-Sep-04	16-Sep-04	09/30/2004	0.3	Q	
Frisch's Restaurants Inc	FRS	31-Aug-04	24-Sep-04	22-Sep-04	10/08/2004	0.11	Q	
Fuller (HB) Company	FUL	30-Sep-04	14-Oct-04	12-Oct-04	10/28/2004	0.115	Q	
Fulton Financial Corp	FULT	20-Jul-04	22-Sep-04	20-Sep-04	10/15/2004	0.165	Q	
Gallagher (Arthur J) & Co	AJG	22-Jul-04	30-Sep-04	28-Sep-04	10/15/2004	0.25	Q	
Gannett Co Inc	GCI	04-Aug-04	10-Sep-04	08-Sep-04	10/01/2004	0.27	Q	Increased
General Dynamics Corp	GD	04-Aug-04	08-Oct-04	06-Oct-04	11/12/2004	0.36	Q	

DIVIDEND ACTIONS OF DIVIDEND-ACHIEVING COMPANIES *(Continued)*

Name	Ticker Symbol	Declared	Record Date	Ex-Dividend Date	Date Payable	Amount, $	Quarterly/ Semi/ Annual	Dividend Action
General Electric Co	GE	17–Sep–04	27–Sep–04	23–Sep–04	10/25/2004	0.2	Q	
General Growth Properties Inc	GGP	20–Aug–04	15–Oct–04	13–Oct–04	10/29/2004	0.36	Q	Increased
Genuine Parts Co	GPC	16–Aug–04	10–Sep–04	08–Sep–04	10/01/2004	0.3	Q	
Glacier Bancorp Inc	GBCI	29–Sep–04	12–Oct–04	07–Oct–04	10/21/2004	0.17	Q	
Golden West Financial Corp	GDW	26–Jul–04	15–Aug–04	11–Aug–04	09/10/2004	0.1	Q	
Gorman–Rupp Co	GRC	22–Jul–04	13–Aug–04	13–Sep–04	09/10/2004	1.25	Q	
Grainger (WW) Inc	GWW	28–Jul–04	09–Aug–04	05–Aug–04	09/01/2004	0.2	Q	
Harley–Davidson Inc	HDI	04–Aug–04	15–Sep–04	13–Sep–04	09/29/2004	0.1	Q	
Harleysville Group Inc	HGIC	03–Aug–04	15–Sep–04	13–Sep–04	09/30/2004	0.17	Q	
Harleysville National Corp	HNBC	16–Aug–04	27–Aug–04	25–Aug–04	09/15/2004	0.18	Q	Increased
Haverty Furniture Cos Inc	HVT	29–Jul–04	13–Aug–04	11–Aug–04	08/27/2004	0.0625	Q	
Health Care Property Investors Inc	HCP	23–Jul–04	04–Aug–04	02–Aug–04	08/19/2004	0.4175	Q	

Company	Symbol					Amount		Status
Healthcare Realty Trust Inc	HR	27–Jul–04	16–Aug–04	12–Aug–04	09/02/2004	0.64	Q	Increased
Heinz (HJ) Co	HNZ	08–Sep–04	23–Sep–04	21–Sep–04	10/10/2004	0.285	Q	
Helmerich & Payne Inc	HP	05–Mar–03	15–May–03	13–May–03	06/02/2003	0.08	Q	Increased
Hershey Foods Corp	HSY	28–Jul–04	25–Aug–04	23–Aug–04	09/15/2004	0.22	Q	Increased
Hibernia Corp	HIB	21–Jul–04	02–Aug–04	29–Jul–04	08/20/2004	0.2	Q	
Hilb Rogal & Hobbs Co	HRH	20–Jul–04	15–Sep–04	13–Sep–04	09/30/2004	0.105	Q	
Hillenbrand Industries Inc	HB	09–Sep–04	16–Sep–04	14–Sep–04	09/30/2004	0.27	Q	
HNI Corp	HNI	02–Aug–04	12–Aug–04	10–Aug–04	09/01/2004	0.14	Q	Increased
Holly Corp	HOC	02–Aug–04	20–Sep–04	16–Sep–04	10/04/2004	0.08	Q	
Home Depot Inc	HD	06–Aug–04	02–Sep–04	31–Aug–04	09/16/2004	0.085	Q	
Hormel Foods Corp	HRL	20–Sep–04	23–Oct–04	20–Oct–04	11/15/2004	0.1125	Q	
Hudson United Bancorp	HU	28–Jul–04	13–Aug–04	11–Aug–04	09/01/2004	0.35	Q	Increased
Illinois Tool Works Inc	ITW	06–Aug–04	30–Sep–04	28–Sep–04	10/18/2004	0.28	Q	Increased
Independent Bank Corporation	IBCP	24–Sep–04	05–Oct–04	01–Oct–04	10/29/2004	0.17	Q	Increased
Irwin Financial Corp	IFC	26–Aug–04	10–Sep–04	08–Sep–04	09/24/2004	0.08	Q	

DIVIDEND ACTIONS OF DIVIDEND-ACHIEVING COMPANIES (Continued)

Name	Ticker Symbol	Declared	Record Date	Ex-Dividend Date	Date Payable	Amount, $	Quarterly/ Semi/ Annual	Dividend Action
Jack Henry & Associates Inc	JKHY	30–Aug–04	08–Sep–04	03–Sep–04	09/21/2004	0.04	Q	
Jefferson–Pilot Corp	JP	02–Aug–04	19–Nov–04	17–Nov–04	12/05/2004	0.38	Q	
Johnson & Johnson	JNJ	20–Jul–04	17–Aug–04	13–Aug–04	09/07/2004	0.285	Q	
Johnson Controls Inc	JCI	28–Jul–04	10–Sep–04	08–Sep–04	09/30/2004	0.225	Q	
KeyCorp	KEY	23–Jul–04	31–Aug–04	27–Aug–04	09/15/2004	0.31	Q	
Kimberly-Clark Corp	KMB	02–Aug–04	10–Sep–04	08–Sep–04	10/04/2004	0.4	Q	
Kimco Realty Corp	KIM	15–Sep–04	05–Oct–04	01–Oct–04	10/15/2004	0.57	Q	
Lancaster Colony Corp	LANC	25–Aug–04	10–Sep–04	08–Sep–04	09/30/2004	0.23	Q	
La-Z-Boy Inc	LZB	10–Aug–04	30–Aug–04	26–Aug–04	09/10/2004	0.11	Q	
Legg Mason Inc	LM	20–Jul–04	07–Oct–04	05–Oct–04	10/25/2004	0.15	Q	Increased
Leggett & Platt Inc	LEG	04–Aug–04	15–Sep–04	13–Sep–04	10/15/2004	0.15	Q	Increased
Lilly (Eli) & Co	LLY	28–Jun–04	13–Aug–04	11–Aug–04	09/10/2004	0.355	Q	
Lincoln National Corp	LNC	09–Sep–04	08–Oct–04	06–Oct–04	11/01/2004	0.35	Q	
Linear Technology Corp	LLTC	21–Jul–04	30–Jul–04	28–Jul–04	08/18/2004	0.08	Q	
Lowe's Companies Inc	LOW	13–Sep–04	15–Oct–04	13–Oct–04	10/29/2004	0.04	Q	

M & T Bank Corp	MTB	27–Jul–04	02–Sep–04	31–Aug–04	09/30/2004	0.4	Q	
Marsh & McLennan Companies Inc	MMC	14–Sep–04	15–Oct–04	13–Oct–04	11/15/2004	0.34	Q	
Marshall & Ilsley Corp	MI	19–Aug–04	31–Aug–04	27–Aug–04	09/10/2004	0.21	Q	
Masco Corp	MAS	13–Sep–04	08–Oct–04	06–Oct–04	11/08/2004	0.18	Q	Increased
May Department Stores Co	MAY	20–Aug–04	01–Sep–04	30–Aug–04	09/15/2004	0.2425	Q	
MBIA Inc	MBI	10–Sep–04	24–Sep–04	22–Sep–04	10/15/2004	0.24	Q	
MBNA Corp	KRB	22–Jul–04	15–Sep–04	13–Sep–04	10/01/2004	0.12	Q	
McCormick & Co Inc	MKC	28–Sep–04	08–Oct–04	06–Oct–04	10/22/2004	0.14	Q	
McDonald's Corp	MCD	14–Sep–04	15–Nov–04	10–Nov–04	12/01/2004	0.55	A	Increased
McGrath RentCorp	MGRC	20–Sep–04	15–Oct–04	13–Oct–04	10/29/2004	0.22	Q	
McGraw-Hill Companies Inc	MHP	28–Jul–04	26–Aug–04	24–Aug–04	09/10/2004	0.3	Q	
MDU Resources Group Inc	MDU	12–Aug–04	09–Sep–04	07–Sep–04	10/01/2004	0.18	Q	Increased
Medtronic Inc	MDT	26–Aug–04	01–Oct–04	29–Sep–04	10/29/2004	0.08375	Q	
Mercantile Bankshares Corp	MRBK	14–Sep–04	23–Sep–04	21–Sep–04	09/30/2004	0.35	Q	
Merck & Co Inc	MRK	27–Jul–04	03–Sep–04	01–Sep–04	10/01/2004	0.38	Q	Increased
Mercury General Corp	MCY	02–Aug–04	15–Sep–04	13–Sep–04	09/30/2004	0.37	Q	

DIVIDEND ACTIONS OF DIVIDEND-ACHIEVING COMPANIES *(Continued)*

NAME	TICKER SYMBOL	DECLARED	RECORD DATE	Ex-DIVIDEND DATE	DATE PAYABLE	AMOUNT, $	QUARTERLY/ SEMI-ANNUAL	DIVIDEND ACTION
Meredith Corp	MDP	11–Aug–04	31–Aug–04	27–Aug–04	09/15/2004	0.12	Q	
Meridian Bioscience Inc	VIVO	22–Jul–04	02–Aug–04	29–Jul–04	08/09/2004	0.1	Q	
MGE Energy Inc	MGEE	20–Aug–04	01–Sep–04	30–Aug–04	09/15/2004	0.34167	Q	Increased
Middlesex Water Co	MSEX	26–Apr–04	14–May–04	12–May–04	06/01/2004	0.165	Q	
Midland Co	MLAN	29–Jul–04	21–Sep–04	17–Sep–04	10/05/2004	0.05125	Q	
Mine Safety Appliances Co	MSA	28–Jul–04	20–Aug–04	18–Aug–04	09/10/2004	0.1	Q	
Myers Industries Inc	MYE	21–Sep–04	10–Dec–04	08–Dec–04	01/03/2005	0.05	Q	
NACCO Industries Inc	NC	11–Aug–04	01–Sep–04	30–Aug–04	09/15/2004	0.4525	Q	Increased
National City Corp	NCC	01–Oct–04	11–Oct–04	06–Oct–04	11/01/2004	0.35	Q	
National Commerce Financial Corp	NCF	20–Jul–04	31–Aug–04	27–Aug–04	09/15/2004	0.2475	Q	Increased
National Fuel Gas Co	NFG	09–Sep–04	30–Sep–04	28–Sep–04	10/15/2004	0.28	Q	
National Penn Bancshares Inc	NPBC	25–Aug–04	10–Sep–04	01–Oct–04	09/30/2004	1.25	Q	
National Security Group Inc	NSEC	17–Jul–04	02–Aug–04	29–Jul–04	08/31/2004	0.21	Q	
NICOR Inc	GAS	15–Jul–04	30–Sep–04	28–Sep–04	11/01/2004	0.465	Q	

Company	Ticker					Amount		
Nordson Corp	NDSN	04-Aug-04	27-Aug-04	25-Aug-04	09/15/2004	0.16	Q	Increased
Northern Trust Corp	NTRS	19-Jul-04	10-Sep-04	08-Sep-04	10/01/2004	0.19	Q	
Nucor Corp	NUE	09-Sep-04	30-Sep-04	18-Oct-04	10/15/2004	2	Q	
Nuveen Investments Inc	JNC	05-Aug-04	01-Sep-04	30-Aug-04	09/15/2004	0.18	Q	
Old National Bancorp	ONB	22-Jul-04	01-Sep-04	30-Aug-04	09/15/2004	0.19	Q	
Old Republic International Corp	ORI	12-Aug-04	03-Sep-04	01-Sep-04	09/15/2004	0.13	Q	
Otter Tail Corp	OTTR	02-Aug-04	13-Aug-04	11-Aug-04	09/10/2004	0.275	Q	
Pacific Capital Bancorp (New)	PCBC	01-Jul-04	20-Jul-04	16-Jul-04	08/10/2004	0.18	Q	Increased
Park National Corp	PRK	19-Jul-04	24-Aug-04	20-Aug-04	09/10/2004	0.88	Q	
Parker-Hannifin Corp	PH	23-Jul-04	20-Aug-04	18-Aug-04	09/03/2004	0.19	Q	
Paychex Inc	PAYX	08-Jul-04	02-Aug-04	29-Jul-04	08/16/2004	0.12	Q	
Pennichuck Corp	PNNW	14-Jul-04	16-Aug-04	12-Aug-04	09/01/2004	0.215	Q	
Pentair Inc	PNR	17-May-04	30-Jul-04	28-Jul-04	08/13/2004	0.11	Q	
People's Bank	PBCT	15-Apr-04	01-May-04	28-Apr-04	05/15/2004	0.435	Q	Increased
Peoples Energy Corp	PGL	04-Aug-04	22-Sep-04	20-Sep-04	10/15/2004	0.54	Q	
PepsiCo Inc	PEP	23-Jul-04	10-Sep-04	08-Sep-04	09/30/2004	0.23	Q	
Pfizer Inc	PFE	24-Jun-04	13-Aug-04	11-Aug-04	09/03/2004	0.17	Q	

DIVIDEND ACTIONS OF DIVIDEND-ACHIEVING COMPANIES (Continued)

NAME	TICKER SYMBOL	DECLARED	RECORD DATE	EX-DIVIDEND DATE	DATE PAYABLE	AMOUNT, $	QUARTERLY/ SEMI/ ANNUAL	DIVIDEND ACTION
Piedmont Natural Gas Co Inc	PNY	27–Aug–04	11–Oct–04	01–Nov–04	10/29/2004	2	Q	
Pier 1 Imports Inc	PIR	30–Sep–04	03–Nov–04	01–Nov–04	11/17/2004	0.1	Q	
Pinnacle West Capital Corp	PNW	16–Jul–04	02–Aug–04	29–Jul–04	09/01/2004	0.45	Q	
Pitney Bowes Inc	PBI	12–Jul–04	20–Aug–04	18–Aug–04	09/12/2004	0.305	Q	
Popular Inc	BPOP	17–Aug–04	13–Sep–04	09–Sep–04	1–Oct–04	0.16	Q	
PPG Industries Inc	PPG	15–Jul–04	10–Aug–04	06–Aug–04	09/10/2004	0.45	Q	
Praxair Inc	PX	27–Jul–04	07–Sep–04	02–Sep–04	09/15/2004	0.15	Q	
Procter & Gamble Co	PG	13–Jul–04	23–Jul–04	21–Jul–04	08/16/2004	0.25	Q	
Progress Energy Inc	PGN	17–Sep–04	11–Oct–04	06–Oct–04	11/01/2004	0.575	Q	
Progressive Corp	PGR	20–Aug–04	10–Sep–04	08–Sep–04	09/30/2004	0.03	Q	Increased
Protective Life Corp	PL	02–Aug–04	20–Aug–04	18–Aug–04	09/01/2004	0.175	Q	
Quaker Chemical Corp	KWR	22–Sep–04	15–Oct–04	13–Oct–04	10/29/2004	0.215	Q	
Questar Corp	STR	10–Aug–04	20–Aug–04	18–Aug–04	09/13/2004	0.215	Q	
Quixote Corp	QUIX	12–May–04	07–Jun–04	03–Jun–04	07/02/2004	0.17	S	
Raven Industries Inc	RAVN	20–Aug–04	24–Sep–04	22–Sep–04	10/15/2004	0.11	Q	

Company	Symbol							
Regions Financial Corp	RF	16-Jul-04	02-Aug-04	29-Jul-04	08/16/2004	0.3334	Q	
Republic Bancorp Inc	RBNC	18-Jun-04	10-Sep-04	08-Sep-04	10/04/2004	0.11	Q	Increased
RLI Corp	RLI	03-Aug-04	30-Sep-04	28-Sep-04	10/15/2004	0.13	Q	
Rohm & Haas Co	ROH	24-Sep-04	05-Nov-04	03-Nov-04	12/01/2004	0.25	Q	
Roper Industries Inc	ROP	17-Aug-04	15-Oct-04	13-Oct-04	10/29/2004	0.09625	Q	
Rouse Co	RSE	29-Jul-04	16-Sep-04	14-Sep-04	09/30/2004	0.47	Q	
RPM International Inc	RPM	02-Jul-04	12-Jul-04	08-Jul-04	07/30/2004	0.14	Q	
S & T Bancorp Inc	STBA	20-Sep-04	01-Oct-04	29-Sep-04	10/25/2004	0.27	Q	
Sara Lee Corp	SLE	24-Jun-04	01-Sep-04	30-Aug-04	10/01/2004	0.1875	Q	
SBC Communications Inc	SBC	24-Sep-04	08-Oct-04	06-Oct-04	11/01/2004	0.3125	Q	
SEI Investments Co	SEIC	25-May-04	08-Jun-04	04-Jun-04	06/24/2004	0.1	S	Increased
ServiceMaster Co (The)	SVM	30-Apr-04	09-Jul-04	07-Jul-04	07/30/2004	0.11	Q	Increased
Sherwin-Williams Co	SHW	21-Jul-04	20-Aug-04	18-Aug-04	09/03/2004	0.17	Q	
Sigma-Aldrich Corp	SIAL	10-Aug-04	01-Sep-04	30-Aug-04	09/15/2004	0.17	Q	
Simmons First National Corp	SFNC	30-Aug-04	15-Sep-04	13-Sep-04	10/01/2004	0.14	Q	
SJW Corp	SJW	29-Jul-04	09-Aug-04	05-Aug-04	09/01/2004	0.255	Q	
SLM Corp	SLM	30-Jul-04	03-Sep-04	01-Sep-04	09/17/2004	0.19	Q	

DIVIDEND ACTIONS OF DIVIDEND-ACHIEVING COMPANIES (Continued)

NAME	TICKER SYMBOL	DECLARED	RECORD DATE	EX-DIVIDEND DATE	DATE PAYABLE	AMOUNT, $	QUARTERLY/ SEMI/ ANNUAL	DIVIDEND ACTION
Smith (AO) Corp	AOS	13–Jul–04	30–Jul–04	28–Jul–04	08/16/2004	0.16	Q	Increased
Sonoco Products Co	SON	21–Jul–04	20–Aug–04	18–Aug–04	09/10/2004	0.22	Q	
SouthTrust Corp	SOTR	21–Jul–04	20–Aug–04	18–Aug–04	10/01/2004	0.24	Q	
Stanley Works	SWK	22–Jul–04	03–Sep–04	01–Sep–04	09/28/2004	0.28	Q	Increased
State Auto Financial Corp	STFC	09–Aug–04	15–Sep–04	13–Sep–04	09/30/2004	0.045	Q	Increased
State Street Corp	STT	16–Sep–04	01–Oct–04	29–Sep–04	10/15/2004	0.16	Q	
Stepan Co	SCL	03–Aug–04	31–Aug–04	27–Aug–04	09/15/2004	0.1925	Q	
Sterling Bancshares Inc	SBIB	26–Jul–04	06–Aug–04	04–Aug–04	08/20/2004	0.05	Q	
Sterling Financial Corp	SLFI	24–Aug–04	15–Sep–04	13–Sep–04	10/01/2004	0.16	Q	Increased
Stryker Corp	SYK	21–Apr–04	03–May–04	17–May–04	05/14/2004	2	A	
SunTrust Banks Inc	STI	10–Aug–04	01–Sep–04	30–Aug–04	09/15/2004	0.5	Q	
Superior Industries International Inc	SUP	02–Aug–04	01–Oct–04	29–Sep–04	10/15/2004	0.155	Q	
Supervalu Inc	SVU	11–Aug–04	01–Sep–04	30–Aug–04	09/15/2004	0.1525	Q	Increased
Susquehanna Bancshares Inc	SUSQ	21–Jul–04	02–Aug–04	29–Jul–04	08/20/2004	0.22	Q	

Company	Ticker					Amount		
SWS Group Inc	SWS	18–Aug–04	15–Sep–04	13–Sep–04	10/01/2004	0.1	Q	
Synovus Financial Corp	SNV	19–Aug–04	17–Sep–04	15–Sep–04	10/01/2004	0.1733	Q	
Sysco Corp	SYY	03–Sep–04	01–Oct–04	29–Sep–04	10/22/2004	0.13	Q	
T Rowe Price Group Inc	TROW	09–Sep–04	27–Sep–04	23–Sep–04	10/08/2004	0.19	Q	
Tanger Factory Outlet Centers Inc	SKT	15–Jul–04	30–Jul–04	28–Jul–04	08/16/2004	0.625	Q	
Target Corp	TGT	08–Sep–04	20–Nov–04	17–Nov–04	12/10/2004	0.08	Q	
TCF Financial Corp	TCB	03–Aug–04	13–Aug–04	07–Sep–04	09/03/2004	2	Q	
Teleflex Incorporated	TFX	04–Aug–04	25–Aug–04	23–Aug–04	09/15/2004	0.22	Q	
Telephone and Data Systems Inc	TDS	03–Aug–04	16–Sep–04	14–Sep–04	09/30/2004	0.165	Q	
Tennant Co	TNC	18–Aug–04	31–Aug–04	27–Aug–04	09/15/2004	0.22	Q	Increased
TEPPCO Partners LP	TPP	16–Jul–04	30–Jul–04	28–Jul–04	08/06/2004	0.6625	Q	
Tootsie Roll Industries Inc	TR	21–Sep–04	01–Oct–04	29–Sep–04	10/15/2004	0.07	Q	
Transatlantic Holdings Inc	TRH	23–Sep–04	26–Nov–04	23–Nov–04	12/10/2004	0.1	Q	
Trustmark Corp	TRMK	20–Jul–04	01–Sep–04	30–Aug–04	09/15/2004	0.19	Q	
UGI Corp (New)	UGI	27–Jul–04	31–Aug–04	27–Aug–04	10/01/2004	0.3125	Q	
United Bankshares Inc	UBSI	23–Aug–04	10–Sep–04	08–Sep–04	10/01/2004	0.26	Q	Increased

DIVIDEND ACTIONS OF DIVIDEND-ACHIEVING COMPANIES (*Continued*)

NAME	TICKER SYMBOL	DECLARED	RECORD DATE	Ex-DIVIDEND DATE	DATE PAYABLE	AMOUNT, $	QUARTERLY/ SEMI/ ANNUAL	DIVIDEND ACTION
United Dominion Realty Trust Inc	UDR	24–Sep–04	15–Oct–04	13–Oct–04	11/01/2004	0.2925	Q	
United Mobile Homes Inc	UMH	01–Oct–04	15–Nov–04	10–Nov–04	12/15/2004	0.24	Q	Increased
United Technologies Corp	UTX	09–Jun–04	20–Aug–04	18–Aug–04	09/10/2004	0.35	Q	
Universal Corp	UVV	05–Aug–04	11–Oct–04	06–Oct–04	11/08/2004	0.39	Q	
Universal Health Realty Income Trust	UHT	01–Sep–04	15–Sep–04	13–Sep–04	09/30/2004	0.5	Q	
Unizan Financial Corp	UNIZ	31–Aug–04	14–Sep–04	10–Sep–04	09/28/2004	0.135	Q	
Valley National Bancorp	VLY	05–Aug–04	03–Sep–04	01–Sep–04	10/01/2004	0.225	Q	
Valspar Corp	VAL	11–Aug–04	01–Oct–04	29–Sep–04	10/15/2004	0.18	Q	
Vectren Corp	VVC	28–Jul–04	13–Aug–04	11–Aug–04	09/01/2004	0.285	Q	
VF Corp	VFC	21–Jul–04	10–Sep–04	08–Sep–04	09/20/2004	0.26	Q	
Vulcan Materials Co	VMC	09–Jul–04	26–Aug–04	24–Aug–04	09/10/2004	0.26	Q	
Walgreen Co	WAG	14–Jul–04	20–Aug–04	18–Aug–04	09/11/2004	0.0525	Q	Increased
Wal-Mart Stores Inc	WMT	02–Mar–04	19–Mar–04	17–Mar–04	04/05/2004	0.13	Q	Increased

Company	Ticker					Amount	Freq	Note
Washington Federal Inc	WFSL	27-Sep-04	08-Oct-04	06-Oct-04	10/22/2004	0.21	Q	
Washington Mutual Inc	WM	21-Jul-04	30-Jul-04	28-Jul-04	08/13/2004	0.44	Q	Increased
Washington Real Estate Investment Trust	WRE	04-Aug-04	16-Sep-04	14-Sep-04	09/30/2004	0.3925	Q	
Webster Financial Corp	WBS	20-Jul-04	02-Aug-04	29-Jul-04	08/16/2004	0.23	Q	
Weingarten Realty Investors	WRI	26-Jul-04	03-Sep-04	01-Sep-04	09/15/2004	0.415	Q	
Wells Fargo & Co (New)	WFC	27-Jul-04	06-Aug-04	04-Aug-04	09/01/2004	0.48	Q	Increased
Wesbanco Inc	WSBC	19-Aug-04	10-Sep-04	08-Sep-04	10/01/2004	0.25	Q	
Wesco Financial Corp	WSC	16-Sep-04	03-Nov-04	01-Nov-04	12/01/2004	0.345	Q	
West Pharmaceutical Services Inc	WST	24-Aug-04	20-Oct-04	18-Oct-04	11/03/2004	0.11	Q	Increased
WestAmerica Bancorporation	WABC	22-Jul-04	02-Aug-04	29-Jul-04	08/13/2004	0.28	Q	
Weyco Group Inc	WEYS	26-Jul-04	01-Sep-04	30-Aug-04	10/01/2004	0.11	Q	
WGL Holdings Inc	WGL	29-Sep-04	08-Oct-04	06-Oct-04	11/01/2004	0.325	Q	
Whitney Holding Corp	WTNY	25-Aug-04	15-Sep-04	13-Sep-04	10/01/2004	0.33	Q	

Dividend Actions of Dividend-Achieving Companies* *(Continued)*

Name	Ticker Symbol	Declared	Record Date	Ex-Dividend Date	Date Payable	Amount, $	Quarterly/ Semi/ Annual	Dividend Action
Wiley (John) & Sons Inc	JWA	15–Sep–04	01–Oct–04	29–Sep–04	10/18/2004	0.075	Q	
Wilmington Trust Corp	WL	16–Apr–04	03–May–04	29–Apr–04	05/17/2004	0.285	Q	Increased
Wolverine World Wide Inc	WWW	09–Jul–04	01–Oct–04	29–Sep–04	11/01/2004	0.065	Q	
WPS Resources Corp	WPS	08–Jul–04	31–Aug–04	27–Aug–04	09/20/2004	0.555	Q	Increased
Wrigley (William) Jr Co	WWY	18–Aug–04	15–Oct–04	13–Oct–04	11/01/2004	0.235	Q	

*As of September of 2004.

Notes

Chapter 1

1. William Gale, "About Half of Dividend Payments Do Not Face Double Taxation," Tax Policy Center, 2002.

Chapter 2

1. H. Kent Baker, Gary E. Powell, and E. Theodore Veit, *Review of Financial Economics*, 2002.
2. Prof. Kathleen Fuller and Prof. Michael Goldstein, Dividend Policy and Market Movement, 2003.
3. "Equity Ownership in America," Investment Company Institute and the Securities Industry Association, January 2002.
4. U.S. Congress, Joint Economic Committee Study, April 2000.
5. Leonard E. Burman and David L. Gunter, Urban Institute, May 26 2003, and U.S. Federal Reserve.
6. U.S. Census Bureau 1900–1980, 1980 Census of the Population, General Population Characteristics, United States Summary (PC80-1-B1); 1990, 1990 Census of the Population, General Population Characteristics, United States Summary (CP-1-1); 2000, Census 2000, Summary File 1; and Projections of the Population by Age, Sex, Race and Hispanic Origin for the United States: 1999 to 2100; published January 2000.
7. Organization for Economic Cooperation and Development (OECD) figures.

8. U.S. Social Security Administration, *Income of the Aged Chartbook*, 2001.

9. Luis Correia de Silva, Marc Goergen, and Luc Renneboog, Dividend Policy and Corporate Governance, 2004.

Chapter 3

1. Internal Revenue Service, "Investment Income and Expenses," Publication 550, 2003.

Chapter 4

1. Standard and Poor's and *JeremySiegel.com*.

2. E.F. Farma and K.R. French, "Disappearing Dividends: Changing Firm Characteristics or Lower Propensity to Pay?," *Journal of Financial Economics*, 2001.

3. Standard and Poor's.

4. H.K. Baker, P.L. Gallagher, and K.E. Morgan, "Management's View of Stock Repurchase Programs," *Journal of Financial Research*, 1981.

5. J. W. Wansley, W. R. Lane, and S. Sarkar, "Managements' View on Share Repurchase and Tender Offer Premiums," *Financial Management*, 1989.

6. G. P. Tsetsekos, D. J. Kaufman, and L. J. Gitman, "A Survey of Stock Repurchase Motivations and Practices of Major U.S. Corporations," *Journal of Applied Business Research*, 1991.

7. American Shareholders' Association, 2003.

8. Michael Barclay and Clifford Smith, "Corporate Payout Policy: Cash Dividends versus Open Market Re-Purchases," *Journal of Financial Economics*, 1998.

9. Scott Lee, Wayne H. Mikkelson, and Megan Partch, "Managers' Trading Around Stock Repurchases," *The Journal of Finance*, 1992.

Chapter 5

1. *Stocks, Bonds, Bills and Inflation 2003 Yearbook,* Ibbotson Associates Inc; Data from 1926–2002, as represented by the Standard & Poor's 500 Index.

2. Prof. Kathleen Fuller and Prof. Michael Goldstein, Dividend Policy and Market Movements, 2003.

3. Peter O'Shea analysis, July 2004.

Chapter 6

1. Marc L. Lipson, Carlos P. Maquieira, and William L. Megginson, "Why Do Public Companies Begin Paying Dividends? A Reevaluation of Dividend Signaling," *Financial Management*, 1998.

2. Edward A. Dyl and Robert A. Weigand, "The Information Content of Dividend Initiations: Additional Evidence," *Financial Management*, 1998.

Chapter 7

1. "The Roots of Broadened Stock Ownership," Joint Economic Committee Study, April 2000.
2. *Mergent Dividend Achievers*, Spring 2004.
3. Matej Blasko, Is The Dividend Puzzle Still Out There? Large Minority Shareholders and the Agency Cost Explanation of Dividends, 1998.

Chapter 8

1. "Equity in America," Investment Company Institute and the Securitites Industry Association, 1992.
2. Federal Reserve, "Flow of Funds Accounts of the United States," September 16, 2004.

Chapter 9

1. *Investment Company Research in Brief*, Vol. 4, No. 12, October 2003.
2. Closed-End Fund Association, July 2004.
3. Ramon P. DeGennaro, "Direct Investments in Securities: A Primer," *Economic Review*, Atlanta; January, 2003.
4. "Equity in America," Investment Company Institute and the Securities Industry Association, 1992.
5. Mergent Analysis, 2004.

Index

A

American Depository Receipt
  (ADR) index, 87–90
Announcements, dividend, 72

B

Better performance of dividend
    stocks
  better performance over time,
    42–43
  dividend companies can outper-
    form major indexes, 43–46
  myth that dividend stocks don't
    grow, 46–49
  overview, 41, 49
Bottom-up approach to identifying
    dividend achievers, 55–56
Buffett, Warren, 38, 63
Bull market of 1980s to 2000,
    32–33

C

Closed-end funds, 94–97
  tax treatment of dividends, 97
  yields of some U.S. funds, 96

Comeback of dividend stocks
  change in mood in 2003
    dividend funds came back into
      vogue, 36–37
    dividend yields rose again, 35
    more companies increased
      dividends on a consecutive
      basis, 35–36
    overview, 34–35
  greater focus on dividends in the
    past, 28–29
  overview, 27–28, 40
  reasons for comeback
    impact of national and world
      events, 37–38
    scandals, 38
    share buybacks discredited,
      38–39
  reasons interest in dividend
    investing subsided
    bull market of 1980s to 2000,
      32–33
    day trading phenomenon,
      33–34
    dot-com craze, 33

Comeback of dividend stocks
(Continued)
overview, 29–30
share buybacks captivated
attention, 30–32
Common stock, 6

D
Day trading phenomenon, 33–34
Debt-to-equity ratio, 79–80
Direct purchase plans, 98–101
Direct reinvestment plans
list of companies with, 102–119
overview, 101
Dividend achievers
identifying, 54–56
NASDAQ dividend achievers,
86–87
overview, 125–126
top 10 dividend achievers by
consecutive years of dividend
increases, 179–199
top 10 dividend achievers by
yield, 127–147
top 14 household name dividend
achievers, 149–177
what dividend achievers have
in common, 56–57
Dividends
announcements of, 72
better performance of dividend
stocks. *See* Better performance of dividend stocks
comeback of dividend stocks.
See Comeback of dividend
stocks
dividend actions of dividend-
achieving companies,
203–224
dividend investment options.
See Investment options

Mergent dividend investing
strategy. *See* Mergent
dividend investing strategy
myth that dividend stocks don't
grow, 46–49
overview. *See* Dividends,
introduction to
as percentage of individual
income, 11–12
real estate investment trusts
(REITs).
See Real estate investment
trusts (REITs)
selected dividend achievers.
See Dividend achievers
tax environment and.
See Tax environment
what makes a good
dividend stock.
See What makes a good
dividend stock
yields and ratios.
See Yields and ratios
Dividends, introduction to, 1–4
common stock, 6
definition of dividends, 5–7
importance of dividends.
See Importance of dividends
reasons companies pay dividends,
7–11
Dividend yield, 68–69
Dot-com craze, 33

E
Exchange-traded funds, 97–98
Ex-dividend dates, 98

F
Fees, warning about, 92–93
Foreign companies, investing in
stocks of, 87–90

G
Grootwassnik, Sara, 65

H
Holding periods, 23–25
Household name top dividend
achievers, 149–177

I
Importance of dividends
dividend payments lead to good
corporate management, 18
dividends are a valuable future
income source, 14–17
dividends indicate stability and
lower risk, 17–18
dividends provide current income,
11
high-yield dividend companies
are undervalued, 18
profile of stock ownership, 11–13
Indexes
Mergent index, 83–84, 87–90
outperformance by dividend
companies, 43–46, 85
Inflation, 67–68
Investment options
closed-end funds, 94–97
direct purchase plans, 98–101
direct reinvestment plans
list of companies with,
102–119
overview, 101
exchange-traded funds, 97–98
fees, warning about, 92–93
mutual funds, 93–94
overview, 91–92
IRS (Internal Revenue Service)
definition of dividends by, 5
filing dividend information with,
20. *See also* Tax environment

J
Jobs and Growth Tax Relief
Reconciliation Act (2003),
19

M
Mergent dividend investing
strategy
how consistency can outperform
key indices, 85
investing in stocks of foreign
companies, 87–90
mitigating risk by identifying
consistency, 82–84
NASDAQ dividend achievers,
86–87
overview, 81–82, 90
Mutual funds, 93–94
yields of selected dividend
mutual funds, 95

N
NASDAQ dividend achievers,
86–87
National and world events, impact
on dividends, 37–38
New Market Wizards, 53

P
Payout ratio, 70–71
Pistell, Tim, 64
Price-to-earnings (PE) ratio
overview, 72–75
for selected stocks, 75–77
Price-to-sales ratio, 79

Q
Qualified dividends, 21–23
IRS explanation of what is *not* a
qualified dividend, 21–22

R

Real estate investment trusts
(REITs)
overview, 23, 121–122
top-yielding, list of, 123–124
Return on equity (ROE), 78–79
Risk, mitigating by identifying
consistency, 82–84

S

Scandals, financial, and dividends,
38
Schwager, Jack, 53
Share buybacks, 30–32, 38–39

T

Tax environment
changes to how dividends are
taxed
holding periods, 23–25
implications for investors,
25–26
overview, 21
qualified dividends, 21–23
consideration by companies
issuing dividends, 10
filing dividend information with
the IRS, 20
overview, 19–20
Top-down approach to identifying
dividend achievers, 54–55

W

What makes a good dividend stock
choosing your own dividend
investments, 52–54
disciplined management is
critical, 63–65

dividend companies are larger and
more mature, 59
dividend companies are past their
growth phase, 60–61
dividend companies found
in particular industries,
57–59
dividend companies have low
levels of research and
development expenditure,
61–62
dividend growth requires strong
earnings growth, 62–63
dividends require strong cash
flow, 62
identifying dividend achievers,
54–56
overview, 51–52
what dividend achievers have
in common, 56–57

Y

Yields and ratios
debt-to-equity ratio, 79–80
dividend announcements, 72
dividend yield, 68–69
higher yields are not always
better, 69–70
inflation, 67–68
overview, 67
payout ratio, 70–71
price-to-earnings ratio
overview, 72–75
for selected stocks, 75–77
price-to-sales ratio, 79
return on equity, 78–79
top 10 dividend achievers by
yield, 127–147